Reaching Out:

Music education with
'hard to reach' children
and young people

Edited by Chris Harrison and Phil Mullen

The authors of all chapters have been most generous in contributing to this book and we are very grateful to them.

The *UK Association for Music Education* – **Music Mark** supports quality music education for all and aims to provide a unified voice for all those involved in music education and to improve the learning and personal outcomes for children and young people in and out of schools and is the lead music subject association.

The organisation:

- advocates, celebrates and challenges on behalf of children and young people locally, regionally and nationally;
- supports professional development within the national community of music education;
- provides rich opportunities for debate, learning and the sharing of best practice to drive standards and achieve high quality in music education;
- connects all those who contribute to the music education of children and young people in different contexts, unlocking the potential to raise standards and improve outcomes.

ISBN 978-0-9566545-3-3

Designed, typeset and printed by:
Addison Design Ltd. Salisbury, Wilts, UK
www.addisondeign.co.uk 01722 329 777
©2013

Copyright of each chapter remains with the authors

CONTENTS

Notes on the contributors — ii

Introduction — vii

Engaging the hard to reach: issues and challenges – Randall Allsup — 1

Why music? A research rationale for making music with children and young people experiencing additional challenges – Douglas Lonie — 3

Challenges and possibilities: Engaging 'hard to reach' families with young children – Deborah Albon, Kim Allen, Sumi Hollingworth and Jayne Osgood — 13

Participation, Inclusion, Diversity and the Policy of English Music Education – Gary Spruce — 23

Hard to Reach, Harder to Let Go: a practice of social action through music inspired by Venezuela's 'el Sistema' – Jonathan Govias — 32

How many pedagogies does it take to train a community musician? – Kathryn Deane — 41

The role of hubs in reaching the 'hard to reach' groups: experiences and reflections from Gloucestershire – Mark Bick — 53

Social *and* Artistic – a reflection on balancing outcomes – Jess Abrams — 62

Music and Looked After Children – Helen Chambers — 67

Beyond access – towards equality of outcome: the challenge for instrumental music educators – Evelyn Grant — 80

Debussy and/or dubstep: non-discriminatory approaches to choosing musical repertoire within a broad and balanced curriculum – Robert Legg — 88

Music Mentoring – Notes from a seaside project – Phil Mullen — 97

Why Technology with hard to reach kids? – Gawain Hewitt — 104

Singing and the body – Beth Allen — 113

Music group work with LGBT youth – Catherine Pestano — 117

Developing a grassroots international community music network serving people with disabilities – Donald DeVito — 127

Developing inclusive instrumental musicking through a Primary School Orchestra – Andrew M Lindley — 135

Focus on 'Harder to Reach' young people: the work of Wigmore Hall Learning's resident outreach ensemble, 'Ignite' – Kate Whitaker and Ursula Crickmay — 141

A Lily of a Day – Andy Murray — 147

Reaching Ben – Emily Sahakian and John Finney — 151

Al's journey – Graham Dowdall — 158

'I am the Moon' – Ros Hawley — 162

NOTES ON THE CONTRIBUTORS

Jess Abrams is a musician and music practitioner who has been living in Scotland for nearly 20 years. She holds an MSc in Music in the Community from the University of Edinburgh, but was a practitioner long before she held the degree! As well as working in the community facilitating projects in music-making and recording, Jess is the Development Manager for the Edinburgh Youth Music Forum, working with music practitioners to explore, develop and share good practice. She also lectures at Edinburgh College. Originally from New York, she performs as a vocalist in the UK and Europe whenever she can.

Deborah Albon is Senior Lecturer in Early Childhood Studies at London Metropolitan University in the Faculty of Social Sciences and Humanities. Her research and publications focus on a broad range of issues pertaining to early childhood practice and to exploring innovative ways of researching with very young children. Deb was a nursery nurse, then nursery teacher and senior manager for many years, primarily in West London, prior to working in Higher Education.

Beth Allen trained initially as an opera singer at the Royal Scottish Academy and then as a music therapist and voice specialist, gaining an MA in Voice. She co-founded the successful children's music theatre company 'The Happy Gang', whose work included the filming of three series of programmes for the BBC. More recently, she has been a voice coach with various performing arts companies. She was Creative Leader for Lancashire's Sing Up initiative for four years and is now Head of Voice for the Lancashire Music Hub, as well as a visiting voice coach at the Liverpool Institute of Performing Arts. She is part of a comedy duo called Doolally.

Kim Allen worked as a Senior Research Fellow with the Institute of Policy Studies at London Metropolitan University and is now a Research Fellow at the Education and Social Research Institute (ESRI) at Manchester Metropolitan University. A sociologist of education and youth, Kim's research focuses broadly on inequalities and identities of social class and gender within education; and representations of class and gender in popular culture.

Randall Allsup is Associate Professor of Music Education at Teachers College, Columbia University, where he teaches courses in creativity and problem solving; democracy and music education; philosophies of music education; and doctoral seminar. In 2006, he hosted and organised the first ever International Conference on Music Education, Equity, and Social Justice at Teachers College. He writes about the challenges of reconceptualising music pedagogy, with a special interest in instrumental and popular music, and his articles have appeared in many journals worldwide.

Mark Bick is CEO of Gloucestershire Music Makers, core partners in Make Music Gloucestershire, the County Music Education Hub. Mark leads the Hub inclusion strategy and also manages a successful music mentoring programme. He has been freelance for 20 years and before that ran Community Music Wales. His first job after qualifying as a secondary music teacher was in a youth project with unemployed young people in Cardiff. He has led the New Horizons training course for Birmingham and other Midlands music services over the last 13 years. He is currently Chair of Sound Sense, the National Community Music Association.

Helen Chambers is an associate of the National Children's Bureau and the Centre for Understanding Social Pedagogy at the Institute of Education, University of London, with specialist interest in the arts and culture in the lives of looked after children. She manages a range of projects to demonstrate how access to arts and culture promotes the well-being of looked after children, young people and their carers, and supports good care. Helen was national manager for the DH/DCSF funded Healthy Care Programme, and Well-being Creativity and Play work at NCB. Earlier MSc research focused on the creative arts to promote health and well-being.

Ursula Crickmay is Director of Learning at Wigmore Hall where she has led the development of a programme of community and education events over the last decade, including work with families, young people, schools, nurseries, hospitals, social care and other community centres, as well as programming a series of study events, masterclasses and lectures at Wigmore Hall. Ursula trained in music at the University of York, and combines her work at Wigmore Hall with freelance project management and consultation for other arts organisations.

Kathryn Deane has run Sound Sense, the UK association for community musicians, since 1995. She was an author of the Music Manifesto report 'Making Every Child's Music Matter'; and co-architect of the notion of music education hubs. She writes extensively on community music, including in NAME publications, edits the UK Journal of Community Music, Sounding Board and sits on the editorial board of the International Journal of Community Music. She evaluates community music practice, and is an adviser to undergraduate and postgraduate courses. She is consultant, contributor and deviser of national occupational standards, codes of practice, and accredited qualifications.

Donald DeVito is a music and special education teacher at the Sidney Lanier Center in Gainesville, Florida and the 2011 U.S. National Council for Exceptional Children (CEC) Teacher of the Year. The Sidney Lanier Music Program is global in scope and linked with universities and music programmes that assist underserved populations internationally through research, grants, cooperative projects and lessons. Examples include projects in Haiti, Pakistan, Guinea, England, China, Australia, Ireland and Brazil. DeVito was the 2010-2012 Chair of the International Society for Music Education's Community Music Activity Commission - practitioners and researchers who research into and develop programs for underserved populations around the world.

Graham Dowdall is an experienced musician, music leader and trainer. For the last twenty years he has worked with young people in a variety of challenging circumstances, including those outside mainstream education, those at risk of or already offending and those with a wide variety of disabilities. One of his specialisms is using music technology. He is an active performer, touring and recording regularly as a member of acclaimed bands including Pere Ubu, Roshi ft. Pars Radio, as well as with his solo electronic project Gagarin. He is also the convenor and tutor on the Certificate in Music Workshop Skills course at Goldsmiths College.

John Finney was Senior Lecturer in Music Education in the Faculty of Education, University of Cambridge, until 2010. Teaching music in four secondary schools prepared the way for teaching the next generation of music students to teach music in secondary schools. John's most recent research interest is in dialogic approaches to pedagogy and in particular the role of talk in shaping a critical pedagogy.

Jonathan Govias is a conductor, educator and writer who is also the recipient of fellowships in Social Entrepreneurship, Arts Leadership and Social Action through Music. As a conductor he has worked with some of the most distinguished ensembles in the world, including the Cincinnati Symphony, the National Arts Centre Orchestra of Canada, and the Zurich Tonhalle Orchester. His articles on *el Sistema* practice have been been published worldwide in multiple languages, and he is a teaching and leadership coach for Sistema-style programs on four continents. He is currently on the full-time faculty of the University of North Carolina, Charlotte, as Director of Orchestras.

Evelyn Grant graduated from the Hochschule fur Musik in Essen, Germany in 1979. She lectured in Flute and, later, in Community Music Studies at CIT Cork School of Music until 2009. Involved in outreach projects for over 30 years, she was the first Irish person to receive a Master's degree in Community Music (University of York.) She was awarded a PhD from University College Cork for her research on 'Social Inclusion in Music Education in Ireland.' A regular broadcaster on RTÉ lyric fm, she researched and presented a 6-part documentary series entitled 'Passions and Policies - Music Education in Ireland.'

Chris Harrison is a music education consultant whose recent work includes teaching on ITE courses, running courses for teachers and young musicians, writing educational materials and advising local authorities on their music provision. A former teacher and music adviser, he is a past Chair of the National Association of Music Educators, for whom he has edited a range of publications. His musical tastes are wide-ranging and he performs with a number of groups and ensembles. He is particularly interested in the role of improvisation as a vehicle for learning music, and in developing musical activities in the wider community.

Ros Hawley is a clarinettist, trainer and workshop leader specialising in the use of music in healthcare and special educational needs settings. She has worked with Mark Fisher and Holly Marland since 2005, developing a pioneering programme, Music for Health, involving students from the Royal Northern College of Music in Manchester in training placements at The Royal Manchester Children's Hospital and Booth Hall Hospital. The team are looking forward to further developing their work this year at The Royal Manchester Children's Hospital in collaboration with Lime (a Manchester arts charity) and linked to Therapeutic and Specialised Play Services.

Gawain Hewitt has been working as a community musician since 2003. Having trained at Community Music, in 2005 he co-founded Skillz, a social enterprise working with children in Pupil Referral Units. At CM, he was a tutor and part of a team developing teaching resources, becoming Creative Director from 2008-2010. Now freelance, Gawain specialises in working with young people in challenging circumstances and in music technology. Clients include Drake Music, where he is the Associate National Manager for research and development; Serious, leading on work in Pupil Referral Units; and Trinity Laban, as a technology lead for the Animate Orchestra and Sound Connections.

Sumi Hollingworth is a Senior Research Fellow at the Weeks Centre for social and policy research at London Southbank University and formerly worked as a researcher at the Institute for Policy Studies in Education (IPSE) at London Metropolitan University. She is a sociologist of youth and education and she specialises in research which explores intersecting inequalities of social class, race and gender. Sumi is currently completing her doctoral research on social mixing and friendship formation among urban youth.

Robert Legg is senior lecturer in music education and pedagogy at Te Kōkī New Zealand School of Music, a joint facility of Massey University and Victoria University of Wellington. His previous academic post was at Oxford Brookes University, where he led the institution's secondary teacher education provision and co-launched its EdD programme. Robert's research interests occupy various intersections between music education and concepts of social justice, and include music and gender, adolescent singing participation, narrative inquiry and critical social theory. In addition to his regular involvement in music theatre education, Robert is active as a choral conductor and as a composer of music for young voices.

Andrew M Lindley left industry to work in music education, initially as a teacher of upper strings. For the last twenty-five years, he has taught in a primary school in East Durham, establishing and developing an innovative primary school orchestra whilst maintaining an active performing life in various orchestras and as the violist in the Kildale Quartet. Andrew is committed to lifelong learning and recently began learning the trumpet and flugelhorn in order to explore an interest in jazz. He holds an MA in Music and Music Education from Newcastle University.

Douglas Lonie is responsible for conducting and commissioning research and programme evaluations, covering every aspect of the National Foundation for Youth Music's work. Prior to joining the organisation, Douglas was based at the Medical Research Council in Glasgow, where he completed his doctoral studies exploring how music affects young people's health. Douglas has also taught Social Research Methods and Sociology of Music and has experience in a broad range of research methods across music education projects.

Phil Mullen has trained Community Musicians at Goldsmiths College, University of London, since 1990. He is also a freelance Community Musician and trainer specialising in working with children and young people in challenging circumstances. Phil has given presentations on Community Music in 24 different countries around the world and is a former chair of the International Society for Music Education's Community Music Activity Commission. He has an MA in Community Music from York University and is currently a PhD student at Winchester University.

Andy Murray graduated with a first class honours degree in music and quickly became a secondary Head of Music. Top 20 and TV soundtrack successes encouraged him to become an early adopter of technology in the music classroom. This led to various advisory, consultancy and authoring roles with a range of national institutions and government agencies. Andy has enjoyed teaching a broad spread of pupils in a variety of situations, including one-to-one GCSE maths interventions for a local authority and musically gifted and talented students at Wells Cathedral School. He is currently involved in producing online music learning apps with Charanga Ltd.

Jayne Osgood is Professor of Education at London Metropolitan University. She is a sociologist of education focusing specifically on early years and is particularly concerned to research issues of inequality relating to gender, social class and 'race' and to critically engage with educational policy as it affects the workforce, families and children in this context. As a feminist she is committed to developing and applying critical post-structuralist, post-colonial and feminist theorisations to her work.

Catherine Pestano is a community musician and social worker using music in her work in diverse settings with young people and adults. She trained with Frankie Armstrong (Natural Voice Network), Phil Mullen (Goldsmiths College) and Rod Paton (Life Music). Training as a music educator also included the PGCE at the University of Greenwich on the innovative course 'Musicians in Education'.

Emily Sahakian teaches music in a Somerset comprehensive school to the whole 11-18 ability and age range as well as dance to year 7. As a musician-dancer she has a special interest in the role of kinaesthesia in music learning and enjoys the synergies that exist between music and dance. Her samba classes dance the music and all classes sing from the heart. Emily is in the fourth year of teaching. Prior to this she was a student of Cambridge and Bristol universities.

Gary Spruce is Senior Lecturer in Education at The Open University and subject leader for the university's music teacher education course. Prior to his appointment at the university he was a head of music in two large comprehensive schools in Birmingham. He has published widely, including co-editing a number of key texts on music teacher education as well as presenting papers at national and international conferences. Until recently he was co-editor of the *British Journal of Music Education*. He is a practising musician with a particular interest in music for the theatre.

Kate Whitaker is the Project Manager for two of Wigmore Hall Learning's outreach projects: Ignite, described in this book, and Music for Life, working with people living with dementia. She has also managed a successful Community Choir in Paddington and performs regularly as a drummer and percussionist. Kate studied for a BA in Music and Philosophy and an MMus in Music Technology at the University of Leeds and is currently continuing her studies in Developmental Psychology at the Institute of Education, University of London.

Introduction

'Hard to reach', children in challenging circumstances, vulnerable, marginalised, disadvantaged, at risk, beyond the mainstream: these are just some of the many labels for the children and young people talked about in this book. All the phrases seem to give a sense of trouble, of a problem. And yes there is a problem. Far too many of these children are not being treated as children, as individuals, with the right to cultural access[1], to sonic fun, to the musical learning that we all should have.

The International Society for Music Education Commission on Community Music Activity (ISME CMA) mission statement says that 'everyone has the right and the ability to make, create and enjoy their own music'[2] but in far too many countries access to music-making is only for those with money to pay for lessons, or in some more fortunate countries those who attend mainstream school classes and have the capacity to learn music in large groups.

This book is about other children, those who have intellectual challenges, physical disabilities, behavioural, emotional and social difficulties, children who don't live with their parents, who are in hospital, who have had lives full of trouble and even those who cause trouble themselves. They are all children, they can all enjoy and grow through music, they can all learn and develop musically if we, the adults, give them appropriate support and nurture their abilities.

In England it is the role of the relatively newly-formed music education hubs to ensure that all children get a high quality and engaging music education. The National Plan for Music Education includes a section on overcoming potential barriers to engagement[3], and charges the hubs with the responsibility to ensure equality of access to opportunities:

> Through hubs, every child should be able to experience enjoyment and success ... including those who do not have the encouragement or support from their parents/carers, or who need additional support for other reasons[4].

Some hubs are comfortable with this role and are forging ahead with work that is building on years of previous initiatives. Others have wisely brought in experts to help them develop and implement inclusion strategies, while some have been somewhat slower to respond, perhaps because of the magnitude of the changes facing them. It is hoped that this book will be of use to stimulate ideas, develop some knowledge and understanding or perhaps just act as an affirmation to the work developing all across England with children and young people who were previously 'hard to reach'.

The book focuses on a range of issues from questions of equity and social justice (Randall Allsup, Evelyn Grant, Gary Spruce) to questions on what is the pedagogy for working with 'hard to reach children' (Kathryn Deane, Jonathan Govias). Some of our authors focus on specific groups and settings (Catherine Pestano, Helen Chambers, Deb Albon *et al.*, Ros Hawley and others) and others describe how they work with these young people (Gawain Hewitt, Beth Allen, Phil Mullen). There are also many stories of individuals, some of positive transformations and some not (Graham Dowdall, Andy Murray, Emily Sahakian and John Finney). There are accounts of structuring the work (Mark Bick, Andrew Lindley) and of individual projects and methods (Jess Abrams, Kate Whittaker and Ursula Crickmay). There is also a chapter from Doug Lonie of Youth Music on the impact and importance of the work and several chapters on public policy and education and the need to not move backward in our approach (Gary Spruce, Robert Legg). Pointing towards possibilities, Don DeVito recounts his experiences connecting musicians and children around the world to strengthen and deepen the musical engagement of his group of children with intellectual challenges from Florida.

We would like to extend our sincere thanks to all the authors who have given their time and expertise to contribute chapters to this publication. We have deliberately aimed at covering a broad range of issues and practices, though there are inevitably aspects of this work which we have been unable to cover within the space of a single book. We hope that this book will act as an encouragement towards building a world of music educators who work inclusively with all children, whatever their backgrounds or circumstances.

Chris Harrison

Phil Mullen

---

1 UN Universal Declaration of Human Rights, article 27 (1): Everyone has the right freely to participate in the cultural life of the community, to enjoy the arts and to share in scientific advancement and its benefits. http://www.un.org/en/documents/udhr/ (accessed 10.09.2013)

2 http://www.isme.org/cma (accessed 10.09.2013)

3 The Importance of Music: a national plan for music education, paras 36-41. https://www.gov.uk/government/publications/the-importance-of-music-a-national-plan-for-music-education (accessed 10.09.2013)

4 Ibid., para 12.

Engaging the 'hard to reach': issues and challenges

Randall Allsup

This is a summary of answers to some questions posed by the editors.

Hard-to-reach citizens are disempowered persons, whether they are the working poor, the homeless, those alienated and unemployed for whom the structures of government have failed, or in our case the students who have removed themselves from the expectations of schools, youth who find the work associated with school meaningless, alienating, or oppressive. Teachers represent the kinds of middle-class values that have marginalized those individuals who are outside looking in. Youth may be saying, "I don't look or talk like you, I don't like you, what do you want from me?" The problem for hard-to-reach citizens, whether they have been left behind or whether they have removed themselves from societal obligations, is that *disengagement harms everyone*. A participatory democracy is enriched by diversity. The refusal to engage with all citizens, no matter how difficult or costly, no matter how out of reach, is inherently uneconomical; such positioning deprives our collective and individual future of the fullest richness that human interaction makes possible.

Dewey (1900) criticized teachers who only teach facts and figures or who only teach from one point of view. In *School and Society,* he writes that all learners come with certain impulses and interests, and that these needs are a kind of natural resource. These include: 1) social impulses, like the need to communicate and share; social impulses are capable of infinite expansion. 2) constructive impulses – the need to make things that are meaningful and self-reflective. 3) knowledge gathering impulses – the need to find things out; to question and enquire. 4) expressive impulses – the longing to be unique, to make art, to refine and communicate. Failure to teach in such a way that any of these are not activated is like 'leaving money on the table'.

Dewey, of course, was talking about social capital and the enlarging of individual powers, talents, and abilities. He was not referring to neoliberal discourses that see students as future resources for work and employment in an advanced capitalist society. Nonetheless, our lives are defined by meaningful engagement with objects in the world, by work in which we are valued and in which we find personal reward. Schools for Dewey are places where we can find life-enhancing employment, not mere job training sites for post-industrial society.

Hard-to-reach students appear to be idle or removed from social life, I think, because our mostly homogeneous middle-class teaching force cannot see the fullest range of student interests and desires that are present around us. Most schools are not designed to be places where the fullest range of learner identity and employment is valued or sought after; nor is space allotted for the discovery of new desires and identities. The problem for Lisa Delpit (1995) is that most teachers are teaching 'other people's children.' Most teachers are products of a very narrow trajectory that has emphasized obedience and extrinsic reward. They come from a middle-class culture that is decidedly not sexy! Students who are disobedient and unmotivated by grades and teacher approval are unlikely to reveal their own particular fascinations and objects of interest. Nor are they likely to seek out inclusion or to trust that inter-generational dialogue will enhance their needs or approve of their lifestyle.

Even basic concepts that music teachers consider their starting points need interrogation. Even seemingly benign objectives can be ideologically laden. "I just want my students to be musical. All I care about is musicianship. I want my students to be expressive and to use music to communicate." These are worthy goals if hard-to-reach students can have a say in defining what it is to be a musician, and what it is that one wants to communicate. In my mind, musicianship is about the demonstration of known musical codes and an understanding of how to bring a particular musical grammar to life. Today's youth are multi-modal and aesthetic rights and wrongs are often contingent and intentionally unstable. It deserves asking, are teachers trained to work in spaces where the four categories Dewey referred to above are negotiated? Or are we trained to explain and clarify? This is a problem that is larger and more complex than learning popular music or teaching the guitar. I have seen examples in the United States where classes in popular music are taught in the exact same way one would teach a Methodist church choir.

I don't think we are doing a very good job of being inclusive for a variety of reasons. I think that music teachers still see this problem as one of genre. There is this feeling that, if I can only find the right music to bring these multicultural and hard-to-reach students, I will finally break through. Another misconception is that whatever the historical style or cultural genre, we keep thinking that music education is about performing – performing this piece or that, performing this instrument in this style. What if we were to change the discourse altogether and say that music education is *not* about performing but making: constructing, exploring, expressing, and sharing? Making music alone on the computer or phone, sharing it with others, or composing in a group. What if learning instruments was secondary to composing? What if performing was secondary to exploring? What if we learned instruments so we can share what we have made, rather than performing music that some else has made for us?

I am struck by conversations that always end with the same questions. Conversations about multicultural classrooms, culturally-appropriate curricula, and hard-to-reach students always lead to this question: *What should I teach?* In other words, what music do I *bring* to these kids? What if the questions were, what can we make together? What can this class do, with these participants, in this unique combination? What if the outcome of these collaborations did not lead to a performance, but to *more* collaborations and classroom experiments. Of course, there would be classroom performances all the time, but what if quality were contingent, mistakes were laughed off, and the recital hall exchanged for the rug on the floor? What if the goal was invention more than application?

We need to let go of our obsession with pre-approved standards and competitive ratings. We need to stop assessing students on a linear scale from low to high. We need to understand that all musical experiences are valuable – that there may be advanced and beginner experiences and all manner in between, but there are no lower or higher experiences. A classroom of making and doing (rather than applying and performing) would contain such a mixture of experiences that a right versus wrong or low-to-high framework would be a distraction to larger aims.

References

Dewey, J. (1900) *The School and Society*. Chicago: University of Chicago Press. Available at http://ia700306.us.archive.org/12/items/schoolsociety00dewerich/schoolsociety00dewerich.pdf (accessed 09.09.2013)

Delpit, Lisa (1995). *Other Peoples' Children: Cultural Conflict in the Classroom*. New York: New Press

Why music? A research rationale for making music with children and young people experiencing additional challenges

Douglas Lonie

Introduction

This chapter presents a review of recent research literature from across the academic and third sectors exploring the impact of participatory music making for children and young people experiencing additional challenges. These challenges range from socio-economic deprivation, educational exclusion, physical disability, special educational needs, behavioural difficulties and social isolation. Many studies on the wider (i.e. non-musical) effects of music education have focused on mainstream and formal settings. More recently there has been increasing investment in participatory music-making by state and third sector agencies and a broad 'inclusion' agenda has been adopted by music education providers. This has encompassed many learning styles and contexts across a wide range of musics, and significantly expanded the corresponding research and evidence base. There are three broad 'outcome areas' that this research relates to across children and young people's development: the musical, the personal, and the social. These issues are explored in greater detail through relevant published literature and with reference to one large scale participatory music programme, Youth Music Mentors. This review presents a timely analysis of the recent field of practice of music education with 'hard to reach' children and young people whilst acknowledging the continuing need for further empirical evidence relating to the topic.

Non-Formal Music Education in England: A different approach?

Hallam (2010) reviewed a number of studies on the effects of music education on children and young people's musical progression, as well as broader effects on learning and personal development. However, one limitation of published research thus far has been a focus on in-school groups and mainstream settings where participation in music education and research is easier to control and measure. Higgins (2012) and Hallam and MacDonald (2009) report a significant growth in the number of opportunities for music-making and learning taking place outside of formal education for people of all ages and backgrounds, however empirical investigations of these initiatives tend to be more *ad hoc* and sporadic.

The National Foundation for Youth Music (Youth Music) is a funder distributing £10 million of National Lottery money in England annually since 1999. Youth Music has funded more than 3,000 projects working with children and young people aged 0-25, predominantly outside of school hours and focusing on young people facing additional challenges. In addition to funding participation for children and young people, a number of evaluation and research studies have been generated by Youth Music in recent years, often focusing on the development and achievements of those considered to be experiencing 'challenging circumstances'[1]. This type of music-making is broadly referred to as 'non-formal' music education, referring to structured and progressive music-making activities that are facilitated by one or more educators in specific contexts and settings. This type of learning is different to 'formal' music education which relates to more traditional pedagogic approaches (such as didactic learning and master-apprentice models), and 'informal' learning which largely takes place without the guidance of a third-party educator and is less explicitly intentional. Further discussion of the distinctions between formal, informal and non-formal education are provided by the Library of the European Parliament (2013) and, with more specific reference to music education, by Folkestad (2006) and Hargreaves, Marshall and North (2003).

Hargreaves *et al.* (2003) propose that the purpose of all music education, wherever it takes place and however it is structured, is to advance skills in music, but also to develop *self-identity*. They propose an overlapping model for the aims of music education that encompasses musical-artistic, personal and social-cultural outcomes. Group performance and ensemble activities, for example, can develop outcomes across all three domains. It could therefore be argued that the role of the music educator is to explore and have an awareness of how their approach to the learning situation may have an effect on any of these domains. Swanwick (2008) extends these arguments when discussing the qualities and skills required by non-formal music educators, or 'music leaders' as these practitioners are defined in the article. Swanwick's work suggests that music leaders negotiate the learning outcomes on an individual basis that is flexible to the needs of the learner and the learning context, compared to classroom and formal music teachers who often have a set of pre-designed and curriculum-based learning outcomes guiding their interactions with learners. Similarly, the relationships that are developed between music leaders and non-formal learners are reported as being based on the exchange of skills between musicians, rather than as a didactic model where one individual imparts knowledge and skills to the other. In an extension of Hargreaves *et al.* (2003), Swanwick also discusses how the goal of these non-formal music education opportunities is equally and explicitly about the development of personal, social and cultural skills and abilities as it is about the musical development of participants.

Saunders and Welch (2012) published the findings of direct observation of three non-formal settings and concluded that the shift towards 'horizontal' rather than 'vertical' learning styles in non-formal settings was one key difference from music education in formal contexts, reiterating Swanwick's notion of non-formal learning providing greater opportunities for equality in the learning situation. The authors also observed that the communication between facilitator and learner featured less 'teacher talk' and greater instances of modelling technique and 'musical ways of being' (Saunders & Welch, 2012: 116). Their study extends the observations of Folkestad (2006), Hargreaves *et al.* (2003) and Swanwick (2008) by empirically analysing the practices of non-formal educators and learners, albeit across a relatively modest sample.

These findings demonstrate that within music education it is crucial to consider environments and approaches appropriate to the individual needs of learners if they are to develop according to their potential. If we accept Hargreaves *et al.'s* (2003) assertion that the aim of all music education is for personal-social development, as well as musical development, then it is logical to extend the exploration into how music education can function for those individuals with additional personal-social development needs. Indeed, focusing on the social and psychological impact of music education provides the opportunity to understand the broader functions of musical learning and extend that enquiry across broader subjects and disciplines.

Musical, Personal and Social Outcomes in Non-Formal Music-Making

As reviewed by Hallam (2010) there are a number of non-musical effects of music education, and some of these are particularly relevant for children and young people experiencing additional challenges. Motivation is linked to self-perceptions of ability and self-efficacy (i.e. how able a person feels to carry out tasks), and therefore, the higher a person's motivation, the bigger the gains in achievement. Hallam (2010: 9) reports that musical practice is well placed to increase and nurture motivation in children and young people, citing evidence that the motivation and commitment required in instrumental practice is transferred to other learning contexts and subjects.

Self-image, self-awareness and positive attitudes are also related to motivation and success. Better attitudes towards learning and the peer group can also create an increase in social cohesion and improved behaviour, and using music as central to this process can be especially useful for children and young people at risk of disengaging from other aspects of education (Spychiger *et al.*, 1993). Commitment, respect, responsibility and trust have been highlighted as key factors in the success of musical groups, and are recognised as essential skills to be developed through structured music-making (Davidson & Good, 2002).

By providing a way for children and young people to express themselves, music making can also develop emotional intelligence and well-being. Research shows how the physical act of singing can improve mood, increase relaxation and reduce physical and emotional stress (Clift *et al.*, 2008). Importantly, many of the personal and social outcomes described above are also related to improvements in emotional intelligence and well-being. Increased social and cultural capital and increased feelings of self-efficacy and agency are strongly related to psychological well-being and reduced stress (Almedom, 2005). These studies have demonstrated some of the broader effects of music education, but have also tended to focus on mainstream settings and formal models of delivery.

More recent evidence relating to non-formal settings and models is emerging which aims to explain how music can function especially well for those young people facing additional challenges. Dillon (2010) reviewed Youth Music evaluation findings and published evidence relating to the effects of music-making on looked after children and young people, supplementing the findings with a small number of interviews with music leaders and local authority care teams. Dillon notes the caveats associated with this type of review, namely that the reports provided to Youth Music are part of a funding process and therefore may be biased and over-report positive effects. Whilst noting this potential bias, analysis of the reports and interviews revealed a consensus in the types of musical, personal and social outcomes achieved through non-formal music making with looked after children.

Musical outcomes related to instrumental technique and ability, group and ensemble performance skills, singing, solo performance, composition, lyric writing and music technology. Improved personal outcomes reported by participants in these programmes related to increased trust, self-efficacy, self-discipline and commitment. Social outcomes related to improved relationships with peers, carers and practitioners, improvements in teamwork, and greater understanding of opportunities for cultural participation. Combining these three outcome areas together, it was also reported that commitment to projects and the self-actualisation of musical achievement led to participants reporting improved attitudes towards education and an increase in motivation generally. Whilst the models of delivery varied between projects, there were common aspects identified by Dillon, including: clear opportunities for the young people to direct the content and scope of the sessions, providing context on where and how the young learners could progress beyond the project, and ensuring music leaders were equipped with listening skills and an understanding of the broader contexts of the young learners' lives (Dillon, 2010). Crucially, the projects were described as developing in young people those skills that make them more resilient to some of the additional challenges they are facing.

'Resilience' describes 'a set of qualities that helps a person to withstand many of the negative effects of adversity... Bearing in mind what has happened to them, a resilient child does better than he or she ought to do' (Gilligan, 2000). There is a wide range of qualities associated with resilience that develop through a young person's life, including self-esteem, self-efficacy, initiative, faith and morality, trust, attachment, a secure base, meaningful roles, autonomy, identity, insight and humour (Maclean, 2003). While not specifically focused on music education, Gilligan's work (2008) shows that recreational activity can support resilience in a number of ways, for example by offering children in care opportunities to develop a sense of mastery in certain spheres of activity; broadening their social networks; cultivating a set of social roles that may enhance their health and well-being; and developing positive and important social relationships with peers or adults.

Daykin, Moriarty, de Viggiani and Pilkington (2011) conducted a systematic review of evaluations and empirical research relating to music projects with young offenders and those attached to the youth justice system. The authors noted levels of inconsistency in the methods applied to the evaluation of these projects, and highlighted the limitations of generalising the findings as a result. Whilst this made it difficult to make significant claims about the impact of music-making with these groups of young people, the authors did offer a number of trends in the approaches of projects and their self-reported effects. The authors reported that music-making with young offenders offered an opportunity for 'expression and release as well as resources for coping with difficult emotions' and noted how the opportunities offered were designed to meet the musical cultures and identities of the participants. This latter observation was linked to the higher instances of rap and hip hop reported within the projects which the authors reported were used to 'acknowledge their backgrounds and respect 'their' music' (Daykin *et al.* 2011: 5). By working with genres and musical cultures that were familiar to the participants, the projects engaged young people on their own terms and gave them the capacity to direct their learning through lyrical and rhythmic practices that built on their existing musical knowledge. Music was reported as aesthetically engaging young people, encouraging them to explore their identities and participate more fully in the immediate communities in which the activity was taking place (ibid).

These findings were extended by Dickens and Lonie (2012) who conducted a series of focus groups and interviews with young participants taking part in a hip hop project on a deprived housing estate in South East England. Drawing on the political concepts of 'voice' and participation (Couldry 2009, 2010) in musical practice (Toynbee, 2000), the authors explored how young people's voices were developed and amplified through musical participation and lyrical composition. Through working with an experienced facilitator and respected rap musician, the young people were encouraged to explore their emotions and their relationships with each other and with their community through lyrical practice. The findings suggested that following this process of exploring rhythm, tone and structure, as well as achieving high quality musical outputs (e.g. recording and performance opportunities) allowed the young people to develop their own emotional literacies and make a positive contribution to their local community. By validating their musical identities and supporting them to progress musically, the practitioner enabled the young people to transform their perceptions and understanding of their musical and wider selves. Indeed, 'The young participants' accounts... offered vital understandings of the affective qualities of the spaces of musical production in such non-formal educational contexts, but further, showed how the emotional geographies of their everyday lives extended and unfolded through such contexts.' (Dickens & Lonie, 2012: 11).

Dickens and Lonie (in press) explored the significance of space and place in non-formal music projects, contrasting an urban and a rural approach to facilitating rehearsal spaces for young musicians. As with much of the literature thus far reviewed, the findings suggested that despite the physical space in which music making was taking place, it was the pedagogy and the approach of practitioners that led to the positive musical, personal and social outcomes being achieved. In both the urban and the rural settings the main music leaders based their practice on the existing musical identities and experiences of the learners and built the provision from there. Rather than approaching the learning environment as one where the knowledge and skills of the practitioner were to be imparted wholesale to the participants, the music leaders in these contrasting projects approached the learners as existing musicians in their own rights. Dickens and Lonie describe the rehearsal studios as a place where all musicians (i.e. practitioners and participants) shared their practice and mutually reflected on the composition and performance process. The setting was designed as a place where musical experimentation could occur in a safe environment and participants were encouraged to innovate and direct their own musical learning, free from a pre-designed curriculum. Whilst high quality learning experiences and high quality musical outputs were still the explicit aim and intention, what counted as 'quality' was critically engaged in and negotiated by all present, not judged or dictated by the educator or a third party. This egalitarian approach meant that communities of learners emerged and positive relationships were built between participants and with practitioners.

These findings will now be contextualised with a more detailed exploration of a national programme explicitly seeking to develop the musical, personal and social abilities of young people at risk of exclusion.

Youth Music Mentors

Youth Music Mentors (YMM) was a music mentoring programme aiming to improve the life chances of young people, specifically those engaged in or at risk of criminal behaviour and educational exclusion. It was delivered by 18 community and voluntary music organisations across England from March 2006 to March 2011. The programme objectives were:

- to deliver high quality music-based mentoring provision for young people in challenging circumstances
- to provide links to high quality music-making experiences
- to engage and train inspirational music mentors appropriate to the needs of the participants
- to provide young people with opportunities to develop their resilience, social and emotional skills, and enable them to lead successful and fulfilling lives
- to help motivate and prepare young people for routes into education, employment or training

In order to achieve these objectives, each delivery organisation was provided with a handbook describing the ways in which 'at risk' young people could be recruited and engaged in music mentoring. The handbook also described how one-to-one and small group tuition could be provided in order to improve young people's musical development according to their chosen genre or instrument. Each young person was provided with at least ten hour-long music mentoring sessions over a period of at least three weeks, with some interventions lasting up to a year. The mentors were supported financially by Youth Music to take part in training, reflection and practice-sharing sessions, which also provided regular opportunities for learning between the educators to take place.

Youth Music commissioned an independent external evaluation of the YMM programme (Deane, Hunter & Mullen, 2011) which employed a qualitative methodology to explore programme delivery and outcomes. Youth Music also designed and implemented quantitative research tools intended to explore the effects of music mentoring on mentees' musical ability, agency, and active citizenship (Lonie, 2010, 2011).

Lonie (2011) presents a range of dimensions where statistically significant positive changes were observed using a repeated measure design over the course of the programme (i.e. musical ability, awareness of opportunities to make music, mentees feeling listened to, mentees feeling like they make good decisions, and mentees feeling like they have control of their lives). These findings were observed in children and young people experiencing a range of challenging circumstances and support the achievement of the overall objectives of the programme. They are also consistent with previous research into the potential benefits of mentoring programmes in general (Bamford, 2006; Phillip & Spratt, 2007). On this evidence alone it could be argued that the aims of the programme were successfully achieved and that the mentees were now closer to being active citizens better enabled to 'lead successful and fulfilling lives'.

In support, the evidence presented by Deane *et al.* in the external evaluation identified a distinct symbiosis in the nature of personal and musical development achieved (Deane,

Hunter, & Mullen, 2011). Based on 150 interviews with participants, mentors and project managers, the authors argued that the aim and method of each delivery organisation, across all mentees, was primarily musically driven but explicitly framed around personal and social development as per the programme objectives. The authors suggest that the relationships that emerged between the music mentors and the participants were based on the exchange of musical knowledge, and through the development of mutual respect and encouragement further creativity and expressivity were also developed. This process of increasing musical confidence and the resulting ability to be creative and expressive manifested itself in young people becoming more engaged in musical practice within the host organisations as well as wider cultural and community participation.

In relation to outcomes, across all interviews and research sites Deane *et al.* observed music mentoring as having ten main effects:

1. *Engagement* - music as a 'hook', to get young people into the programme
2. *Trust* - the shared interest of music-making; the credibility of the mentor as a respected musician
3. *Transferable skills* - communication skills, giving and receiving criticism, increased confidence, developing resilience
4. *Success* - doing something well and getting praise for it; stepping out into the professional world
5. *A safe place* - developing a community with peers and adults
6. *Social pedagogy* - room for a more equal relationship between mentor and mentee
7. *Telling the tale* (expressing yourself) - most directly with rap lyrics, but seen in music generally
8. *Therapeutic aid* - music not as therapy, but as therapeutic
9. *Creative cooperation* - not only in group projects but also creating music with the help of a mentor
10. *Personal reflection* – on life challenges, understanding of self, and the art they do

(Deane *et al.* 2011:12)

Deane *et al.* suggest that rather than music being merely an 'instrument' for personal or social change, music-making is the intrinsic process through which change occurs. Through developing their musical expression and creativity, mentors and mentees were able to develop a range of externally measurable social and personal outcomes. Mentees were not 'done to' or 'instructed' in how to become more active or employable citizens, but through the process of having their creativity nurtured and facilitated in a trusting relationship, began to recognise the validity of their 'voice' and the range of ways in which it could be heard (Deane *et al.* 2011; Lonie 2010, 2011).

Consequently, it is suggested that musical and personal or social outcomes of non-formal music education in such contexts are inexorably related. As Deane *et al.* note:

> There is a higher level on which music works. Music is a communication system, an art beyond words. Recognition of development can be a look or just knowing. In

music groups people change, become more competent, become cool, realise a different identity: this can be known by a group even if not necessarily verbalised. This concept is that the act of making music is intrinsically a mentoring one (2011: 50)

Alongside the developmental value of gaining music skills, the manner in which mentoring relationships developed was also a key success factor. Mentors were instrumental in motivating the mentees and encouraging them to recognise the value of their own creativity. Lonie (2010, 2011), following Hallam (2005), discusses how intrinsic motivation is one of the key elements fostered in music mentoring and how this allows young people to validate their experiences and perspectives. He argues that it is in providing mentees with a safe space to acknowledge and develop their expressive abilities (building on trust and personal knowledge) that music mentoring flourishes.

The evidence from the Youth Music Mentors project suggests that music learning in this context is a key way to enable genuine decision making. Rather than disengaging through participation in an enforced model, these young people took the opportunity to make themselves heard, with music providing the device through which this happened. The mentors enabled the young people to identify their own agency and supported the mentees to validate their opinions and self-efficacy. As Deane *et al.* (2011) describe, this is a form of agency facilitated through the act of music making.

Discussion

The research discussed above highlights a growing field of enquiry relating specifically to participatory music-making outside of the school classroom, often with children and young people experiencing additional challenges in their lives. Following the work of Hargreaves *et al.* (2003) it has been argued that such music education is *explicitly* linked to the development of self-identity, as opposed to some more formal styles of music education through which self-identity is developed *implicitly*. Indeed, as suggested by Folkestad (2006), the impact of non-formal music education on outcomes other than musical ability may be directed more by the intentionality of the educator and the setting in which it takes place than by the basic facts of learning new musical skills.

Music education in the examples discussed above is providing the tools by which young people, particularly those in challenging circumstances, can alter their understandings of their identities and their situations. Rather than explicitly tackling the conditions of material poverty, physical illness, or disability often experienced by young people facing additional challenges, the music project serves as a way of raising consciousness and expressive ability, facilitating a deeper understanding amongst the young people of their own abilities and providing opportunities to communicate and connect with other people. Since many of these young people are disengaged from some of the more formal aspects of education and mainstream cultural participation, projects like those discussed above highlight the importance of validating the musical identities and cultural forms that young people of all backgrounds embrace and encourage deeper thought and wider development amongst music education providers. At the heart of non-formal pedagogy and many of the opportunities provided to young people experiencing additional challenges is a recognition of the validity of that person's voice, and developing musical mechanisms by which to understand, amplify and validate that voice.

The notion of separating out and isolating outcomes and effects of music education is challenging and must be approached with caution. As much of the literature discussed above suggests, it is in the very act of music making and the development of musical skills, technique and understanding, that broader personal and social effects take place. Whilst some studies have aimed to focus on 'other than' musical development for young people, this is not instead of, or at the expense of, musical development. Indeed, to value one 'set' of outcomes over another is to devalue the richness of musical development itself. It may also risk the situation that for some young people there can be a focus on musical development, whereas for others, expectations of musical ability, and ultimately excellence, are compromised as personal and social outcomes are given greater weight in the learning opportunities offered and reported. This false dichotomy may then dictate which musical opportunities are offered to which young people, perpetuating a stratified offer of music education based on false perceptions of their musical potential and identity.

The theory and practice discussed above goes some way towards developing an understanding of how pedagogy is one of the main elements of engaging young people experiencing additional challenges in musical learning. However, there is an ongoing need for further empirical research relating to the topic, and also a need for many in music education to challenge their own perceptions and engage in such discussions.

References

Almedom, A. (2005) Social capital and mental health: An interdisciplinary review of primary evidence. *Social Science & Medicine* 61(5): 943-964.

Bamford, A. (2006) *The Wow Factor: Global research compendium on the impact of the arts in education*. Münster : Waxmann Verlag.

Clift, S., Hancox, G., Staricoff, R. & Whitmore, C. (2008) *A systematic mapping and review of non-clinical research on singing and health*. Sidney De Haan Research Centre for Arts and Health, Canterbury: Canterbury Christ Church University.

Couldry, N. (2009) Rethinking the politics of voice. *Continuum e-Journal of Media & Cultural Studies 23(4): 579-582*.

Couldry, N. (2010) *Why Voice Matters: Culture and Politics after Neoliberalism*. London: Sage.

Davidson, J. & Good, J. (2002) Social and musical co-ordination between members of a string quartet: An exploratory study. *Psychology of Music 30(2): 186.*

Daykin, N., Moriarty, Y., de Viggiani, N. & Pilkington, P. (2011) *Evidence Review: Music Making with Young Offenders and Young People At Risk of Offending*. London: Youth Music.

Deane, K., Hunter, R. & Mullen, P. (2011) *Move On Up: An evaluation of Youth Music Mentors*. London: Youth Music.

Dickens, L. & Lonie, D. (2012) Rap, Rhythym and Recognition: Lyrical Practices and the politics of voice on a community music project for children experiencing challenging circumstances, *Emotion, Space and Society,* http://dx.doi.org/10.1016/j.emospa.2012.11.003

Dickens L. & Lonie, D. (in press) Rehearsal Spaces as Children's Spaces? Considering the place of non-formal music education. In S.Mills & P. Kraftl (eds.) *Informal Education and Children's Everyday Lives: Geographies, Histories and Practices*. Basingstoke: Palgrave Macmillan.

Dillon, L. (2010) *Looked After Children and Music Making: An Evidence Review*. London: Youth Music.

Folkestad, G. (2006) Formal and informal learning situations or practices vs formal and informal ways of learning. *British Journal of Music Education* 23(2): 135-145.

Gilligan, R. (2000) Adversity, resilience and young people: the protective value of positive school spare time experiences. *Children and Society* 14(1): 37-47.

Gilligan, R. (2008) Promoting resilience in young people in long-term care – the relevance of roles and relationships in the domains of recreation and work. *Journal of Social Work* 22(1): 37-50.

Hallam, S. (2010) The Power of Music: its impact on the intellectual, personal and social development of children and young people. In S. Hallam & A. Creech (Eds.), *Music Education in the 21st Century in the United Kingdom* (pp. 2-17). London: Institute of Education, University of London.

Hallam, S. & Creech, A. (Eds.). (2010) *Music education in the 21st century in the United Kingdom: achievements, analysis and aspirations.* London: Institute of Education, University of London.

Hallam, S. & MacDonald, R. (2009) The effects of music in community and educational settings. In S. Hallam, I. Cross & M. Thaut (eds.), *The Oxford Handbook of Music Psychology.* (pp.471-80) Oxford: Oxford University Press.

Hargreaves, D., Marshall, N. & North, A. (2003) Music education in the twenty-first century: a psycholgical perspective. *British Journal of Music Education,* 20(2): 147-163.

Higgins, L. (2012) *Community Music: In Theory and In Practice,* Oxford: Oxford University Press

Lamont, A., Hargreaves, D. , Marshall, N. & Tarrant, M. (2003) Young people's music in and out of school. *British Journal of Music Education,* 20(03): 229-241.

Library of European Parliament. *Validation of non-formal and informal learning.* http://libraryeuroparl.wordpress.com/2012/12/07/validation-of-non-formal-and-informal-learning/ [accessed 01.08.2013]

Lonie, D. (2010) *Attuned to Engagement: The effects of a music mentoring programme on the agency and musical ability of children and young people.* Paper 1. London: Youth Music.

Lonie, D. (2011) *Attuned to Engagement: The effects of a music mentoring programme on the agency and musical ability of children and young people.* Paper 2. London: Youth Music.

Maclean, K. (2003) Resilience: What is it and how children and young people can be helped to develop it. *The International Child and Youth Care Network,* 55.

Phillip, K. & Spratt, J. (2007) *A Synthesis of Published Research on Mentoring and Befriending.* Mentoring and Befriending Foundation/University of Aberdeen.

Saunders, J. & Welch, G. (2012) *Communities of Music Education.* London: Youth Music/iMerc, Institute of Education.

Spychiger, M., Patry, J. Lauper, G., Zimmerman, E. & Weber, E. (1993) Does more music teaching lead to a better social climate. In R. Olechowski & G. Svik (eds.) *Experimental research in teaching and learning.* Bern: Peter Lang.

Swanwick, K. (2008) The 'good-enough'music teacher. *British Journal of Music Education,* 25(1): 9-22.

Toynbee, J. (2000) *Making Popular Music: Musicians, Creativity and Institutions.* London: Arnold.

Notes

[1] *Children and young people in 'challenging circumstances' are defined by Youth Music as those who are often marginalised by society, vulnerable, may be 'hard to reach', or have fewer opportunities to participate in mainstream cultural opportunities.*

Challenges and possibilities: Engaging 'hard to reach' families with young children

Deborah Albon, Kim Allen, Sumi Hollingworth and Jayne Osgood

This chapter will report on some of the findings of a Youth Music funded study which we conducted in order to examine the engagement of 'hard to reach' families with children under five years in early years' music making, and aimed to establish what components of early years' music-making could be replicated in other contexts in order to encourage greater participation of parents and their young children. The study consisted of three main strands of enquiry: a review of the existing literature; an investigation of practice in relation to engaging 'hard to reach' families with young children; and finally, an action research strand. For the purposes of this short chapter we will not elaborate on the methodology of the study but refer the reader to the full report (Osgood *et al.*, 2012) for further detail. However, of particular interest was one of the strategies employed in the study, which involved interviewing a range of parents living in low income areas (mostly working class families, not all of whom attended formal music-making activities) about their families' engagement with music and music-making. In presenting data, all references to parents, music educators, and other professionals in the study use pseudonyms.

Following a brief consideration of the notion of 'hard to reach' in relation to families with young children as well as some situating of the research within the wider early years' context, our intention is to focus on a few of the challenges of working with families deemed 'hard to reach', emphasising that organisational settings and programmes can be alienating or 'hard to reach' for some families (Landy & Menna, 2006). In the final part of the chapter we examine some of the implications for practice of the study's findings, drawing on data from the action research phase of the project.

The early years' context

Engaging 'hard to reach' families in the UK has its roots in policy developments enacted under successive Labour governments from the late 1990s. In essence, the central aim was to improve the life chances of children from disadvantaged families through targeted investment into early years' programmes: a position which is premised on the idea that children's earliest years are of *particular* significance to their later outcomes (Marmot *et al.*, 2010; Field, 2010). Indeed Gulløv (2012) argues that the work of early childhood settings is seen as a panacea for addressing an ever-widening range of social problems.

As a result of this, there has been a growth in programmes aimed at both increasing parental involvement in their children's education as well as improving parenting skills. In such a context, the notion of families being 'hard to reach' is considered by policy makers to relate to those families in need of assistance in order to lift themselves out of deprivation (Boag-Munroe & Evangelou, 2010). A key initiative in this area has been the Sure Start programme, which has at its core the aim of supporting families with young children with a particular emphasis on those families living in areas of deprivation. The notion that some families are 'hard to reach' evolved in recognition of the challenges statutory services experience when trying to engage families who have significant needs (ibid).

So, who is considered to be 'hard to reach' in such a context? Generally, the term refers to those groups who occupy a marginal or excluded position outside the mainstream of society and this may include young parents, travellers, lone parents, and families living in poverty, to name but a few. Criticism of the notion of 'hard-to-reachness' can be levelled at the way the term suggests a deficit view of particular groups as 'vulnerable' or 'having complex needs' which can somehow be 'fixed' easily. In such a context it is families themselves, as opposed to services which aim to engage with them or indeed *wider issues of inequity*, that come to be regarded as problematic (Archer *et al.*, 2010). As a result – if we take the example of working class families –they are regarded as requiring 'support' with and surveillance of their parenting skills, unlike their middle-class counterparts, and the underlying economic source of their disadvantage is left unchanged (Gillies, 2013).

But to re-imagine services and institutions as exclusionary as opposed to the families they work with involves a shift in thinking (Landy & Menna, 2006). In the early years' context especially, the idea of the 'parent-as-partner' is pervasive, but as Reay (2005) has shown, it is often white, middle-class parents who dominate education services and are seemingly 'more engaged' than parents who do not share their background. Similarly – as we will see in the next section - in early years' music-making contexts, our study found that despite their best efforts, there is a tendency for music educators to privilege white, British, middle-class norms and practices in relation to music making (Osgood *et al.*, 2012, 2013).

This brief overview of the wider context in which early years' music-making provision is positioned suggests that this provision faces many challenges when trying to engage with families deemed 'hard to reach'. Drawing on some data from the Youth Music study, we will now examine some of these challenges further.

Key challenges

In this section, we first aim to draw on interview data from parents in our study. The data indicates a keen interest in music amongst these families, which was sometimes at odds with the kinds of music and interactional style favoured by some music educators. Secondly, we will draw on data from music educators to highlight the challenges they face when trying to work in partnership with professionals who work with children and families.

Contrary to the idea that music-making is a middle-class activity, our study found that music-making was embedded in the daily routines of the homes of each of the families we interviewed as opposed to being a structured activity requiring dedicated practice such as learning to play an instrument. For the black, minority ethnic and working class families we interviewed, music-making occurred in myriad ways such as listening to CDs in the car, singing along to the radio and, in the case of families who attended church, singing and dancing as part of services.

The music practices of the home sometimes contrasted markedly with those of sessions organised by music educators. In the action research phase of the project (project three –

discussed later), Monica - a Brazilian parent - commented that when at home, she liked 'sexy Brazilian music' and that she liked to 'dance sexy' to it, to the amusement of her children. She laughed at the possibility of such music and dance being introduced into a session at the Children's Centre. Similarly, Vicky - a white British working class parent – described the way her children like to move to pop music: 'shaking, wiggling, laughing and giggling' as well as making fun of their father's playing of heavy metal anthems on his electric guitar (see also Osgood *et al.*, 2013).

Families listened to popular music via a range of mediums such as CDs, radio, Spotify and video. In one family, Vicky talked of her children having their own sections for the music they liked on her iPod. The idea that 'interventions' should be made into families' lives is often premised on the idea that very young children are especially vulnerable (Shallwani, 2010), yet many parents such as Vicky pointed to their children's *competence* as music 'consumers'. Children had their own favourite pop tunes and parents noted how their children sang along to their favourites informally at home, albeit that their parents expressed concern over some of the content. Some parents stressed the potential of incorporating pop music or music from children's television programmes into music-making sessions and contrasted this with the rather dry and 'boring' music choices of some music educators in their programmes for young children.

This finding mirrors Young *et al*'s (2007) evaluation of the Music One-to-One Project, which found that middle-class, white, often older mothers were keen to engage with music-making provision. They found that parents are more likely to engage with music-making provision when it uses and values the kinds of music genres and practices they are familiar with as well as activities in keeping with their own style of parenting.

This sense of the unwritten 'rules' of music sessions being compatible with one's style of parenting was also very evident in our study. For instance Sarah (a white British, middle-class mother) was concerned about her children having:

> …much more of a shorter attention span and they wander off and don't really get the idea of having something structured… now I'd be a pariah from that group *[one she had attended]* because there's no way I could keep my children under control and so no-one would benefit from the session.

By way of contrast, Mark and his partner (also a white British, middle-class family) were less concerned with this even though they too recognised that their child was often the 'least engaged' during music sessions. These parents seemed to favour play-based pedagogies and a more 'relaxed' style of parenting. Mark was not troubled by his child's wanderings during sessions – perceiving these as 'normal' – whereas for Sarah, such wanderings were the cause of anxiety, not least as she felt subject to the scrutiny of other parents in the group. Whilst we found that both middle-class *and* working-class families highlighted the challenges they face in being parents of young children, it is working-class families who come to be labelled by professionals as leading 'chaotic lives' and having problematic parenting styles (Gillies, 2005).

Our study found that parents on low incomes in particular expected music educators to be well-organised and accomplished musicians as well as skilful in engaging very young children in music-making – a point we further develop later in this chapter. This is indicative of the multiple and complex array of knowledge and skills required of music educators working with young children and their families. In order to justify spending money on music sessions and mobilising themselves and their children to attend regularly, parents were keen that this complex set of skills and knowledge should be evident.

Music educators in the study were often acutely aware of how they might be perceived by parents and in an extract from an email blog from the action research phase of the project, James describes the difficulty he faced in engaging with parents in a school setting in a deprived area, recognising both class differences between himself and the majority of the parents coupled with the institutional authority he represents as a professional working in a school context. James also recognises that his relationship with families relates to a particular agenda – in this instance an agenda in which he is expected to engage both children and families – and he regards this as a 'danger' but nevertheless a key factor in forging and maintaining a relationship with families for the life of the project.

> One reception teacher took me out to playground when children were being brought in and introduced me to lots of parents from their class. Next week will do the same thing. Still feels slightly uncomfortable, some obviously more enthusiastic than others, but can feel very much that I'm from a different world: I am like one of the teachers, representing an institution, and that's a difficult barrier to break – I'm obviously different from them [white British, male, and middle class]. In their situation, what would make me want to come in and see what's going on?... With best intentions I could come over as an awfully smiley idiot who is only saying 'hello' because he wants something from them (which is of course true). So have to avoid this danger.

Similarly, in case study two (a university town in S.E. England) the Artist in Residence argued that music leaders and artists need to lose their 'expert persona' and emphasise the *co*-construction of projects. With this in mind, he spent weeks building relationships with families in an early years centre as a precursor to involving them directly in the construction of a Musical Sculpture Garden.

Challenges also present themselves at a more strategic level as music educators working with families and young children are often working in highly complex environments. In our study we found that Children's Centres were often the site in which music sessions were delivered, yet these comprise a complex mix of different professionals, some of whom are not educators; a range of provision on one site – some working more with adults than children; and a mix of universal and targeted provision (a point we develop later). Similarly, at the local authority level, there may be a range of structures for music provision, early childhood education provision (including the voluntary and statutory provision) and family support. The scoping exercise undertaken during the study across England demonstrated that this differs between local authorities and between Children's Centres within a local authority. And these structures change over time. For music educators wishing to engage with young children and their families, we suggest that there is an especially complex and fluctuating array of provision and professionals to navigate.

However, it should not be assumed that similar kinds of provision have similar levels of parental participation. One music provider noted that in the many schools he works across, some actively encouraged parental involvement whereas in others, parents might be expected to leave their children at the gate – keeping their 'involvement' to a bare minimum. As someone providing music sessions once a week for a defined period of a few weeks, it is very difficult to shift the attitudes of such schools towards parental participation if this is not already embedded in their practice.

Another linked difficulty relates to sustaining relationships with other professionals working with families of young children. In West London, two of Jane's music projects are situated in Children's Centres and she consistently invites early years' staff to evaluation meetings about the project as she regards their input as invaluable owing to their knowledge of the children and families as well as early childhood practice. She noted:

> No-one from either group is attending despite my invitation. This is a repeated problem, as with all my projects. Families or centre workers can only commit to the time they have at the site. This meeting is outside the site since we need time away from the children to explore the next step.

We have not done justice to the challenges this poses for educators who aim to work with families of young children deemed 'hard to reach' but there are two points we would stress here in relation to working with other professionals. First, a huge amount of time and effort is needed in order to navigate a path through the vast array of provision that comprises early education and care, music education and family support/services in some areas. Second, in a time of austerity, relationships that are built between music educators and key professionals are often severed when local authorities undergo restructuring exercises with inevitable job losses or changes in role and location. For a project in the South of England aiming to engage with Roma families in the area (outlined later), local authority restructuring meant the Roma support worker, seen as key to establishing and maintaining relationships with this community, was moved to another area. It took a great deal of time and effort to re-negotiate her inclusion into the music project.

Implications for practice

We can see from the previous section that are some significant challenges for music educators to negotiate when trying to engage families with young children regarded as 'hard to reach'. In this final section, we will draw especially on the data from the action research phase of the study as it was during this phase of the project that three settings reflected on their on-going practice. The three projects are as follows:

- **Project 1:** A project in the South of England working from a school and children's centre with the aim of engaging Roma families with young children
- **Project 2:** Two reception classes in two separate primary schools (part of a much larger, well established music project working with children and their parents – notably in areas of deprivation across East London especially)
- **Project 3:** An established music organisation in West London which works with children who are hearing impaired in a children's centre as well as two other children's centres – engaging families with young children

A number of key themes emerged in the study: for the purposes of this brief chapter we will focus on just a few. Although we would emphasise the broader context of inequalities within which some families come to be marginalised and the challenges this presents to music educators trying to engage with them, we do think there are some ideas for practice derived from the projects which might prove useful to others.

Relationships are forged over time

Relationships are of *central* importance to engaging with families. They are forged over time rather than through short term 'interventions', not least as the reputation of projects which have proved popular develops gradually through 'word of mouth'. For new music projects, it can take time to establish relationships with key professionals but more significantly, with families and particular communities. Our study found that music educators who are parachuted in to work with particular communities may lack such connections. And this leads to our next point.

Knowledge of particular communities

Being a recognisable member of the community is important when trying to engage families with young children in music-making. In action research project one, it was regarded as of central importance to work closely with a family worker – Florica - who is also a member of the Roma community, in order to make links with a group who are perceived as especially 'hard to reach' not least as she shares a language with the group.

However, maintaining an open mind as to one's 'knowledge' of a particular community is important. For example, it is vital to avoid making assumptions about the kinds of music families listen to on the basis of their ethnicity and class. In action research project one, the music educators noted that many of the older Roma children enjoyed listening to rap or R&B music like many of their White British peers. In addition, young children's musical interests should not be viewed as automatically synonymous with those of their families – they may well have different musical tastes to their parents and older siblings. Therefore music providers need to be attuned to the children and families that make up the local communities within which they are situated and need to listen to families with regard to the music-making activities that happen within their homes and communities.

Universal or targeted provision?

Music projects steer a fine line between making their project available to all, risking being taken over by middle class families, and targeting families deemed especially 'in need', risking alienation and potentially low attendance. Generally, our study found that services which are universal rather than targeted at particular groups are viewed as less stigmatising. Parents were seen as more likely to attend music sessions when encouraged informally by their *peers* (i.e. other parents) as opposed to being 'referred' by professionals. And this is also linked to the venue chosen for early years' music-making. A wider range of families seemed to be attracted to sessions when on 'neutral territory' such as libraries or other community venues, as opposed to settings such as Children's Centres, whose remit includes targeting, engaging and monitoring particular families in their 'reach'.

But there may be occasions when targeting music sessions can have greater success. In one of the case study projects, the Children's Centre Manager described a music project aimed at young mothers, pointing out:

> Some of the girls have tried other sessions that are open to all but they always come back and say that they felt they were being stared at and judged. This is a very middle-class town so that's got a lot to do with the way people see young mums.

In action research project three, Jane tried to negotiate the notion of universal versus targeted provision by advertising her project on a notice-board *within* the Children's Centre and encouraging the family support worker to urge families regarded as 'harder to reach' to attend on a personal basis. Her prior experience was that when she advertised her project more publicly, her sessions were dominated by middle-class families.

Developing relationships with key professional partners

Relationships with key partners such as Children's Centres are also important. In project two, the music leader worked closely with early years' staff to maximise parent participation at a workshop as his involvement with the setting was on a weekly basis whereas the early years' staff saw families on a *daily* basis:

> I suggested to teachers that the children create invitations for the parents' session, for their own parents. Teachers seemed to think this was a good idea. They will *carry on* talking to the parents about the project.

Working in partnership with other professionals also involves respecting each other's skills and knowledge. As one project leader remarked, 'early years' staff are rarely musically trained and music staff lack the early years training.' In project three, Jane spent time after a session discussing a particular child with a family support worker, Samira. Jane was able to share what she had seen in relation to his musical ability and Samira was able to share her knowledge of working with families of Somali origin as well as her knowledge of this particular child.

Sharing what children have been doing with parents

Whilst strategic planning is important, attention to the minutiae of developing relationships with families can be significant – such as careful consideration of tools for communication. This is exemplified in James' work in project two. In the emailed blog he kept, he states:

> Since previous session, teachers had put pictures up outside classroom of the session for parents to look at. There has been a lot of interest, with parents asking about what had happened. I again went out to meet the parents as they brought their children in for the day, and had a quick chat to a few of them. Feel I'm beginning to know who's who amongst the children a bit more.

Here we can see that displays can be a useful way of encouraging parents to engage with music-making programmes, particularly if they include photographs of children participating in such activity (with the caveat that there is parental approval for the use of photographs). Displays also had the advantage of enabling parents and children to continue their interest in the early years' music-making project when the project leader was not present. Video technology was also used in the project and played as children and parents arrived in the morning to show the work children had been doing. When reflecting on these different strategies, James stressed the importance of the 'personal touch'; celebrating the achievements of children with their parents through informal conversation, displays and video-footage.

Jane (project three) similarly stated that she would:

> ...do a little video film of what they all did, join them all together and have a movie event, to make them [the parents] think "wow, music really is great!" in conjunction with a note book of snippets of what they [the children] can do, did, enjoy, have fun with - not a nasty, prescriptive, corporate looking book that enchants only the back of a reference library stock room.

Whilst ideas such as these offer promising avenues for practice, it is important to remain mindful that some parents may be wary of contributing to a book or display, or may not want to be filmed, and may be unclear as to the expectation of what the children's contributions might be or how they might be regarded by others in the group.

Opportunities to socialise

Building in informal opportunities for socialising with other families alongside music activities is another important avenue that seems to increase engagement. Some projects made a point of offering refreshments during the session, including comfortable seating for mothers who needed to breast-feed. In project three, which targets families in which one of the children is hearing-impaired, parents ran the refreshment break part-way through each session and introduced other non-music making activities, such as sharing a story or more 'active' play. This enabled the music educators to either talk informally with parents or reflect together on how the music session had been received so far and whether any tweaks needed to be made to the planning for the second part of the session. We would suggest that the sense of ownership of the project displayed by these parents is indicative of the many years the project had been running. As noted earlier, relationships take time to develop.

The structure and formality of the session

Parents interviewed in the study stated a preference for sessions that were informal and flexible, that did not require a long-term commitment or payment long in advance. Sarah, for instance, valued music sessions where there were some other activities available for the children, notably for babies who might accompany their families to sessions. In project three, Jane was happy for children to run up and strum her guitar and would follow the children's musical lead if their musical explorations led away from the planned ideas for the session.

The study found that overly structured sessions and an expectation that families adhere to 'rules' of punctuality and 'active' participation from children and parents throughout sessions can be off-putting for some families. In project two, James noted that whilst children readily picked up percussion instruments left out to play, parents were usually reluctant to do this and often seemed embarrassed when this was suggested.

Engaging children and their parents

The final point we wish to make here relates to the challenges music educators experience when engaging with children *and* their parents. As noted before, parents value music educators who have an appreciation and experience of working with very young children alongside their music competence and organisational ability. Music educators need to be able to engage with very young children as well as those (usually adult family members) who care for them. And this can pose some interesting dilemmas. James (project two), for instance, noted the degree to which seating arrangements impacted on forging relationships with children and parents:

> Either we are on the floor, working with the children, so it's hard to engage the (standing) parents, or we are standing trying to engage the parents and not working with the children. Seems tricky to find the right balance.

Seating was the focus of much reflection. In the end, one music educator led with the children, seated on the floor, whilst one of the early years' practitioners greeted parents, whilst standing, offering them either a comfortable chair or floor to sit on. Over the weeks, they swapped roles at the beginnings of sessions to enable the music educator to interact with parents more freely.

Conclusion

There are no 'easy answers' to engaging with families with young children deemed 'hard to reach'. Yet at the present time, the thrust of policy is directed towards easy solutions and 'what works' (Gillies, 2013). Whilst our research established some areas of practice that might usefully be disseminated across projects, we do not see these as prescriptions for all music educators to follow uncritically and would stress the need to be responsive to local communities. Crucially, we would emphasise the need for a shift in attitudes towards conceptualising *early years' services* (including music services) rather than *families* with young children as 'hard to reach'. In the latter part of this chapter we have highlighted the practice of music educators who are continuously engaged in reflecting on how they might develop their practice in order to engage with young children and their families as opposed to thinking the 'fault' of lack of engagement resides within families.

In addition, we have emphasised the importance of establishing and sustaining relationships with parents/carers, children and the range of professionals who work with young children and families. This requires careful consideration at the strategic planning stage, at the level of sessional planning, and when responding to children and their parents during the sessions themselves.

Finally, the research and ideas for practice presented here suggest the need for reflexive practitioners, who are willing to re-appraise their attitudes and practice towards *all* the families with whom they work. But as Burman (2006: 324) has persuasively argued in relation to action research, it is important to exercise some caution against reflexive wanderings, not least as 'talk has become the walk: the researcher's reflection on the action *is* the action'. It is, after all, all too easy to reflect on what one might do to improve practice in order to engage with families with young children who are deemed 'hard to reach', but another thing to enact those changes. Both reflection *and* action are important. Therefore, reflexivity needs to be coupled with a commitment to making a difference to the lives of marginalised collectivities, including families deemed 'hard to reach'. With this in mind, we hope that this chapter has stimulated thinking as well as given ideas for ways forward in practice.

Acknowledgements

Thanks go to Youth Music for funding the study and most especially to the parents, music educators and other professionals who gave their time to the study.

References

Archer, L., Hollingworth, S. & Mendick, H. (2010) *Urban Youth and Schooling: The Identities and Experiences of Educationally 'At Risk' Young People*. Buckingham: Open University Press.

Boag-Munroe, G. & Evangelou, M. (2010) From Hard to Reach to How to Reach: A Systematic Review of the Literature on Hard-to-reach Families. *Research Papers in Education* (iFirst Article): 1-31.

Burman, E. (2006) Emotions and Reflexivity in Feminised Action Research. *Educational Action Research*, 14(3): 315-332.

Field, F. (2010) *The Foundation Years: Preventing Poor Children Becoming Poor Adults: The Report on the Independent Review on Poverty and Life Chances*. London: Whitehall Cabinet Office.

Gillies, V. (2005) Meeting Parent's Needs? Discourses of 'Support' and 'Inclusion' in Family Policy. *Critical Social Policy* 25(1): 70-90.

Gillies, V. (2013) From Baby Brain to Conduct Disorder: The New Determinism in the Classroom. Paper given at *Gender and Education Association conference*, London South Bank University, April 25th 2013.

Gulløv, E. (2012) Kindergartens in Denmark: Reflections on Continuity and Change. In A.T. Kjorholt & J. Quortrup (eds.) *The Modern Child and the Flexible Labour Market*. London: Palgrave Macmillan.

Landy, S. & Menna, R. (2006) *Early Intervention with Multi-Risk Families: An Integrative Approach*. Baltimore: Paul H. Brookes.

Marmot, M. (2010) *Fair Society, Healthy Lives*. London: The Marmot Review.

Osgood, J., Albon, D., Allen, K. & Hollingworth, S. (2012) *Engaging 'Hard to reach' Parents in Early Years Music-Making*. London: Youth Music.

Osgood, J., Albon, D., Allen, K. & Hollingworth, S. (2013) 'Hard to Reach' or Nomadic Resistance? Families 'Choosing' Not to Participate in Early Childhood Services', *Global Studies of Childhood 3(3), forthcoming*.

Reay, D. (2005) Mothers' Involvement in their Children's Schooling: Social Reproduction in Action? In G. Crozier & D. Reay (eds.) *Activating Participation: Parents and Teachers Working Towards Partnership*. Stoke on Trent: Trentham.

Shallwani, S. (2010) Racism and Imperialism in Child Development Discourse: Deconstructing 'Developmentally Appropriate Practice'. In G.S. Cannella & L. Diaz Soto (eds.) *Childhoods: A Handbook*. New York: Peter Lang.

Young, S., Street, A. & Davies, E. (2007) The Music One-to-One Project: Developing Approaches to Music with Parents and Under Two-Year-Olds. *European Early Childhood Education Research Journal* 15(2): 253-267.

Participation, Inclusion, Diversity and the Policy of English Music Education

Gary Spruce

Introduction

This chapter will examine English music education policy and innovation over the last thirteen years from the perspective of participation, diversity and inclusion. For the purposes of this chapter, participation, diversity and inclusion are understood as a triumvirate which are fundamental to social justice. Social justice, from a music education perspective, is defined here as the democratic engagement of individuals and communities in music education programmes, curricular documents, projects and initiatives. This democratic engagement is manifest through the involvement of individuals and communities in deciding what is worthwhile musical 'knowledge' and how that 'knowledge' is best learnt. Democratic engagement and hence social justice is dependent on access to what Habermas calls 'emancipatory knowledge' (McLaren, 2012: 7). Emancipatory knowledge enables individuals and communities to recognise and understand the power-relationships that exist in their world and to draw on this understanding as a means of interacting with, and fully participating in, that world.

The premise of this chapter is that the first decade of this century was a period of innovation and initiatives which laid the seeds for a paradigm of music education which was socially just and inclusive. However since 2010 this has given way to a more reactionary policy which has the potential to be exclusionary rather than inclusive. The chapter will begin by attempting to gain some conceptual purchase on what is meant by the terms 'participation', 'inclusion' and 'diversity' in the context of a socially just approach to music education. These terms will then be used to examine music education since the turn of the millennium in terms of its propensity for social justice. The chapter will conclude by considering briefly the implications of this for 'hard to reach' young people.

Participation, Diversity and Inclusion: Conceptual clarifications

> "When I use a word," Humpty Dumpty said, in rather a scornful tone, "it means just what I choose it to mean- neither more nor less."
>
> (Lewis Carroll, *Through the Looking Glass*.)

The discourse around music education and social justice is dominated by the concepts of 'participation', 'inclusion' and 'diversity'. These three terms are regularly appropriated by governments and other legislative and quasi-legislative bodies as a means of rationalising and legitimising policies, and by pressure and interest groups (including organisations representing music education) as part of the rhetoric of advocacy. However as Quick and Feldman (2011) point out, there is typically a lack of clarity about what these terms mean and also in what ways they differ. As they say, 'participation' and 'inclusion' are often understood as being virtually synonymous, with 'diversity' being an inevitable and natural consequence of effective 'participation'. They contend however that 'participation' and 'inclusion' are 'two independent dimensions' (ibid: 272) and that whilst effective participation enriches the input received, inclusion is about creating a community that is able to implement decisions and to 'make connections between people, across issues and over time' (Ibid). Their proposition is that whereas there can be participation without inclusion there cannot be inclusion without participation. They also argue that both elements have distinctive natures and that the presence of both *together* can result in much richer diversity by ensuring that both *diverse representation* and, importantly, *diverse perspectives* are brought to the community discourse.

Although Quick and Feldman were writing about public engagement in policy decision-making, their definitions and distinctions have much to offer education in general and music education in particular. So how might their conceptual definitions be understood in the context of music education?

They define 'participation' as being formed of three aspects:

- 'increasing input' (op. cit: 274) through making a project accessible, inviting people to take part and ensuring that those participating are representative of the particular constituency within which the project is located;
- supporting participants in 'learning the practices, tacit and explicit, intended and unintended, that make one part of a community'(op. cit: 273-4);
- enabling newcomers to play a dynamic role in reconstituting and renewing those practices.

Opportunities for participation are fundamental to an inclusive music education. In order for these opportunities to be to be considered as educational however they need to support the participant in learning and understanding the particular music practices which are being engaged with (this relates to issues of pedagogy) and, from a social justice perspective, for these practices to be dynamic and negotiable, not fixed and immutable - in other words as practices that the participant can act upon. It is thus necessary for particular music practices themselves to be dynamic and open to renewal.

'Inclusion' is different from 'participation' in that it is about the conditions which allow individuals to be able to adopt this dynamic role in reconstituting and renewing practices. Quick and Feldman suggest that a community with a disposition towards inclusion is characterised by:

- a recognition that there are 'multiple ways of knowing';
- the involvement of individuals in constructing process, content and decision-making;
- temporal openness.

'Multiple ways of knowing' recognises that there are multiple musical practices in the world which reflect the various ways in which different individuals and communities engage with music. It also recognises that musical meaning is socially and culturally constructed not just through the inter-relationship of music's sonic materials but in the way music is used in various social and cultural contexts. A socially just music education recognises, values and supports different ways of musical knowing but also seeks to enhance the ways of knowing of those who learn music, firstly through deepening their understanding of the music in which they might be socially embedded and secondly by broadening their knowledge and understanding of other musical practices. What a socially just model of music education does not do is to seek to impose a particular practice or 'way of knowing' on a community or social group as being in some way inherently superior.

'The involvement of individuals in constructing process, content and decision making' involves issues around the extent to which pedagogy promotes a relationship between the learner and the teacher, where the voice of the learner is enabled to be heard in deciding 'what' is to be learnt and 'how' it might be learnt. It is important also to consider *whose* voices are being heard and especially whether the voices are heard of those who experience alienation from, or who are less successfully integrated into, for instance, the school. For example, Arnot and Reay (cited in Flutter, 2007: 350) suggest that teachers can benefit most from listening to those pupils who are less articulate and/or do not achieve particularly well in formal education. This aspect lies at the heart of a socially just approach to music education in that the voice of the learner is key to their involvement in the construction of knowledge through dialectical engagement with teachers and with their own and the teachers' worlds.

'Temporal openness' is Quick and Feldman's perhaps rather opaque way of expressing the idea of a lack of imperative for closure. This is manifest in music education in two ways. The first is through the recognition that many musical practices do not involve musical completion in the sense of the production of an object or piece of music. (Turino, for example, identifies one of the characteristics of 'participatory practices' as music that '… tends to be in open form' (Turino 2008: 37) with 'feathered beginnings and endings' (ibid: 59)). The second, and most important, way is through what Freire (1970: 65) describes as 'The unfinished character of human beings and the transformative character of reality [that] necessitate that education be an ongoing activity'. Thus musical learning in its widest sense is a lifelong, continuing and always incomplete endeavour.

In summary, then, a music education that has a disposition towards social justice will demonstrate some at least some of the following characteristics:

Table 1: A Conceptual Framework for Social Justice in Music Education

Participation	• The opportunity to take part in music
	• The opportunity to learn, understand and engage with the practices of a particular music culture and tradition
	• The openness of music practices to change and for that change to be instigated by 'newcomers' to the practice
Inclusion	The willingness of musical projects, including curriculum design to :
	• Acknowledge and value multiple ways of musical knowing;
	• Involve participants dialectically in constructing knowledge and pedagogy
	• Recognising musical learning as a lifelong endeavour
Diversity	• Diversity of participation
	• Diversity of perspectives

Drawing on these conceptual ideas and the paradigm of social justice set out at the beginning of the chapter, I will now examine the developments in English music from the turn of this century in terms of the extent to which they reflect a disposition towards social justice and a propensity for reaching out to all children.

2000-2010: a renaissance in music education

Writing in 2006, in a chapter updating Bernarr Rainbow's seminal book on the history of music education, Cox (Rainbow with Cox, 2006: 379) noted reasons for 'optimism for music education' and pointed to four developments which he felt justified this view:

1. A research project which indicated that music in the curriculum was highly valued by teachers and young people and that young people were heavily engaged in informal music making beyond the school (Lamont, Marshall, Hargreaves & Tarrant, 2003)

2. A return to government funding for music services through the Music Standards Fund, part of which was to be used to meet David Blunkett's pledge of 2001 that 'over time all pupils in primary schools who want to will be able to learn a musical instrument' (DfES, 2001: para. 2.15)

3. The founding of an organisation, eventually to become Youth Music, whose remit was to support organisations working with young people's informal music making out of school, particularly in areas defined as being of 'social and economic need' (Rainbow with Cox, 2006: 380)

4. The launch of the Music Manifesto whose broad aims were to provide a framework for bringing together the many agencies and organisations involved in music education in England in order to 'deliver a universal music education offer to all children, from early years onwards, where they can take an active part in high-quality music making' (Music Manifesto, 2006: 7)

The Music Manifesto also argued for greater support to be given to singing in schools resulting in £40 million of Government money being invested in a national singing programme, Sing Up, focusing on promoting singing in primary schools.

The second Music Manifesto report had as one of its core aims, to enable 'young people to help shape music provision through consultation, participation and leading the music of others' (Music Manifesto, 2006: 29). There is here an understanding that participation is defined by more than simply the physical presence of young people in a musical project or event. It should also involve including them in decision making about their music education.

Cox describes these initiatives as being indicative of 'an increasing emphasis upon providing wider opportunities for musical *participation*' (my emphasis) (op. cit: 379). He also identifies a greater diversity of performing opportunities for those pupils involved in 'extra-curricular' musical activities in school. He would also have been correct to point to the increasing representation of music from traditions and cultures other than western art music in curriculum music lessons.

Two developments in music education that occurred too late to be considered in any detail by Cox were the National Strategy for Music (DfES, 2006) and Musical Futures.

Both of these in different ways contributed to the embracing of musical diversity and increased opportunities for participation.

The National Strategy for Music was one of a series of 'strategy' documents for all national curriculum subjects which, although non-statutory, sought to influence teachers' pedagogy. It aimed to address a 'perceived lack of significant improvement in practice and ... a general unresponsiveness to the curriculum set out in 1999'. (Finney, 2011: 125). As Finney goes on to say, 'underpinning the Strategy was a central focus on developing musical understanding, understanding of musical conventions as they exist within musical traditions, genres and styles and as experienced through and referenced to musical activity' (ibid: 127).

Although not explicitly stated, the kind of pedagogies promoted by the Strategy broadly reflected a 'praxial' view of music which holds that music cannot be understood exclusively - or even primarily - in terms of its sonic materials but rather 'in relation to the meanings and values evidenced in actual music-making in specific circumstances' (Elliott, 1995: 131). A 'praxial' approach to music education thus has the *potential* to be 'inclusive' in Quick and Feldman's terms in that it allows for 'multiple ways of knowing' through engagement with, and recognition of, the multiple musical practices, values and processes that are present in the world's music.

This praxial approach provided an opportunity to address a long-term issue in music education relating to participation, inclusion and diversity. Although the music curriculum in many schools had for some years included the *products* of popular, traditional and non-western musics, some teachers' pedagogies ignored the musical practices and values which lay at the heart of their production and reception, continuing instead to teach according to the values and procedures of western art music. In short, although the music curriculum included a wider variety of music it often valued only one learning process, or 'way of knowing', and therefore limited participation (as defined here) to those for whom that way of learning and knowing was familiar. Thus, although the Strategy had the potential to allow for 'multiple ways of knowing' it remained tied to the idea of the pupil as 'a recipient of a top down managed curriculum' (Finney, 2011: 131).

An alternative and more democratic approach to the learner/teacher relationship came with the 'Musical Futures' project. Funded by the Paul Hamlyn foundation, Musical Futures was rooted in Lucy Green's work on informal learning and the ways in which popular musicians learn music. Both Green's work and the Musical Futures project sought to address many young people's disillusionment with formal music education by supporting teachers in introducing informal pedagogies into the classroom. According to Green (2008: 10), these informal pedagogies are characterised by:

- allowing learners to choose the music themselves
- learning by listening and copying recordings
- learning in friendship groups with minimum adult guidance
- learning in personal, often haphazard ways

Informal pedagogies significantly reconfigure the conventional relationship between 'the teacher', 'the learner' and 'what there is to be learnt', with the learner becoming a key agent in the construction of knowledge. Musical Futures thus addresses the second characteristic of Quick and Feldman's definition of inclusion - that of involvement of individuals in 'constructing process, content and decision-making' (op. cit).

From the perspective of temporal openness, the breaking down of barriers between 'school' music and music in society as a whole and the rooting of music education in 'real' musical practices resulted in a growing recognition of music education as not being bounded by the formal curriculum but continuing beyond school both temporally (beyond school hours and beyond the years of formal schooling) and spatially (taking place in arenas other than the school). In addition, in many documents of the period, the importance of music education as a lifelong endeavour was consistently emphasised.

Considering, finally, the two aspects of 'diversity' identified by Quick and Feldman, evidence of diversity of participation could be witnessed by the increasing numbers of young people who were beginning to engage with music education in its broadest sense and the different perspectives brought both by these young people and the increasingly diverse range of teachers and musicians who, in and out of school, were supporting their music education.

Over the course of the decade, music education in England had passed through a period of arguably unprecedented change. There had been a significant increase in funding for music education from both government and independent organisations and a concomitant increase in the range and numbers of people involved in music education including formally qualified teachers, musicians in the community and performing musicians. In addition there was a growing commitment to increasing participation of young people in music and music education tied, importantly, to an increasing role for the voice of the learner and recognition of the multiple ways of knowing, understanding and engaging with music offered by the diversity of musical practices in society and beyond the school. The synergy between participation, inclusion and diversity held out hope for a music education which might justifiably lay claim to being democratic and embodying social justice. Cox's reasons for optimism remained.

The National Plan for Music Education – a policy of exclusion?

The beginning of the second decade was marked by the publication, in November 2011, of 'The importance of music: A national plan for music education.' (DfE, 2011, hereafter referred to as the NPME). The NPME not only reconfigures the way in which music education is structured and organised, but also establishes a new relationship between external music and music education organisations and schools and articulates a philosophical and ideological framework for music education both within and beyond school.

In analysing the language of the NPME, I have pointed to its almost exclusive focus on performing, with 'progression … almost always framed within the context of developing performing skills and more often than not exemplified with reference to groups most closely associated with western music practices: typically, choirs, bands and orchestras – the latter being mentioned twenty times' (Spruce, 2012b). Fautley (2012: 6) makes a similar observation when he writes that 'composing-related words occur in single digit counts, listening likewise, whereas performing-related words are well into double-digits, whilst improvising and creativity warrant hardly a mention'. Also unmentioned are informal pedagogies/learning and 'inclusion'. Although the NPME acknowledges the existence other musical traditions its examples and case studies are almost exclusively those of western art music.

The NPME thus privileges and promotes a relatively limited way of musical knowing, rather than the multiple ways of knowing which characterise inclusive music education practices. Furthermore, this particular way of musical knowing, rooted in the practices of western classical music, does not readily allow for the 'the involvement of individuals in constructing process, content and decision making' (Spruce, op. cit) or the deployment of informal learning pedagogies.

To understand fully the ideological underpinning of the NPME, it perhaps needs to be seen as part of the government's wider education policy agenda. One of the key aspects of this agenda is the promotion of particular types of knowledge as being inherently of greater worth than other types of knowledge and the 'distancing' of knowledge from many children's social context such that they are unable to make connections between their learning and their lived experiences. This 'distancing' is achieved either temporally through, for example, the proposed emphasis on Romantic poets in the GCSE English literature specification, or by the abstraction of knowledge from 'real life' situations/social contexts e.g. removing the debates around climate and atomic energy from, respectively, the geography and science national curricula.

It is arguable that the intention in promoting this kind of abstract, distanced knowledge is to resist learners' acquisition of 'emancipatory knowledge' (McLaren, 2012:7). Emancipatory knowledge poses a particular threat to the status quo in that it is knowledge which McLaren suggests 'helps us to understand how social relationships are distorted and manipulated by relations of power and privilege' (ibid). This understanding then leads to what Freire (1974) calls 'conscientisation' which is the process whereby an individual comes to see the world not as fixed and immutable but 'as a dynamic phenomenon upon which, and within which, a person consciously acts in the construction of knowledge and understanding' (Spruce, 2012a: 191). Emancipatory knowledge is also central to 'participation' and 'inclusion' as defined within this chapter. For it is through acquiring emancipatory knowledge that individuals can become involved in 'reconstituting and renewing practices' and develop an awareness of 'multiple ways of knowing'. Where knowledge is distanced from the lives of the learners, education then becomes simply a process of induction into the value systems of dominant groups with inclusion taking place only 'under the terms of those with the power to decide the nature of [that] inclusion' (Rix, 2013: 251).

In promoting a narrow concept of music making and music education (limited ways of musical knowing) the NPME has the potential to provide a framework, rationale and legitimation for a curriculum where 'other' musics are included only under the terms of the western art music paradigm. This then excludes the musical histories and identities of those social and cultural groups whose musical practices do not reflect the practices of western art music, resulting in the 'distancing' of many young people from musical 'knowledge' as it is presented in formal music education contexts. Music education then becomes primarily a process for inducting young people into the hegemonic practices of western art music thus returning music education to the exclusionist practices described by Green (2008) earlier in this chapter.

Conclusion

In this chapter I began by attempting to gain some conceptual clarity around those terms (participation, inclusion and diversity) that are so often associated with the discourse of social justice and then to use this to identify some characteristics of socially just and unjust approaches to music education. In focusing on music education policy since the turn of the millennium and the dangers to an inclusive and socially just approach to music education posed by the NPME, I have tried to demonstrate that a socially just approach to music education is a prize hard won but easily lost. The chapter should not be read as an 'attack' on the place of western art music in music education. Rather its argument is that western art music ought not take for itself an hegemonic position within music education whereby it becomes the 'sun' around which all other musics orbit. Jorgensen (2003: 121) ponders whether Suzanne Langer's view that 'There are no happy marriages in art - only successful rape' holds equally true with musical genres and traditions, concluding that it probably does.

Cassell and Nelson (2013) suggest that as part of the neo-liberal agenda, institutional education (by which they mean state-promoted education) becomes '…an apparatus of society …[that]…function[s] to isolate, transform and eradicate the expression of cultures of resistance'; in other words, perhaps, to eradicate emancipatory knowledge. There is a danger that the NPME, with its strong support for initiatives such as In Harmony and the particular way of 'musical knowing' that these programmes promote, will have the effect of 'eradicating' from music education the *practices* of those musical traditions and cultures which 'resist' the hegemonic domination of western art music. If we are to learn what history would teach us, then what proceeds from this is the alienation from music education of many young people who see what they prize in music as not being valued or respected.

In striving for a socially just approach to music education we should perhaps keep at the forefront of our thinking Regelski's view that the core purpose for music education should be something that adds value so 'that students are *newly able or better able to "do" music*' as a result of that education' and that 'this approach implies, then, building on the music backgrounds students bring with them to school, not "redeeming" them from their existing musical dispositions and practices' (Regelski, 2005: 21).

References.

Cassell, J.A. & Nelson, T. (2013). Exposing the Effects of the "Invisible Hand" of the Neoliberal Agenda on the Process of Sociocultural Reproduction. *Interchange* 43: 245-264.

DfE (Department for Education) (2011) *The Importance of Music - A National Plan for Music Education*. London: DfE.

DfE (2013) The National Curriculum: in England: Framework document for consultation. London: DfE.

DfES (Department for Education and Skills) (2001) *Schools Achieving Success*. London: DfES.

DfES (2006) *National Strategy: Foundation Subjects: Key Stage 3* Music. London: DfES.

Elliott, D. (1995) *Music Matters*. Oxford: Oxford University Press.

Fautley, M. (2012) Music Education Hubs and CPD. *National Association of Music Educators Magazine* (36): 6-8.

Finney, J. (2011) *Music Education in England 1950-2010: The Child-Centred Progressive Tradition*. Farnham: Ashgate.

Flutter, J (2007) Teacher development and pupil voice. *The Curriculum Journal* 18(3): 343-354.

Freire, P. (1970) *Pedagogy of the Oppressed*. London: Penguin.

Freire, P. (1974) *Education for Critical Consciousness*. London: Continuum.

Green, L. (2003) Music Education, Cultural Capital and Social Group Identity. In M. Clayton, T. Herbert & R. Middleton (eds.) *The Cultural Study of Music: a critical introduction*. London: Routledge.

Green, L. (2008) *Music, Informal Learning and the School: A New Classroom Pedagogy.* Aldershot: Ashgate.

Jorgensen, E (2003) *Transforming Music Education.* Bloomington and Indianapolis: Indiana University Press.

Lamont, A., Hargreaves, D., Marshall, N. & Tarrant, M. (2003) Young people's music in and out of school. *British Journal of Music Education* 20(3): 229-41.

Lave, J. & Wenger, E. (1991) *Situated learning: Legitimate peripheral participation.* Cambridge: Cambridge University Press.

McLaren, P. (2013) Critical Pedagogy. In J. Soler, C.S. Walsh, A. Craft, J. Rix & K. Simmons (eds.) *Transforming Practice: critical issues in equity, diversity and education.* Stoke on Trent: The Open University and Trentham Books.

Music Manifesto (2006) *Making every child's music matter: Music Manifesto Report 2. A Consultation for Action.* London: Music Manifesto.

Philpott, C (2010) The Sociological Critique of Curriculum Music in England: Is Radical Change Really Possible. In R. Wright (ed.) *Sociology and Music Education.* Farnham: Ashgate.

Quick, K. & Feldman, M. (2011) Distinguishing Participation and Inclusion. *Journal of Planning Education and Research* (31): 272-290.

Rainbow, B. with Cox. G. (2006) *Music in educational thought and practice.* Woodbridge: The Boydell Press.

Regelski, T.A. (2005) 'Music and Music Education: Theory and praxis for 'making a difference'. In D. Lines (ed.) *Music Education for the New Millennium - Theory and Practice: Futures for Music Teaching and Learning.* Oxford: Blackwell.

Rix, J. (2013) From equality to diversity? Ideas that keep us quiet. In J. Soler, C. Walsh, A. Craft, J. Rix & K. Simmons (eds.) *Transforming Practice: critical issues in equity, diversity and education.* Stoke on Trent: The Open University and Trentham Books.

Spruce, G (2012a) Musical Knowledge, critical consciousness and critical thinking. In C. Philpott & G. Spruce (eds.) *Debates in Music Teaching.* London: Routledge.

Spruce, G (2012b) Unanswered Questions: A Response to the National Plan for Music Education. *National Association of Music Educators Magazine* (35).

Turino, T. (2008) *Music as Social Life: The Politics of Participation,* Chicago: The University of Chicago Press.

Hard to Reach, Harder to Let Go: a practice of social action through music inspired by Venezuela's el Sistema.

Jonathan Govias

> *For Releife of aged impotent and poore people, some for Maintenance of sicke and maymed Souldiers and Marriners, Schooles of Learning, Free Schooles and Schollers in Universities, some for repaire of Bridges Portes Havens Causwaies Churches Seabankes and Highwaies, some for Educacion and preferment of Orphans, some for or towards Reliefe Stocke or Maintenance of Howses of Correccion, some for Mariages of poore Maides, some for Supportacion Ayde and Helpe of younge tradesmen Handicraftesmen and persons decayed, and others for reliefe or redemption of Prisoners or Captives, and for aide or ease of any poore Inhabitantes concerninge payment of Fifteenes, setting out of Souldiers and other Taxes. (Jones, 1969)*

With this grand preamble, the Statute of Charitable Uses of 1601 legally defined the extraordinary range of charities in Elizabethan England, setting the stage to enact the means for their oversight. Even in 1601, oversight was overdue: a nineteenth century commentator noted that by the time of the law, 'A self-regarding system of relief had superseded charity, and it was productive of nothing but alms, large or small, isolated and unmethodic, given with a wrong bias and thus almost inevitably with evil results.' (Loch, 1910)

Plus ça change: today, in the face of massive government deficits, so-called austerity programming has renewed attention on social policy, its outcomes, and how rarely the two are connected. In 2012, forty-eight years after Lyndon B. Johnson declared his 'War on Poverty' the American federal and state governments collectively spent nearly $1 trillion (£650 million) on anti-poverty measures (Tanner, 2012). If disbursed directly, that sum would provide an instant cash payment of over $20,000 to each of the forty-six million Americans living in privation, yet poverty in the nation remains endemic. More to the point, there's no evidence that such a handout, aside from its political or philosophical unpalatability, would be any more effective in the long term. In an era of large alms and small results, the great challenge of the social sector is not finance: it's reaching the right people the right way.

The idea of a population being 'hard to reach' goes far beyond the obvious issues of financial or physical accessibility. The very process of applying for social services may be intrusive and humiliating, sometimes deliberately so, with the intention of creating psychological barriers. Cultural or spiritual hurdles can manifest if the nature of the services offered conflicts with traditionally held beliefs or values, especially in the spheres of health care and education. Finally, once all other obstacles have been surmounted, the final "reach" problem, the effectual barrier, remains: whether the social service actually delivers the benefits or impact that it promises.

The Venezuelan national youth orchestra network, known internationally as *el Sistema*, stands as a fascinating effort to solve the multiple "reach" problems. With over 400 music schools offering free ensemble-based instruction across the country, the Fundación Musical Símon Bolívar has made huge strides in reducing the barriers of finance and geography. Psychologically, its participants see their association with its ensembles as a source of genuine pride and socio-cultural capital. With its focus on musical activities alone, the Fundación has no direct religious or political messaging or connotations. At the human level, its programming is expanding to encompass special needs groups and other marginalized populations, including the incarcerated. Its activities now integrate multiple musical art forms beyond the Western European, including jazz and indigenous traditions. But what is most intriguing and ambitious about the organization – and the many emulations it has inspired internationally – is its self-identification primarily as a social service. In making explicit an association between ensemble music and positive social development, *el Sistema* promises a new approach to music education with the potential to transcend the final reach problem too.

It is an extravagant claim, but one not without foundation. In *The Power of Music*, essentially an annotated bibliography of utility research, Susan Hallam presents the various established individual and social benefits of group music making. The paper mentions 'discipline, teamwork, co-ordination, development of skills, pride, lifetime skills, accomplishment, cooperation, self-confidence, sense of belonging, responsibility, self-expression, creativity, performance, companionship, building character and personality, improving self-esteem, social development and enjoyment' as just a partial cross section of the outcomes (Hallam, 2010). The list is remarkable, but in strengthening *Sistema's* fundamental premise, it simultaneously reveals a critical weakness. The benefits Hallam cites are those associated with established modes of music education, not specific or unique to *Sistema*. Yet even while enumerating the advantages, Hallam concedes that the reach problem for conventional methods remains unsolved, and that the research fails to take 'account of those who have not found [music making] an enjoyable and rewarding experience.'

There are therefore major questions facing *Sistema*-style music education. In light of the established impact of conventional models, can *Sistema* offer something in addition, or something different? Moreover, in offering something different, can *Sistema* programmes close that final 'reach' gap?

In order to answer those questions, some definition or description of the practice within *Sistema* is necessary. This is a surprisingly challenging task. The Fundación in Venezuela operates in a pedagogically decentralized manner, allowing its faculty to address local challenges as they see fit, and has as a matter of policy resisted any efforts to formalize or systematize the national activities. This has resulted in an extremely varied practice particularly between programmes beyond Venezuela describing themselves as modeled after or inspired by *Sistema*. From a research perspective, external efforts to deconstruct the work of the Fundación therefore parse the structural attributes, the perceived philosophical principles, or some combination of the two. The model I proposed in 2011, entitled 'The Five Fundamentals of El Sistema' (Govias, 2011) was an attempt to differentiate the work in Venezuela from the conservatory-style or private sector approach to music education on a purely organizational level. In the article I advanced five critical areas of distinction, the first being the declared objective of the Fundación Musical Símon Bolívar to achieve social transformation through the pursuit of musical excellence. The remaining four constituted the following: a focus on group music making; high frequency of contact; the elimination of the twin barriers of aptitude and finance; and the creation of a broad network of opportunities to allow students long-term involvement in the programme. While the framework succeeds in capturing accurately the operational characteristics of the programme in Venezuela, what it does not do is define specifically any mechanics that produce social action. This element is communicated solely by intention, via the first Fundamental. Remove the expression of intent and the word 'music' from that Fundamental, and the remaining bullet points may well describe the operational premise of the average state-funded school system. Intention is critically important, but on its own it is insufficient to distinguish the practice of *Sistema*, or social action through music, from current in-school music education models.

If the *Five Fundamentals* and similar deconstructions might be considered 'operational' in nature, the contrasting approach may best be described as 'aspirational.' While citing many of the same structural attributes, these latter models often place further emphasis on intangible objectives, such as the need for music-making to be a joyful pursuit in which passion for the art should take precedence over technical considerations. A group of *el Sistema* advocates at Boston's New England Conservatory also addressed the function of program leadership, identifying what they believed to be a new professional archetype in which teachers assume the multiple roles of 'Citizen, Artist, Teacher and Scholar.' (ElSistemaUSA.org, 2010). Individually or collectively these aspirations are laudable, but they become problematic, if not offensive, if they are proposed as qualities unique to the practice in Venezuela or within *Sistema* programmes, as sometimes happens. In such a context they could be taken to imply that conventional music educators have no interest in cultivating a lifelong love of the discipline in their students, or possess no desire to develop their personal craft as performers and pedagogues. Both assertions are patently false, and even if presented as a philosophical code to which every teacher in every discipline should aspire, they too remain statements of intention only. Like the *Five Fundamentals,* they fall far short of describing the mechanics in any specific manner, like listing the ingredients for a cake without supplying measurements, the mixing order or the bake time and temperature.

The failure of both models to outline a workable theory for the practice of *Sistema* or to define a unique result raises an extremely difficult question. If structurally *Sistema* is no different in its activities from school music education systems, how can it claim a different outcome? And if the intention is only to intensify or refine the existing benefits of music education, results in fact borne out by some of the formal evaluations of Sistema programmes, could the ends then be better and more cost-effectively served through improvement and expansion of the existing systems?

The absence of a testable hypothesis of *Sistema* does not dispel the idea that something more, something special might still be accomplished. One final model of some popular traction is the belief that *Sistema* entails some element of magic. If this is truly the case, then by definition it requires the intervention of the supernatural for the purposes of explanation or reproduction, and thus lies beyond the purview of most music educators and researchers. (Just don't call it voodoo, as one British scribe had the temerity to do, thereby inciting the cyber wrath of some inconsistent *Sistema* adherents. (Toronyi-Lalic, 2012)) There is something ineffably inspiring about the Venezuelan orchestras in performance, particularly their physical intensity, but the idea of *Sistema* as magic is in practicality an expression of the failure of our imagination, a concession that the mechanics or even the potential of the practice are not yet understood. As the third of Arthur C. Clarke's Three Laws states, 'Any sufficiently advanced technology is indistinguishable from magic.' (Clarke, 1962) Perhaps *Sistema* is simply too new a technology.

Certainly, the children in Kalkaji, a slum in suburban New Delhi, must have originally considered the Windows desktop they found embedded in a wall in 1999 to be of supernatural origin and functionality. Its capacity to capture ideas graphically or in text, deliver entertainment in the form of interactive games, or retrieve knowledge via its internet connection would have seemed miraculous to a demographic group entirely bypassed by the early information era. Yet the machine was conquered, its magic demystified over the course of the experiment as the children playing with it developed a real understanding of the tool *and* the knowledge to which it connected them. In the absence of any formal teacher or guide, the learning processes for these youth were those of exploration and experimentation, driven by the children's natural instinct to share and show, if not show off to one another. The brainchild of researcher Sugata Mitra, this combined social, technological and educational experiment and its subsequent iterations offer an intriguing insight into the vast potential of new modes of learning in which the primary vehicle is informal social interaction, instead of formal instructor intervention. (Mitra, 2003)

Mitra's experiments do more than reintroduce the social element to the process of learning: they reveal the critical importance of time. In a subsequent, more controlled version of his original experiment, researchers observed that over an average two hour daily session of *shared* computer usage, the children devoted only twenty percent of the time (barely twelve minutes!) to the available academic content, using the remainder for activities such as gaming or browsing. (Mitra & Dangwal, 2010) Such a perceived waste of time would drive any teacher to distraction, even though the educational outcomes were eventually measured as equivalent or superior to those of the public school system over the 150 days of the study. Mitra's research established that with the right setting and the right balance of resources, children instinctively organize informal learning environments that can be as effective as classrooms with qualified teachers.

At their heart, Mitra's experiments may reflect a technology unfamiliar not through its modernity but through its antiquity, if not its centuries-long institutional renunciation: the innate, longitudinal nature of learning. Humans are biologically hardwired to acquire knowledge through frequent, long-term social interactions with competence models: in short, we learn best through observation, imitation and repetition. This simple rubric forms in part the basis of Albert Bandura's *Social Learning Theory,* in which he ascribes learning to the four codependent elements of attention, retention, repetition and motivation (Bandura, 1971). Bandura's choice of terminology is not just an academic paraphrasing, but an effort to emphasize the cognitive processes involved over the physical, hence his inclusion of the critical element of motivation.

Bandura's psychological framework for learning stands in stark contrast to the reality of most musical or academic teaching. The predominant modus operandi is one of 'telling,' a model rooted in millennia of tradition. A respected elder talks, the supplicants listen; a teacher instructs, the students obey. Whether in the lecture hall or music studio this method retains the benefit of tremendous efficiency, assuming a sufficiently advanced and self-motivated student body. But as a means of schooling, this model is in fact an entirely artificial construct, bearing no resemblance to how children naturally learn things like how to walk, talk, play games, or interact with their environment. This is why the school system, for all its frequency, group classes, accessibility and connectivity (Four out of Five Fundamentals), generally produces negligible or occasionally negative social impact: the socialization process requires passive obedience, not active collaboration. The relationship that is habitually modeled by teachers is authoritarian, rather than cooperative. No criticism of teachers should be inferred from this statement. In an era marked by a paucity of resources and an excess of high-stakes testing, educators often have very few alternatives.

It is through Bandura's lens that we see the potential convergence of the worlds of music and Mitra. What Mitra proposes, in his words a 'Self Organized Learning Environment' (SOLE) (Mitra & Dangwal, 2010), could well also be called a *Social Learning Environment* (SLE), although the respective managerial and cognitive emphases of each title remain relevant, and warrant combination. Self-Organized Social Learning Environments are a natural extension of how children instinctively learn: by first watching others model a behaviour or action, then remembering it, and finally trying it repeatedly on their own – a process to which music is eminently suited. For example, a sectional rehearsal, in which a small group is engaged in exactly the same activity or mastering the same skill, offers perfect conditions for social learning to take place. The forum encourages focused observation, but also facilitates informal, non-hierarchical demonstration, exchange and adoption of ideas. Full rehearsals extend this process, but the integration of the musical product adds both purpose and enjoyment, providing the essential motivation required to drive those characteristics of attention, retention and repetition identified by Bandura. Social learning environments can be effected in many disciplines, but ensemble music is the only one that can easily accommodate many students, is fundamentally physical, and inherently motivational thanks to the repertoire.

Unfortunately, the reality often falls far short of such an ideal. Contrary to current *Sistema*-sector thought, the use of an orchestra or other ensemble does not in itself automatically create the optimal context for social learning or impact. Historically the orchestra is perhaps the most anti-social model of group action and cultural expression, both nature and source of the problem elegantly captured in the title of David Ewen's book *Dictators of the Baton*. But the tyranny of the orchestra is ultimately no different than the tyranny of the classroom, both products of the extreme premium placed on time. Conversely, *Sistema* programmes are justifiably proud of the immersive nature of the experience they offer students, with contact several hours a day, multiple days a week over the year. This luxury of time presents a tremendous opportunity, as yet unrealized, to create a true practice of social action through music, rooted first and foremost in social learning.

Such a practice entails unfamiliar, and at times more challenging roles and responsibilities for teachers. Contrary to what the phrase 'social learning' might imply, a degree of hierarchy is always essential; there must be some variance in expertise as a necessary condition of the modeling process. The critical corollary to that point is that the hierarchies that form are implicit, dynamic and highly context-sensitive, with right of leadership granted on the basis of knowledge or ability to meet a specific need. In the words of Mitra, they should be 'self-organized' instead of externally dictated. In the past, a number of *Sistema* commentators have proposed the concept of 'peer instruction' as an important element of the programme, but the terminology they choose accurately reflects their very different vision of the practice, one of 'teacher substitution.' In implementation, this idea, reflecting the adage that 'the student who knows five notes teaches the one who only knows four,' has become a rationale for placing children in temporary or long-term positions of explicit authority over their colleagues. They are often given roles, or even titles such as 'mentor,' in which they serve exactly the same function as a teacher, but without possessing the requisite training or maturity. Apart from subverting the social and self-organizing processes, this bestowing of preference or creation of hierarchies is not just unnecessary in nations with developed music education infrastructure, but it could conceivably have many more negative outcomes than positive.

At the most simple end of the spectrum of teacher responsibility, Mitra's research established the need for what he described as a 'mediator,' an observer whose sole function is to inquire about the progress of the activities, or to supply an appreciative audience for learner demonstrations. This model of minimal intervention, which helps keep students on task without dictating their activities or externally imposing a hierarchy, may work best in an environment where the content can be pre-moderated through technology, or in small groups of focused physical activity such as instrumental practice. However, as the contexts change, so do the exigencies of the leadership role. The addition of more individuals to the environment means simply that the processes of social learning must be modelled and illuminated, if not carefully scaffolded.

In defense of the orchestra as a medium of social change, its problems, or that of any musical ensemble, are inherently social problems. Issues of intonation, balance, or synchronization all imply a failed relation; a musician must be out of tune or too loud or soft *in comparison to* another musician, a section must be rushing or dragging *in contrast* with another. It is the manner in which the problems are resolved that makes the difference. The function of a mediator, or more accurately, a facilitator, is to re-establish failed connections both aurally and visually – the latter not by demanding obedience and obeisance to the focal point of the baton, but by clarifying textures or isolating groups whose successful integration lays the foundation for a cohesive performance.

If the specific nature of the problem is clarified through strategic temporary alterations in dynamics, instrumentation, numbers of performers (on a single part) and creation *or elimination* of visual cues, performers of almost any ability will instinctively arrive at the optimal solution extremely quickly, without the problem ever having to be verbally articulated. This is a more subtle and complex process than may be initially apparent. In this pursuit, it is insufficient to diagnose that a performer's intonation is faulty: the facilitator must also discern the root cause, and identify precisely what variables require adjustment within the ensemble setting in order for the musician to hear and thus resolve the intonation issue. The most common approach to solving this situation, the bald and efficient statement of "You're flat," will have the player produce a randomly higher pitch without ever having identified the underlying cause or having understood precisely how much modification of pitch is required. In effect, this approach is akin to treating a symptom, rather than curing a disease.

More serious or multifaceted ensemble problems may require a more sophisticated, measured approach to deconstruction and reintegration. A passage of great rhythmic complexity might entail starting with the principal players, and having them perform *without a conductor,* compelling them to rely on their visual and aural connections to each other until they achieve both comprehension and cohesion. The numbers of performers can then be increased, stand by stand or row by row, until the full ensemble is entirely locked in with full understanding of each part's contribution. Here the relation to social learning theory is even clearer. While the principals are playing, the remainder of the musicians have the opportunity to observe, then imitate them. As the size of the ensemble is gradually increased, the musicians repeat the passage, thereby reinforcing the new technical and aural skills it demands. This process can be extremely time-consuming, much more so than a simple demand to follow the baton, but as in the case of the intonation problem, the results are often significantly better and last longer. With patience and the right approach, some diseases can be cured.

Although the above scenarios do not describe the general practice in Venezuela, there are unique qualities of the work there that strongly suggest some innate understanding of social learning principles. The incredibly physical vitality with which the Venezuelan orchestras perform is not a spontaneous expression of passion and engagement, but a choreography that is trained in the musicians from an early age until it becomes natural and organic – like any instrumental technique. With a mode of learning based on observation of motions, it simply makes sense to make those motions larger and easier to observe. The gestures may also help students connect better with the repertoire as well as each other: research has demonstrated that a two-way relationship between external physicality and internal emotion exists (Davis, Senghas, Brandt, & Ochsner, 2010), and that the mere act of synchronizing movements can produce a social bonding effect. (Wiltermuth & Heath, 2009) It is also important to remember that for the first three decades of its existence, the Fundación operated and grew largely in a vacuum, without the music education or conservatory training infrastructure found in many developed nations, and yet was still able to build a national orchestral programme that is the envy of the world. Clearly much can be accomplished musically just with time, freedom, and great sense of purpose. Should the Fundación incorporate social learning principles scientifically and strategically across its network, the results would strain the imagination.

The idea of minimal teacher or conductor intervention may not be original, nor by itself does it constitute the practice of social action through music, but an emphasis on social learning represents the most logical first step towards any pro-social objective. Social learning also provides a rudimentary potential answer to the two questions posed earlier: how is *Sistema* different, and in being different, can it address the 'reach' problem? A practice of *Sistema* rooted primarily in social learning could offer its participants a desperately needed counterpart, if not counterpoint, to deeply embedded, ineffective forms of schooling. *Sistema* in this incarnation could have the potential to offer children the rare chance to learn and grow in the most cognitively consonant way, closing a 'reach' gap that has been institutionalized for generations.

Reaching students cognitively may simultaneously help them connect as a community. As the musicians listen to each other, as they model for each other, as they move into a space in which they rely on each other rather than on a teacher or conductor, they begin to understand implicitly their interdependence at an extremely tangible level, and appreciate their collective strength and capacities when working in concert. This is collective efficacy, the group counterpart to self-efficacy, and it represents a powerful non-politicized experience in the complex and dynamic interrelation between individual autonomy and the needs of the community.

The trouble with the epithet 'hard to reach' is that it implicitly places the responsibility for programme shortcomings on the target population, rather than on the programme mechanics. This is akin to blaming students in Yorkshire for not understanding the most well-meaning instructions in Mandarin. Teachers have an innate desire to help, share and show – to intervene. These are extremely positive, if not essential, attributes within the restrictions of most standard educational systems, but in social learning environments, they must be sublimated by equal or greater impulses to prioritize music over speech, to create space for listening, to build invisible scaffolds and to accept mistakes and pedagogical blind alleys. This is much harder than it sounds. In its 2012 report on music education in the UK, the independent Office for Standards in Education, Children's Services and Skills (Ofsted) neatly summarized the tendencies of the pedagogical culture. Ofsted noted that while much excellent work was being done, 'in too many instances there was insufficient emphasis on active music-making or on the use of musical sound as the dominant language of learning. Too much use was made of verbal communication and non-musical activities. Put simply, in too many cases there was not enough music in music lessons.' (Ofsted, 2012)

Educators will always be an essential part of the learning processes, within social learning environments and beyond. What remains critical is the degree and nature of their involvement. No simple rubric exists as to how much verbal communication or direct intervention is required in any situation: maintaining a focused social learning environment requires significantly more skill and judgment – and humility – than issuing directives from centre stage. The processes of social learning are also far less impressive to the untrained eye, and appear far less efficient. David Russell, Distinguished Professor of Violin at the University of North Carolina Charlotte, once humorously compared them to the American sitcom *Seinfeld*. After seeing the processes in action, Russell stated "It's as if you do nothing!" referring to the comedy's deliberate lack of premise. But then he continued: "but they [the musicians] keep getting better and better!" expressing an appreciation for the effective mechanics he saw at work. (D. Russell, personal communication, March 18, 2013.)

As apt as Russell's comparison might be, music educators might understandably be quite reluctant to repeat it. A more poetic perspective on the nature of social learning comes from Lao-Tzu in the 6th Century BCE:

> *Therefore the Master*
> *acts without doing anything*
> *and teaches without saying anything.*
> *Things arise and she lets them come;*
> *things disappear and she lets them go.*
> *She has but doesn't possess,*
> *acts but doesn't expect.*
> *When her work is done, she forgets it.*
> *That is why it lasts forever.*
> (Mitchell, 1999)

Sistema is only of value, only justifiable if it is different in every meaningful way from that which already exists. When coexisting with any music education infrastructure, when *Sistema* shares or competes for resources, the bar must necessarily be set much higher. As hard as its stakeholders may be to reach, *Sistema* as an educational philosophy may reach furthest when it lets go.

References

Bandura, A. (1971) *Social Learning Theory*. New York: General Learning Press.

Clarke, A. C. (1962) *Profiles of the Future: an inquiry into the limits of the possible*. New York: Harper & Row.

Davis, J. I., Senghas, A., Brandt, F. & Ochsner, K. N. (2010) The Effects of BOTOX Injections on Emotional Experience. *Emotion* , 10 (3): 433-440.

ElSistemaUSA.org. (2010) Retrieved July 12, 2013, from ElSistemaUSA.org: http://elsistemausa.org/el-sistema/u-s-a/what-distinguishes-an-el-sistema-inspired-program-in-the-u-s/

Ewen, David (1943) *Dictators of the Baton*. Chicago / New York: Alliance Book Corporation. Available at http://archive.org/stream/dictatorsoftheba001489mbp#page/n9/mode/2up (accessed 09.09.2013)

Govias, J. A. (2011) The Five Fundamentals of El Sistema. *Canadian Music Educator,* September 2011: 21-23.

Hallam, S. (2010) The power of music: its impact of the intellectual, personal and social development of children and young people. *International Journal of Music Education* , 38 (3): 269-289.

Jones, G. H. (1969) *History of the law of charity, 1532-1827*. Cambridge: Cambridge University Press.

Loch, C. S. (1910) *Charity and Social Life: A short study of religion and social thought in relation to charitable methods and institutions*. London: MacMillan & Co. Ltd.

Mitchell, S. (1999) *Tao Te Ching, from a translation by S. Mitchell*. London: Frances Lincoln.

Mitra, S. (2003) Miminally invasive education: a progress report on the "hole-in-the-wall" experiments. *British Journal of Educational Technology* , 34 (No. 3): 367-371.

Mitra, S., & Dangwal, R. (2010) Limits to self-organising systes of learning - the Kalikuppam experiment. *British Journal of Educational Technology* , 41 (No. 5): 672-688.

Ofsted. (2012) *Music in schools: wider still, and wider*. Manchester: Ofsted.

Tanner, M. (2012, April 11) The American Welfare State: How We Spend Nearly $1 Trillion a Year Fighting Poverty - and Fail. *Policy Analysis*: 1-22.

Toronyi-Lalic, I. (2012, June 27) *theartsdesk.com*. Retrieved July 12, 2013, from theartsdesk.com: http://www.theartsdesk.com/classical-music/sim%C3%B3n-bol%C3%ADvar-symphony-orchestra-dudamel-royal-festival-hall

Wiltermuth, S. S. & Heath, C. (2009) Synchrony and Cooperation. *Psychological Science* , 20 (No. 1): 1-5.

How many pedagogies does it take to train a community musician?*

Kathryn Deane

*Answer at the end. Community musicians don't talk much about pedagogy. But they talk a lot about quality work and the qualities they bring to it. How is that quality, and those qualities, determined?

The importance of music

The answer starts with another question. Why is it important to reach hard to reach young people with music? Community musicians take two approaches.

First, there is equity: 'Everyone has the right freely to participate in the cultural life of the community, to enjoy the arts' says the United Nations (1948) in Article 27 (1) of the Universal Declaration of Human Rights. But access to the arts is patchy at best, and disadvantaged people often miss out. Becko (2012), in mapping provision in London, showed there were multiple areas where little or no non-formal music provision was taking place – but yet where socio-economic disadvantage was highest.

Second, there is pragmatic benefit. The Centre for Economics and Business Research (2013) noted that formal education in the arts was associated with improvements in transferrable skills leading ultimately to improving the likelihood of young people gaining employment. Other reports have come to similar conclusions. More, these effects may be particularly marked in disaffected young people (Spychiger *et al.* 1993, quoted in Hallam, 2010).

These two approaches synthesise into Sound Sense's description of community music:

> Community music involves musicians from any musical discipline working with [...] people to enable them to develop active and creative participation in music; it is concerned with putting equal opportunities into practice; and it happens in all types of community [...] where it reflects the context in which it takes place. (Macdonald, 1995)

That is to say, there has to be active music creation, equality is central, and the music making itself somehow tells the tale of the community that's making it. This is about what music *does* as well as what music *is*. In that sense, community music is 'an active intervention between a music leader or facilitator and participants' (Higgins, 2012: 5) As an 'intervention' the activity is clearly designed to make change in the participants. Of course, that is what teaching of all sorts is designed to do – but community music goes further, and by its definition is designed to make change on a personal or social level *through* the music making.

Community musicians therefore make all sorts of change in all sorts of people. And this article is about the qualities (in the broadest sense) they need for working with hard to reach young people.

Recruiting hard to reach young people

The first challenge for community musicians and community music organisations is to reach the hard to reach young people. Though this appears somewhat oxymoronic, it does occupy much attention, both at strategic and at practical levels. Techniques for recruiting hard to reach young people can be straightforward if you work in closed institutions. A pupil referral unit (PRU), for example, provides a literally captive market. In other cases a cohort might have to be created, and the first action might be to research areas of deprivation, both social and cultural: Becko's mapping has already been highlighted as a detailed and comprehensive way of carrying out such research.

Deane, Hunter & Mullen (2011) describe a range of recruitment methods used in a music mentoring programme, including building strong holistic links with a young person's carers. Student 'O', a young man with autism, was referred to one organisation by a charity with which they had longstanding links; and the musician involved established links with O's mother in order to develop a fully-informed joint strategy. All the music team took autism training in preparation for the work (p46). In other examples, launch events, at which young people interested in music production could meet each other and the music leaders, had been used: music leaders working in schools, PRUs, and so on could spot students who might benefit from programmes the leaders knew about (pp44, 49).

Islington Music Forum ran a creative music programme for young adult mental health service users, in partnership with the local NHS Mental Health Foundation Trust with referrals from the trust's Early Intervention services, Community Mental Health Teams and Highgate and St Pancras hospitals. Each young person had an initial interview which was also a mental health and risk assessment, and ongoing clinical contact was maintained with referral partners (p47).

These examples of recruiting practices make clear two things. First, some of the best practice arises when musicians are involved in recruiting, rather than this issue being left to the employing organisation. Second, working with hard to reach young people is a care issue at least as much as it is a music issue. These points have implications for the range of skills that a musician needs for this work – not only particular *music* skills (the skills you need for music performance, or even for music teaching, are not sufficient for participatory work) but equally a set of *personal* and *social* skills. Where is such a skill-set laid out, and how is it interpreted?

Skills, knowledge and understanding

The generic skills, knowledge and understanding, behaviours and values needed to work as a community musician have been described consistently for more than two decades now (see e.g. Keith, 1992) mostly from the view of the practitioner. But in community music the usual model of operation is that of an organisation leading on a project and hiring (whether on a self-employed or employed basis) a musician to carry out the music work – with the extent of negotiation between the two over the form, content and outcomes of the work varying from a pure contract, where the musician does what's bid by the employer, to a fully musician-led model, where the employer agrees to a musician's plan for the work.

Deane (2013) examined how employers hired, using a form of expert questioning called Delphi technique (see e.g. http://en.wikipedia.org/wiki/Delphi_method). For these producers of community music activities, the music was certainly important:

> high quality music opportunities ... with an emphasis on those who are experiencing barriers to accessing music.

But so too were personal, social, or community developments in the participants:

> Our work covers the whole spectrum of musical and social interventions
>
> it can be curriculum (but usually in this case we'd be working with young people who are not meeting the standards of their peers), or a social justice purpose (that the group are denied these opportunities in mainstream) or a socialising purpose (to re-engage with learning) (Deane, 2013: 3)

Musical skills

Where does this leave musical skills, then? Sometimes they are highly-specified ("musicians who have ideas for group activities for a range of ages and abilities up their sleeves as flexibility is essential in our groups"), sometimes vaguely, described using words like 'versatile' and 'musicianship.' (Deane, 2013: 4)

The new Level 4 Certificate for Music Educators (CME) (ACE, 2013), which has been developed for musicians involved in musical learning activities for children and young people, avoids the issue by not addressing musical skills at all, saying only that music educators taking the qualification should have:

> a level of competence in music practice and knowledge, which is appropriate to the learning settings in which they are working [and] appropriate musical [...] skills that enable them to inspire confidence in, and elicit musical responses from, children and young people with whom they work.

The community arts National Occupational Standards (NOS) (descriptions of what would make you a competent performer in your job) take us no further forward. Standard CCSCA25 (UK Standards, 2013) says merely:

> You must be able to [...] demonstrate sufficient knowledge and experience of using your art form in your sessions that enable individuals and groups to engage in the arts activity [...] provide appropriate guidance and support to ensure that participants grow in confidence and competence in their chosen art form.

Full disclosure: I was on the working groups devising both the qualification and the standard; and may indeed have suggested those vague-sounding forms of words. This was not so much an attempt to get home early from the meetings as to try to ensure that *in*appropriate musical qualities or qualifications were not asked of community musicians.

'Appropriate' means, for one thing, fluency ('good-enough' playing) on relevant instruments – and for many community musicians that translates as music technology, as the go-to instrument for engaging hard to reach young people. It might also mean taking musicality on trust, especially where the 'instrument' is the latest fashionable micro-genre of urban music style:

> Our experience is that people who have learned these skills tend to have learned very informally, and professional work in this area (as a performer, or producer, or whatever) is in no way connected to qualifications. ...Which is fine, until it comes to delivering workshops; we can't tell a good musician from a poor one, and it is a very specialist area of practice. ... So for us, this is a live issue – we have to take the word of people who know more about it than we do (Deane, 2013: 8).

Or it might mean *hiding* your musicianship:

> There is a world of difference between a drummer sitting at a kit and demonstrating a particularly tricky drum roll – with the implied statement that if only the kids would practise they could play like that, too – and a drummer handing over a pair of sticks and saying 'The hardest thing is walking across the room to the kit – once you've made that step, everything else is easy.' (Wingate, 2012: 12)

Or avoiding technical language:

> One really nice guy ran a workshop for a group of adults with learning disabilities but wanted them to count and come in at a certain number – yes, well, many of them couldn't count, it took quite a while for him to realise this. (Deane 2013: 4)

Saunders and Welch (2012) observed a limited number of community music workshop sessions in detail, looking at a range of 'micro-events' in the session at one-minute intervals, and producing colour-coded timelines mapping out activities (p37). They found 'striking' similarities across different community music organisations and different community musicians; and commonalities between these workshops and formal education: 'good teaching, irrespective of the subject, can be characterised by empathy, enthusiasm, explanation, clarity, structure, an appropriate level and pace' (p85).

But they also found differences between these non-formal practices and practices found by Ofsted (2009) in its report on schools' music. There was less teacher talk (more music making); more use of modelling (playing by the practitioner alongside the young people) and scaffolding (supporting the next steps in the young person's playing). And there were examples of dialogic work rather than transmissive teaching, such as peer-led activities on the peripheries of a session. A practitioner showing how, and the young person assessing and then adopting, 'was found to be a common way of working and often a process without words. It was often carried out within the musical performance, a learning conversation reliant on the young person's ability to absorb the new information through careful observation and listening' (p91). And of course an emphasis on aural skills. All these would be considered by community musicians as 'appropriate' musical skills both for entry to the new CME and to meet the NOS.

The projects reported on in Saunders and Welch largely involved young people who were not hard to reach. But other studies with hard to reach young people confirm the practices described above. A report by the Sing Up 'Beyond the Mainstream' programme for a range of hard to reach groups at primary age included in its list of good techniques:

- teaching by ear
- listening and responding to the children's needs

- songs with repetition and varying tempos, rhythms and pitches of songs to maintain engagement
- starting with something children engage with and then expanding their range (Sing Up, 2010: 5).

Non-musical skills and qualities – in theory

All of the above could form the basis for the musical elements of a community music pedagogy. The *non*-musical skills and qualities make for an even longer list. The employer above who wanted flexibility went on to enumerate:

> They also need to be able to manage a group of people with learning difficulties and also have some experience in supporting non musical volunteers to work with the groups as well. They also need a sense of fun and energy and enthusiasm (Deane 2013: 4).

And the list of skills demanded also blurred into values: 'humble, passionate, ethical, committed' (ibid.).

No pressure there, then. It certainly seems demeaning to label this range of communicational, organisational, inter- and intra-personal, and value-laden qualities with the usual tag of 'soft skills.' Certainly they take up more attention. The 'arts leadership' suite of NOS referred to above contains just the one standard on artistic skills (CCSCA25), and eight on the non-musical skills required of a community artist (CCSCA20 to 24, 26 to 28) covering:

- identifying a market for your work and understanding its needs and expectations
- designing a programme of work that 'must be clear in its purpose and match your available skills with the needs and expectations of the end user'
- managing expectations (not only of the participants but also of the range of stakeholders involved in a programme)
- safety (of participants and the artist) and professional responsibilities
- engaging participants
- evaluation
- group facilitation
- and finally the artist's own professional development.

The 'units' of the CME provide a similar list:

- understanding children and young people's musical learning
- planning, facilitating and evaluating children and young people's musical learning
- reflective practice and professional development in music education
- promoting children and young people's positive behaviour
- equality, diversity and inclusion in music education
- safeguarding children and young people in music education.

The two lists can be mapped on to each other relatively straightforwardly, and neither would appear outlandish to formal sector educators.

Intents and purposes

The fun begins, however, when we try to interpret the standards and qualifications and apply their broad statements to real-world practice – a task that is made the more complicated when working with hard to reach young people, where the intent, or purpose, of the music work can be complex. Intent has been seen as an important lens through which to view work since at least the late 1990s (Tambling & Harland, 1998).

Deane (2013) identified three broad types of intent in community music work: where the focus was on the music itself; where the music was important, but it was recognised how it would lead to personal, social, or community development; and where the focus was on personal, social, or community development, with the music as a vehicle to deliver this. Lowe (2011: 36) implicitly identifies similar intents through a set of questions. The issue is the extent to which the non-music skills that a community musician needs vary depending on the purpose of the work they are undertaking. As an example: a community musician could work with young people in school to help them with an A-level composition project; or to explore homophobia; or to get them off drugs. The client group and setting is the same in each case, but the specifics of what qualities a community musician might need to deploy in the different cases might vary a lot. In other words, it's about the extent to which 'community' in 'community music' is important.

Non-musical skills and qualities – in practice

An interview with a community music organisation project manager starts to unpick these nuances:

> Music Education according to his understanding was 'not just about learning musical skills but understanding the young people's musical culture.' [which] was largely 'overlooked in the formal sector.' Music, he argued, 'was the vehicle on which to travel to somewhere else.' [...] And while he 'stressed that in every circumstance, the organisation aimed to gain a musical outcome for the young person involved. [he also] argued for 'musical experiences with transferable life skills' (Saunders & Welch, 2012: 48-49)

An evidence review of work with young people not in education, employment or training (QA Research, 2011) identified a number of non-musical skills that community musicians working on such projects would need to possess including:

- spontaneity: being able to change the direction of workshop activities instantaneously in response to creative ideas and preferences
- participant-centred: participants contribute to the decision-making process, influencing the delivery style and techniques used, and so develop the young people's thinking skills and sense of empowerment
- developing community partnerships: working with schools, churches, museums, parish councils and other enterprises
- offering information, advice and guidance: community musicians recognise

their role in harnessing and nurturing talent; and so have a responsibility to offer help about both music related and non-music related careers, qualifications and provision.

This type of list crops up time and again. Sound Sense member Graham Dowdall (2012), convenor of the Certificate in Music Workshop Skills Course at Goldsmiths University of London, described it thus:

> Personally I'm pretty clear about some of the broader skill sets that make up a good community musician: facilitation skills, planning, evaluation, entrepreneurial, observational, communication, project management, research etc [...] Then there's knowledge and understanding. And finally the even more intangible 'qualities' – empathy, understanding, patience, drive, enthusiasm, energy, diligence and more.

Dowdall's 'qualities' can also be described as *behaviours*, difficult to capture in a standard or a qualification. Community musicians have a code of practice (Sound Sense, 2011) which includes behaviours such as valuing people and being "friendly, approachable and professional."

It seems fair to say that the basis of what constitutes quality in community music practice (not only with hard to reach young people but with a wide range of other, largely disadvantaged, groups) is settled between the three documents of the NOS, the level 4 certificate and the code of practice. But how far do the details depend on the type of client group?

Pick your pedagogy

On the one hand, there appear to be differences in approach according to client group or purpose of the work. One respondent thinks working in a healthcare setting is "so unbelievably different to working in a school or youth club setting." (Deane 2013: 7) "There is no manual for working in community music with those on the autistic spectrum," says Sound Sense member Tina Pinder (2009:14) but her description of how she goes about the work – including "dealing with everything from communication systems to toilet needs and special diets" – is manual enough. And there are indeed such guides for working with those with a learning disability, written by yet more Sound Sense members (Paton & Garside, 2010; Mencap, 2009).

On a larger scale and more formal level, Sing Up Beyond the Mainstream championed the use of 'social pedagogy' practice for its work with looked after children. A practice more familiar in mainland Europe, social pedagogy can be seen as addressing social issues by educational means. Social pedagogues see the child as a whole person of equal value to themselves, and bring themselves 'head, hands and heart' to their relationships with the children, rather than as distant professionals. There is a strong emphasis on team work and cooperation with the other professionals and members of the community. Creativity often plays a large part in social pedagogic work, and so it was a straightforward step for the National Children's Bureau (NCB) to develop the notion of the 'artist pedagogue' (Chambers & Petrie, 2009; Chambers, 2009).

An evaluation of Sing Up Beyond The Mainstream projects with looked after children (Petrie & Knight, 2011) explored elements of the projects that displayed artist pedagogic principles. These included not underestimating the musical and creative capabilities of looked after children. At the same time projects were seen not as 'singing classes in miniature, but as pleasant places for adults and children to form warm relationships;' the first consideration being to undertake a musical journey from 'where the children were' rather than following preconceived plans or a rigid curriculum (pp29-30).

Working with children holistically rather than seeing music activities as separate from their other experiences was seen by almost all of the leaders as essential for good practice: 'We are community musicians and we have to work with well-being in a holistic way, about feeling good, positive engagement and finding out what the children are like and are good at' (p33). One project began with everyone eating together, sharing their days in a 'sociable and creative space'; singing started when it was right to do so rather than when the timetable dictated. And good projects valued all children's contributions.

Managing challenging behaviour by young people was, for artist pedagogues, about

> find[ing] other ways, other strategies, to contain them.' Accepting the child as they are, rather than as adults would like them to be [...] 'some of the boys were a bit shouty, so rather than everyone saying 'shush' all the time, he [the music leader] got them to use that [loud voice] in the workshop, so we used it creatively (p38).

The report was keen to distinguish such techniques of managing the social context so that the child feels secure and with less need to behave in ways that may be unacceptable to others from a traditional approach to managing unacceptable behaviour.

It wasn't only young people who could be challenging:

> Teaching staff who were sitting in intervened frequently to control the children, interrupting the creative process and the relationship building between the children and the tutors, and between the children with each other (p38).

Things worked better where all the people present were seen as part of the team, fully included in discussing the ethos of the project and how children were to be valued and made welcome.

Many other examples could have been chosen. Are all these principles and pedagogies different? It seems they are more a case of being divided by a common language. The techniques of artist pedagogy exemplified above fit very neatly into items of the CME – in the order of the elements described above, music educators are required to

- explain how music can benefit the whole child or young person by enhancing their aesthetic, spiritual, social, emotional and intellectual development
- design musical learning activities that meet the learning objectives and which promote a sense of ownership, enjoyment and engagement in participants [and] are appropriate to the setting, learning mode and age of the participants
- select and use appropriate strategies, resources and pedagogical approaches that will support, challenge and inspire children and young people
- implement strategies for promoting positive behaviour [and] demonstrate realistic, consistent and supportive responses to children and young people's behaviour

- build relationships and collaborate with partners and participants, as appropriate [...] agreeing roles and responsibilities of self and others.

This is good news for community musicians and their employers. The alternative theory – that community musicians need wholly different types of training for each different type of work they do – does not bear thinking about.

Core and contextual skills

Certainly respondents in Deane (2013) thought there was no issue. There was a lot of consensus that core skills were transferable between contexts; and that contextual skills could then be added on top (p7). This, of course, raises the question of what counts as core skills; and that of course begs the answer that core skills are those that are common to different types of work. One of the respondents beautifully put this as:

> The common ground is empathy, listening skills, ability to lead in a supportive way, ability to adapt plans in a flexible way as you discover how the participants react to different activities and when you need to change the energy of the workshop for any reason, how to deal with individual needs in a group situation, and how to identify individual learning paths, monitor reactions, and build energy and focus with a group (p7).

That can be rendered more prosaically in the language of the NOS and the CME as (mixing up standards and unit this time):

- understanding children and young people's musical learning
- engaging participants
- planning, facilitating and evaluating children and young people's musical learning; managing expectations
- safety and safeguarding
- group facilitation,
- promoting children and young people's positive behaviour

all underpinned by:

- reflective practice and professional development
- equality, diversity and inclusion

and with the pre-requisites of:

- identifying a market for your work and understanding its needs and expectations
- designing a programme of work that must be clear in its purpose and match your available skills with the needs and expectations of the end user.

Get all of that right – and "right" is as described throughout: community musicians having an underlying ability to understand and be sensitive to the specific needs of any group; with an understanding of their own music making and how they can adapt and develop their ideas for each setting – and you can add on the contextual knowledge (the culture and practical operation of the setting, the users, and the purpose of the work) relatively easily.

So does it work?

The short answer is yes: community musicians working in the sorts of pedagogies described above do enable all sorts of people - including hard to reach young people – to make changes, as a range of case study and quantitative reports make clear.

For example, Deane *et al.* (2011) described various effects of music in a music-based mentoring programme for hard to reach young people (pp71-72), four of which were thought to be found specifically in music programmes:

- telling the tale: an opportunity to express oneself, most often seen in young people's rap lyrics
- therapeutic aid: using music as a way of venting feelings
- creative cooperation: learning how to work together, to improve
- personal reflection.

A quantitative evaluation on the same programme (Lonie, 2011) examined three measures of agency (feeling respected, able, and in control) at the beginning and end of the project and found statistically significant increases in response across all three, particularly strong for a combined measure of agency.

Case study research in community music often produces particularly powerful testimony (Dunkley, 2011). A raft of support workers from various statutory and voluntary services could not help Jake – returning to mainstream education following time spent in a young offenders' institution with no qualifications, no self-esteem and no routine – until Sound Sense member Simon Glenister of Noise Solution stepped in. Glenister's approach 'demonstrate[d] sufficient knowledge and experience of using [his] artform' because it combined musical activity with instant engagement, which is what Jake needed:

> 'We use a practical technique based on shape recognition (rather than theory) that allows anyone, regardless of ability, to play the piano within ten minutes. Enabling them to rapidly build self-confidence doing something new naturally fosters engagement and trust – the two essential ingredients of successful interventions,' advises Simon (ibid: 15).

By the end of a 12-week course with Noise Solution, Jake had written, recorded and produced his own track, tutored someone else in using the production equipment and gained an Arts Award. This award was enough to help win Jake a place on a music course at a local college.

An evidence review (QA Research: 22-23) of 15 reports of Youth Music-funded projects working with young people not in education, employment or training identified a range of positive outcomes from involving such hard to reach young people in music making, including:

- increased motivation – to engage in education, employment, or voluntary activity
- transferrable skill development – including numeracy, listening, concentration, and meeting deadlines
- enhanced emotional well-being – including increased empowerment and sense of achievement

- improved social interaction – including reduced feelings of alienation, trusting others, expanding friendship circles and providing support to peers

and not forgetting:

- improved musicianship – composition, improvisation, music technology, DJ-ing, and performance skills.

Conclusion

The community musician works with people of all ages in all sorts of challenge – including hard to reach young people. S/he has to be a paragon, that's for sure. And their job description and person specification seem endless. A musician – and more; teacher – and more; facilitator, carer, mentor, inspirer, social worker - and much, much more.

But the job is not impossible, as so many good community musicians across the UK are testament to. Quality in, and the qualities of, a community musician have been codified and described in numerous reports, just some of which are described here. We now know what a good community musician is and can be expected to do – and what musical, personal and social results with all sorts of people (including hard to reach young people) they can be expected to achieve.

Community music is often accused of not having a pedagogy. On the contrary: it probably has too many. So how many of the above pedagogies does it take to train a community musician? Any one: all the others are just variants.

References

Arts Council England (ACE) (2013) Level 4 Certificate for Music Educators. http://www.artscouncil.org.uk/what we-do/our-priorities-2011-15/children-and-young-people/new-qualifications-creative-practitioners/updated-certificate-music-educators-faqs/

Becko, L. (2012) *Mapping non-formal music provision and social need in London.* Sound Connections http://www.sound-connections.org.uk/news/mapping-music-in-london (accessed 15.05.2013).

Centre for Economics and Business Research (2013) *The contribution of the arts and culture to the national economy.* Arts Council England http://www.artscouncil.org.uk/news/arts-council-news/economic-contribution-arts-and-culture-report-publ/ (accessed 15.05.2013).

Chambers, H. (2009) *People with passion.* London: National Children's Bureau.

Chambers, H. & Petrie, P. (2009) *A learning framework for artist pedagogues* London: National Children's Bureau.

Deane, K. (2013) *Employing Community Musicians – an ArtWorks Navigator artists lab.* ArtWorks http://www.artworksphf.org.uk/page/resources-and-research (accessed 15.05.2013).

Deane, K. Hunter, R. & Mullen, P. (2011) *Move On Up: an evaluation of Youth Music Mentors.* Youth Music http://network.youthmusic.org.uk/resources/research/move (accessed 15.05.2013).

Dowdall,G. (2012) Showing your worth. *Sounding Board* (2): 7.

Dunkley, S. (2011) A lot done, a lot more to do. *Sounding Board* (4):14-15.

Hallam, S. (2010) The power of music: its impact of the intellectual, personal and social development of children and young people. *International Journal of Music Education* 38(3): 269-289.

Higgins, L. (2012) *Community music: in theory and in practice.* New York: Oxford University Press.

Keith, M. (1992) NVQs and the community musician. *Sounding Board* Autumn pp12-13.

Lonie, D. (2011) *Attuned to Engagement Paper 2: The effects of a music mentoring programme on the agency and musical ability of children and young people.* Youth Music http://network.youthmusic.org.uk/resources/research/attuned-engagement-paper-2-effects-music-mentoring-programme-agency-and-musical-a (accessed 13.07.2013).

Lowe, T. (2011) *Audit of Practice: "Arts in Participatory Settings"* [Audit of Participatory Practice]. ArtWorks North East http://www.artworksphf.org.uk/page/resources-and-research [accessed 20.05.2013].

Macdonald, I. (1995) The Leiston Statement. *Sounding Board,* Spring, pp29-30.

Mencap, (2009) *Music and people with a learning disability: a guide for music leaders.* http://www.mencap.org.uk/sites/default/files/documents/Guide%20for%20music%20leaders_0.pdf (accessed 20.05.2013).

Ofsted (2009) *Making More of Music: An evaluation of music in schools (2005-08).* London: Ofsted.

Paton, R. & Garside, G. (2010) *Doing music.* Mencap http://www.mencap.org.uk/sites/default/files/documents/Doing%20music4.pdf (accessed 20.05.2013).

Petrie, P. & Knight, A. (2011) *I want to sing: Sing Up NCB looked after children programme evaluation.* Centre for Understanding Social Pedagogy, Institute of Education University of London http://www.singup.org/fileadmin/singupfiles/previous_uploads/Sing_Up_Looked_After_Children_full_report.pdf (accessed 17.05.2013).

Pinder, T. (2009) 'Music with respect', *Sounding Board* (3):13-14.

QA Research (2011) *Young People Not in Education, Employment or Training (NEET) and Music Making.* Youth Music http://network.youthmusic.org.uk/resources/research/young-people-not-education-employment-or-training-neet-and-music-making (accessed 17.05.2013).

Saunders, J. & Welch, G. (2012) *Communities of Music Education: a pilot study.* International Music Education Research Centre (iMerc) http://network.youthmusic.org.uk/resources/research/communities-music-education (accessed 18.05.2013).

Sing Up Beyond the Mainstream (2010) *Report on funded programmes 2009* http://www.singup.org/fileadmin/singupfiles/previous_uploads/Sing_Up_BTM_programmes_report.pdf (accessed 17.05.2013).

Sound Sense (2011) *Music Education Code of Practice* http://www.soundsense.org/metadot/index.pl?id=25842&isa=Category&op=show (accessed 14.07.2013).

Tambling, P. & Harland, J. (1998) *Orchestral Education Programmes: intents and purposes* London: The Arts Council of England.

UK standards (2013) CCSCA25. http://nos.ukces.org.uk/NOS%20Directory/NOS%20PDF%20%20Creative%20And%20Cultural%20Skills/NOSProjectDocuments_359/CCSCA25.pdf Or http://nos.ukces.org.uk/andsearchforccsca25 (accessed 15.05.2013).

United Nations (1948) *Universal Declaration of Human Rights.* https://www.un.org/en/documents/udhr/ (accessed 17.05.2013).

Wingate, C. (2012) Training the trainers. *Sounding Board,* (2):12-13.

The role of hubs in reaching the 'hard to reach' groups – experiences and reflections from Gloucestershire.

Mark Bick

Valuing every child equally, equality of opportunities, and inclusion of all children and young people are underlying principles in British society and our education system. They are not always implemented in practice and there can be significant barriers of cost, practicality, attitudes and institutional barriers. Access to music education is currently far from equal.

The National Plan for Music Education (DfE, 2011) is clear that the new Music Education Hubs should be changing this as part of their core roles.

> We expect hubs to … ensure equality of opportunity amongst all children, regardless of the school they attend, their background or personal circumstances – both in the context of ability to pay, their level of musical aptitude, as well as across the spectrum of special educational needs and disabilities, looked after children, race and gender.

Make Music Gloucestershire, our local hub, has contracted my organisation, Gloucestershire Music Makers, to deliver an inclusion strategy over the current period of hub funding. We are an independent charity and we led the development of the strategy, which we based on the National Plan, the ACE funding brief for hubs and our existing work. Initial priorities have been young people out of mainstream education and looked after children.

We see inclusion as developing provision that meets young people's needs and encourages integration. There is an expectation that integration of 'hard to reach' young people into open hub provision will increase over time, with changes needed to the open provision and for the workforce. The starting point has to be working with young people where they are.

There is a long track record across the UK of community music projects having a very positive impact in unlocking re-engagement with learning. Progression for individual participants is now getting a much stronger focus and is the subject of current work by Youth Music, Sound Sense and others. Our aim in Gloucestershire has been both to provide progression routes and consistent long term provision for new students coming into the 'hard to reach' categories. We are operating in challenging times with rapid change in the education system, driven by both the academies programme and restricted resources. What we do has to be cost effective if it is to be sustainable.

We see ourselves as a community music organisation and bring a particular set of values - particularly in valuing creativity, composition and song writing, a bias to the marginalised and a priority of empowerment - which have not traditionally been part of Music Service thinking or provision. What music services have always done well, however, is to provide consistent and regular access to music education for large numbers of young people across the whole of their area. We want to see the best of what our two histories can offer coming together as we work in partnership within the hub.

At the end of the first academic year Gloucestershire Music Makers has delivered a varied programme including:

- 9 hours a week in 3 different Pupil Referral Units (PRUs) and with an independent alternative education provider
- 4 hours a week across two hospital education sites
- a 2-day summer school for 7 young people invited from these settings
- a 15-day Summer Arts College for 10 'high risk' young offenders, leading to Bronze Arts Award
- taster & training sessions with foster carers on encouraging active music making in the home
- an 'urban music room' at a fun day for 200 foster carers and looked after children
- a taster day for looked after teenagers
- a mentoring project with 14 young people who are in 'challenging circumstances'

All this is expected to continue and grow in the new school year. Head teachers and service managers in Hospital Education, Social Services and Targeted Youth Support are increasingly buying in. Young people who have received very little music education are performing with live backing, writing songs, recording, collaborating and behaving (mostly) as young musicians, serious about learning and progressing.

I do not really see any of these young people as particularly 'hard to reach', more ignored, overlooked and sometimes challenging. The complex issues in their lives do sometimes get in the way of the music however. We have to be both supportive and flexible beyond what might be expected with mainstream students, but this is outweighed by their passion for music, engagement and musical progress.

This work has grown out of a history of previous work going back 12 years. It is led by a team with many years of experience mostly from a community music background. We share a set of values, approaches and skills and have positive working relationships with different parts of the statutory sector built over many years. Though we are very pleased with the outcomes of the partnership with our hub so far, we still have a long way to go in fulfilling the full potential of the hub and building genuine partnership working. We are bringing together two very different cultures and the power is still very much with the Music Service.

Engagement through music

One of our experienced music mentors, visiting a PRU for an initial meeting with one young person, noticed a teenage girl listening intently to what was going on, asked if she could speak to her and found she had a huge passion for music. She had been writing lyrics and singing at home, but no one in the education system was aware of this interest. It turned out that the PRU were having huge difficulties engaging her. As a result of this meeting, the PRU funded sessions and we kept working with her as she was moved to different settings. She has since performed for the first time and we are still working with her.

Once a young person is outside the mainstream there can be an increased focus on numeracy and literacy which means that music provision may suffer. At the same time not all traditional music services have had people with the skills or experience to meet the needs of these young people. We regularly experience young people engaging and achieving in ways that amaze the staff that had worked with them. I recently interviewed young people at our summer school and was repeatedly told that music was one of the most important things in their lives but that they had not been able to engage with music in school.

What are the barriers to engaging with these young people?

Structural barriers

We know that amount of engagement of Music Services with some 'hard to reach' groups has varied widely (Hallam, 2012 p31-32). It is more difficult to identify the depth or quality of engagement with these groups. When we started the Gloucestershire Hub inclusion strategy, it was recognised by the head of service that provision had often not matched the needs and interests of 'hard to reach' groups, or been culturally and financially accessible. This was also the most frequent reason given by music coordinators and senior staff in the schools and units we are working with now, for not previously engaging with the music service.

Schools, key workers and managers

One big challenge is engaging with the schools and other settings where the young people are. Local Authority staffing levels have been drastically cut, heads and managers often have multiple responsibilities with almost constant change, plus Ofsted pops up every so often and pushes all other priorities out of the window. In contrast to that, working as part of the hub can open doors, as part of the 'official' services, but we must continue to work carefully to ensure the offer meets every school's need.

Making at least some taster sessions free can be an important starting point, but does not however always ensure engagement. Managers are getting more wary of wasting precious time on initiatives that do not deliver sustainable outcomes. They seem more convinced by an approach that is honest about needing funding to be sustained. Doing thorough research has been another important element (Local Authority Committee papers are a great source) enabling us to go into meetings well informed and make best use of senior managers' time. Ultimately it is about delivering quality outcomes plus making a bit of effort to let managers know how things are going. I find that quick updates of a student's progress by email are highly appreciated. Noise Solution in Bury St. Edmunds use a blog system with their clients that social workers or teachers can access direct to see progress[1].

Professionals not knowing where to refer people

This is not easy to overcome. We have a County children's and families information service which includes details of all our provision, but many people don't seem to use it. We have had instances of staff in children's homes not knowing we existed when their senior manager (based at a different home in the group) had been working with us for a couple of years. We also see clusters of referrals from particular workers, which then drop off when staff change. The hub has developed a web site with a search facility for provision[2] and we are working hard on communications, but there is still a long way to go.

Barriers for students

We experience some common barriers to learning and engagement among children and young people. They are interconnected mostly with strong emotional components.

Disengagement

At some stage in our education, most of us learn to avoid the emotional pain of failing in learning by developing a multiplicity of strategies. The levels of honed skills in procrastination, diversion, distraction, passive disengagement etc. among the students we work with are quite impressive, if not very constructive. For example, one year 11 student had learnt to keep a teaching assistant busy all day trying to get him to write one sentence. He was a naturally active lad and did not enjoy desk work, but could quickly write three or four coherent sentences in an email if he wanted to negotiate with me to get a free recording session in exchange for some voluntary work. A year 9 girl is brilliant at hiding in a room by curling up inside or on top of a cupboard and staying completely silent and has also perfected just saying yes while someone is talking to (or at) her, while completely disengaging.

Low resilience

This is often shown in quite dramatic bursts of "can't do it", giving up easily, switching tasks or being easily distracted.

Refusal to work on things beyond school time

Quite often the young person has reached a level of grudging compliance with the system, often based on extrinsic motivations. Work has become for them a very negative thing, with very little intrinsic motivation. So music done in school time can be labelled work, leading to a conflict between desperately wanting to do music - for example, at a summer school - but not wanting to let go of this boundary.

Low self-esteem

This is both the product of poor learning habits and a driver of poor learning habits. For many young people it is very deep, and not easily shifted. Making a lasting difference takes consistent support, sometimes over years.

Aggression

I have only very rarely experienced aggressive or actively destructive responses, despite working in settings where these behaviours are regularly reported. What I have experienced has almost always been when a student is being emotionally pushed into a corner they cannot cope with, either by staff or other students.

Things that consistently work in overcoming these barriers

Music works

It works because for significant numbers of young people it provides the intrinsic motivation to get started on over-coming the barriers they face.

Music mentoring

This is a fairly new approach to this work, supported over the last seven years by Youth Music (Lonie, 2010). It values the power of a one-to-one engagement based on music, while at the same time giving 'permission' to address other life and learning issues. It involves joint setting of both musical and life goals with the mentee. It is not very different from what many good instrumental and vocal teachers have been doing for years, but it is much safer and more effective if the support element is clearly part of the brief for the teacher or mentor with appropriate training and support. Good music mentoring uses all the approaches and techniques described below.

Finding and connecting with the musician within

This means focusing on what a student can do rather than what they cannot do, using our own musicianship to connect with them wherever possible.

Observation

Learning from the student and those around them. As educators we need to be prepared to take time and effort to rebuild engagement in learning. This involves careful observation of the student, noticing the emotional aspects as well as the cognitive, building mutual understanding and trust and ideally being able to have a frank but sensitive discussion about what is going on. If we attend properly to students we can pick up quickly if someone is not coping. Significant behavioural problems usually only emerge as a defence reaction, if we persist with something a student is uncomfortable with.

We also need to attend to relevant insights from those who know students well. This often means asking - they may not be confident to volunteer information, seeing us as the experts! Teachers, parents, carers, teaching assistants etc. can have hugely useful insights.

Feedback – the oxygen of learning

I come across trained and experienced teachers not using feedback skills as effectively as they could do. Feedback needs to be accurate, constructive and balanced with as much praise as possible. Young people who live in challenging circumstances often have well developed 'bullshit detectors' so it is rarely possible to get away with empty compliments. We have to observe and listen and spot the good things.

It is important to structure the learning to maximise the opportunity for accurate positive feedback. Asking students "What was good and what needs improving" about a particular thing they have just done enables us to give positive feedback for the accuracy of their observation. For example, one student in a PRU loved singing and had the musical ability to hear when things were wrong but would easily panic, get upset and give up. She was encouraged to realise that her ability to hear what was wrong was a good thing – it showed she had a musical ear, and the fact that she got upset showed that she cared about music; these were the two most important starting points to become a good musician. This was real and genuine feedback for a student who had never managed to sing more than the first few lines of a song. Beginning to believe and trust this opened the door to learning. She has since recorded six songs, performed in public, passed a Bronze Arts Award, and is now working on a BTEC composition module.

Breaking learning into the right size steps

After over 30 years of teaching I still get this wrong, usually when I get overexcited at initial progress and make the next step too big, only to see confidence plummet, making it twice as much work to get to the next step. We need to be aware and realistic about where a student is, without placing limitations on what they might achieve. It needs a holistic approach that looks beyond just the obvious instrumental or vocal skills. For example being able to sit behind a drum kit with sticks in your hand and *not* play it is a musical skill – essential if you want other musicians to work with you and important for our sanity as teachers. If this is taught as a skill we can then give praise for getting it right. This is far more effective than just nagging when they don't get it right.

Being co-learners with the students

Basically it is just recognising the reality of the situation; they are learning to learn from us, we are learning to teach them. Admitting when we get things wrong as teachers can make it far easier for students to learn to cope with critical feedback themselves. Coping with the risk of getting things 'wrong' also opens the door to creativity. Part of this attitude is to recognise and value the students' passion for music and their specific musical skills. Young people who listen a lot to music can become very aurally aware and know instinctively when things fit or work and when they don't. It can also be helpful to spot and acknowledge other skills that a student has, even if they are negative. "You said to me that you are not very clever, but you seem to be extremely skilled at winding up the other teachers" (there needs to be a sufficiently good relationship for this to be a point of shared amusement rather than threatening).

Empowering

Students who have been pushed around in various ways in their lives can be very sensitive to issues of power. It is not helpful if the only power left to a student is the power to misbehave or disengage. Giving them control of what kind of music is created, what sounds are used etc. can be central to engagement, motivation and success. This is particularly true of looked after children, those who have been excluded or have experienced repeated failure with education. It is important to acknowledge and work with their knowledge of musical genres and their stylistic sensibilities. The worst thing we can do is to try and push onto them a poor 'teacher's interpretation' of a genre with which they are very familiar.

Giving choice needs to include the choice not to participate. This may be one of the few choices that some vulnerable young people have in their life.

Where low confidence is combined with a powerful desire to engage with music, then the slightest critical comment or even the possibility of success can trigger strong negative emotional reactions. We need to be willing to ride any resultant emotional 'storms', give the student space and assure them that we are willing to persist (but not false hope that we will be there forever, whatever happens).

One of the most empowering things we can do is teach children and young people to reflect for themselves on their music and to give feedback to their peers. At the right time, and with the right tools, leaving students to learn independently can be highly motivating, as is giving the opportunity to teach others. Being a peer leader is highly empowering and a valuable progression route. Working with peer leaders often opens up learning in ways that older "professional" teachers cannot.

When learning is not possible

The skills and approaches I have described will nearly always allow learning to take place, but even when we get everything right as a teacher, there are times when learning is not possible. Challenging behaviour may get in the way, or other things, such as uncertainty about living arrangements, may make it impossible for a student to focus, no matter how important the music is to them (cf. Maslow, 1954). This can happen more often for students with chaotic lives. We need to be willing just to let go and come fresh to the next session with no hard feelings. This also applies to children with mental health issues, such as depression, where if something has gone wrong with a session, or they have missed it, they may need huge reassurance that you will not want to give up on them. Sometimes as educators we need to take active steps to reduce the risks and impact of things going wrong. For example, if we are offering mentoring to someone who struggles to get to places on time, then discussing strategies with them, perhaps agreeing to text them an hour or two before (this needs to be cleared with managers in respect of safeguarding procedures) or making sure we have other productive work to do if they don't turn up so that resources are not wasted.

Allowing (or even encouraging) fun

We all need fun and it helps us learn. It is great to get students to re-connect with the possibility that when music goes wrong it is funny and we can enjoy a good laugh (needs to be initiated by the person who has gone wrong!). This can open up creativity. Well placed humour can be very powerful in defusing tension and connecting with students at a human level.

Flow

We need to create learning environments that allow for creativity and total absorption in the music and foster intrinsic motivation. I do not like interruptions or time constraints when I am working on playing, writing or recording music. There are times when you are blocked and need to take a break and other times when you are in the 'flow' and need to be able to carry on (cf. Csikszentmihalyi, 1990). The structures of a formal education context can be unresponsive to this. When this need for 'flow' is undermined students can give up and retreat to a less demanding context such as computer games to fulfil the same need to be engrossed or disconnected from the world.

At a recent taster day with 7 young offenders, the Youth Offending Team staff had promised MacDonald's burgers for lunch as an enticement to get them there. The whole group got so engaged in creating and recording a track that they refused to stop for lunch. They explained to rather surprised staff that they were not at all concerned that their food was cold, what mattered was that they had completed their track. I have repeatedly experienced this with summer schools where young people with very poor school attendance records are waiting to get in when staff arrive 40mins before the start time.

Setting clear boundaries – and implementing them consistently.

If we are doing all the other stuff right, most problems will be avoided. But there are boundary issues with many students. They often do not have clear limits at home and are used to pushing boundaries. This can turn into a self-destructive power game. At the simplest level we need to be clear with students when it is OK to make noise and talk and when we want them to be totally quiet, we need to be reasonable in our expectations, keep boundaries to a minimum, but it is essential to maintain them. Fair and reasonable boundaries create security. Having started my working life in a city centre project for unemployed young people I quickly developed a view that they have to believe that you will call the police if you need to. If they can see that in your eyes, then you will probably never need to!

Being ourselves

All of the elements discussed above involve us having secure confidence in ourselves and what we bring. This goes beyond our skills as educators. It is having a balanced self-awareness and personal self-esteem, so that we are not threatened by what the student brings and do not get tempted to indulge in negative power games.

Progression

One-to-one work is expensive and for young people who are not from wealthy backgrounds it is unlikely that it can be sustained long term. We work from the beginning to promote independent learning. A key objective is for them to progress and flourish as musicians. For this to happen we need to nurture the students' own intrinsic motivation, respecting and encouraging skills (often already existing) in learning independently through listening to music, watching musicians and finding lessons on YouTube and also just by spending time experimenting and of course, building their learning and practice skills, particularly the ability to reflect on their own performance. Overcoming very practical barriers can also be important. Often there are no opportunities to do music independently at their schools. YouTube and similar sites are blocked by filters (for looked after children this often extends to home settings), so students have no access to internet. It is helpful to find music software that is affordable and runs on the computer they have (we have been using Reaper[3] recently). Some students will progress into mainstream existing hub provision and this is to be hugely encouraged, but much of what is in place at the moment does not really match their needs and interests. The instruments available for hire are often not the ones they want to play.

Accreditation

This is often a high priority of agencies working with young people. I am by instinct an accreditation sceptic, but for individuals who are being told they have no prospect of getting GCSEs it can be important. The primary motivation of a Year 9 student who has just achieved Bronze Arts Award was to "prove to the f*****g teachers that I can do stuff". Seeing the grin on her face as the headteacher presented her certificate was highly rewarding! She is now working hard on a BTEC composition module. Our Summer Arts Colleges – specifically designed & funded by the Youth Justice Board for young offenders - are based around achieving Arts Award.

How is this paid for?

It is significant that this work is resourced primarily through a direct grant for delivery of the inclusion strategy (expected to total nearly £70k by the end of March 2015) from Gloucestershire Music, holders of the Hub funding. In addition to this we have had funding of £28K over the 17 months to March 2014 from Youth Music Inclusion.

We have operated a very simple sustainability model, saying to the various settings 'if you can fund at a per hour rate toward the upper end of what you would pay for a supply teacher, we will find, train and support a good quality music leader to deliver sessions. We will subsidise 1 hour sessions in the hope that you will soon want more'.

Summary and conclusion

- Engaging with so called 'hard to reach' young people is perfectly possible and sustainable
- This broad category of young people includes young people with significant levels of musical potential and musical creativity
- It is highly valued by significant senior staff in the local authority and in schools
- It does require an approach which some might see as different, but at core is just good teaching and the underlying principles will work well with all students
- Partnerships between Music Services and Community Music organisations can be a powerful way forward, but success requires changes of culture and attitude for both

I believe that consistency of provision for these children and young people is essential, for credibility with heads and service managers, to achieve quality outcomes and fulfil the hub brief. It is an ethical imperative when working with those students least able to cope with inconsistency. Inclusion should not and cannot be a marginal part of hub work and cannot be just funded with short term extra bits of funding. I would strongly contend that all hubs should be making this work a priority, making use of external funding where and when it is available, but planning to underwrite provision where it is not. At the same time, community music organisations need to shift attention from high profile one-off projects to consistent long-term work at sustainable costs.

References

Csikszentmihalyi, Mihaly (1990). Flow: *The Psychology of Optimal Experience*. New York: Harper & Row.
DfE (Department for Education) (2011) *The Importance of Music: a national plan for music education*. London: DfE.
Hallam, Richard (2012) *Music Education Grant 2011/2012 Report based on Local Authority data returns May 2012*. http://www.dickhallam.co.uk/articles-publications-and-reports.php (accessed 06.09.13).
Lonie, Douglas (2010) *Attuned to Engagement: The effects of a music mentoring programme on the agency and musical ability of children and young people*. London: Youth Music.
Maslow, A. (1954). *Motivation and personality*. New York, NY: Harper.

Notes

[1] www.noisesolution.org
[2] http://searchtool.gloucestershiremusic.co.uk
[3] http://www.cockos.com/reaper

Social *and* Artistic
– a reflection on balancing outcomes

Jess Abrams

Writing this piece has been quite a reflective process. It has challenged me to review some of my approaches and to reflect on methods that I take for granted. Here I will share my views on working with young people who are hard to reach. This chapter only touches the surface, but highlights some of the motivations and rationale behind the way I work as well as illuminating some of the processes in action. It's important to state at this point that I don't think there is only one way in which to do this work, this is just the way I work in this context. I hope it is useful.

As a music practitioner, many of the groups I work with are in the social care system. I've worked in young offenders' institutions and with ex-offenders, young people who have been excluded from school, homeless young people and those who have been identified by Social Work, for one reason or another, as 'at risk'. I work primarily with groups, but have, on occasion worked one to one. Regardless of the participant group I'm working with, I employ the same basic principle – the participants do the work. By this I mean they make the decisions along the way. Practitioners approach the work from different perspectives. Some feel that by focusing on the artistic outcome the participants will have meaningful and/or transformative social experiences as part of the process, while others focus on the social outcomes using the artistic undertaking as a tool or intervention. I don't think it's a case of social *versus* artistic, but a question of context; who the artist/s are working with and the reason he/she has been hired to do the work. The majority of *my* work is in settings where offering a meaningful musical experience is the tool or intervention by which there can be a range of social outcomes including confidence, the ability to communicate, make decisions, be part of a group and in fact build a community. My goal is to balance social and artistic outcomes, while very consciously ensuring that the process is socially driven. I don't tend to arrive knowing what the artistic outcome will be – the participants will decide - but I have yet to see a project produce a piece of work that the participants are not proud of. Is it an artistic masterpiece? I don't know. But what it *is*, is a meaningful process with a tangible piece of work at the end that people celebrate together with a sense of pride and connection.

Although always a musician, when I am working with a group, I am a music practitioner. While I utilise my musical ears and ability, I am not the one who is making the musical decisions; the group makes them. Working with socially driven outcomes raises three questions I always contend with in workshops: if the group is composing a song and making the lyric, chord and arrangement choices, how and when do I guide or intervene to ensure that the choices lend themselves to a quality musical outcome? A bigger question is: *should* I intervene at all? And the even *bigger* question: what constitutes a quality musical outcome? I try never to direct decision-making as, although it might be in the best interest of the song, I question if it's in the best interest of the participants. Being empowered to make their decisions, discuss, communicate, reason, debate and agree on choices is a key aspect of working with young people who may have had little opportunity to do this in their lives, especially in a creative setting.

I recently ran a project called 'Moving On' with a group of nine teenagers living in an emergency accommodation unit for vulnerable young people. Their chosen goal was to write and record an original song. The group was determined to keep the introduction of their song at 24 bars long. Without blatantly telling them it was too long, I asked them questions about the music they often listened to and how long the introductions usually were. Even after we had listened to several of their favourite tracks and they had all agreed that introductions are usually four to eight bars long, they were adamant that they wanted to keep the 24-bar intro – so we did. After the CD was produced, we had a final celebratory session where we listened to the finished song. It was at this point that more than one participant commented that they wished the intro were shorter. For me, this is not a project failure, but a great success. The participants were empowered to make their own informed decisions during the process yet afterwards were able to notice and reflect on how they would do it differently next time. On a musical level, they heard the impact the prolonged introduction had on the track - the waiting to get to the 'story' or 'meat' of the song. Aside from the music, however, there was an increased ability to be still and listen, to notice, to reflect on and critique their own work. In this particular group we had a range of issues including severe depression, ADHD, low literacy, low self-esteem and general behavioural issues. When we started, focusing and engaging in the music making process for more than a minute or two was challenging and simply being quiet and listening was unheard of. So the fact that by the end they were able to sit and listen to their song for over five minutes and then share their opinions led me, as well as the support team from the emergency accommodation unit, to believe that the process of music-making and decision-making was successful for the participants on many levels.

While I am actively engaging in practices that incur social outcomes, I am, of course, doing this in the context of the musical *outcome* the participants are working towards. After all, the group is *only* focusing on a musical/artistic outcome. This means that I am constantly trying to balance the social outcomes with the artistic. There are often conversations in our 'down-time' in which participants share something personal, sometimes from quite an emotional frame of mind. This is something I believe, and research shows (MacDonald et al., 2012; Juslin & Sloboda, 2003), music can elicit. In these instances, I try to steer that emotion into the musical work. It would be easy to be a sympathetic ear, but I am wary of taking this route too far for two reasons. Firstly, I am not a counsellor or therapist and don't want to take them into a process that I am not equipped to handle. Secondly, in those moments meaningful lyrics are at our fingertips.

One participant in the Moving On project wrote a set of very personal lyrics in response to being out of her anti-depressant medication. Usually very bubbly and energetic, this participant arrived at our third session despondent and unwilling to work as part of the group. While the group worked with my colleague, she and I discussed how she was feeling and went on to explore how we could use her present feelings to write lyrics. By using examples of contemporary artists such as Adele and Rhianna, both of whom she'd mentioned liking, we agreed that some of our darkest times gave us our best lyrics. We then went into the following lyric writing process:

> Me: 'You're missing something (in this case her anti-depressant medication) that's important to you, how does that make you feel?'
>
> Her: *Sad*

Me: 'Without you, I feel?'

Her: 'Without you I feel blue' (sitting up a little at this point)

Me: 'Great, write it down' (pulls out her notebook and pen and writes it down)

Me: 'What else does it make you feel?' 'Without you I feel?'

Her: 'Without you I feel blue, sad inside and angry too' (becomes more animated while writing down the second line)

Me: '**WITH** you I feel?'

Her: 'With you I feel happy, light and new'

At this point, she was animated and enjoying the process. She was no longer hunched in her seat, head down and mumbling but engaged in a creative process that eventually led her back into working with the group. It was a visceral shift. In the end, we did not use the lyrics she had written, but the process was musical and creative and instead of delving into her depression, we used it. Again, bearing in mind my parameters, I feel that this approach outweighed taking her on a path of exploring her feelings of depression which I may not have properly navigated.

I use a range of methods, particularly in terms of ensuring that the project and the music-making process are unintimidating and accessible. Ironically, there is a lot of time in my workshops spent not making music at all, but building rapport. To build rapport, being genuine and transparent is essential. The young people I tend to work with have seen a lot, lived a lot, are often street smart and savvy and distrusting of adults – thinking we either have our own agenda or are not trustworthy. I often explain my way of working with them rather than go ahead with it in a way that may seem manipulative. Sessions always start with the group coming together to share something that has stood out about their week. The purpose of this time together is two-fold: firstly to help each participant to become 'present' and secondly, to give each person – including the leaders - a chance to be heard. We then discuss and agree as a group, what we'd like to happen that day. In a two-hour session with eight participants and two leaders, this process can take around 30 minutes. I do not see this as simply a preliminary activity, but as vital a part of the session as the music-making. At the end of a session we come back together to reflect on how things have gone and confirm what we want to do in the following session.

One of the luxuries I have in working in the non-formal sector is that of a flexible outcome (within reason). Obviously, I'm hired to run a music-making project, but what we actually *do* musically will be up to the group. By offering a series of options such as composing, performing or recording, the participants have their own say very early on, fostering a sense of ownership. While I know that the participants and I will be making music, I don't know what the genre, form and output will be. To some degree, it's dependent on what the commissioning body (the funder!) wants, but in reality it's far more dependent on what the group chooses. In my experience the majority of organizations or local authorities funding this work are also flexible in that they know the value of the arts as an intervention and are looking for the social outcomes as much as, if not more than, the artistic ones. The reason I mention this at this point is to further explain why I allow so much 'non-music-making' time. A perfect example of this was when I worked on a project in a young offenders' institution. Due to various staffing issues, our music sessions were 3.5 hours long, often with as many as 15 young men at once. While a few of them were very musical, none were willing to work solidly on music for 3.5 hours. We would work in 20-30 minute increments interspersed with small groupings of participants carrying on conversations. I sometimes think the greatest work took place in the conversations – when these young men, who often did not interact with each other outside of the music making sessions, would talk quite openly about topics including family, next steps and even their anxieties. There was a sense of community built through playing music together that lent itself to connections and friendships. I did, however, bring them back to music-making as projects are often reasonably short and it's important that the group accomplishes what they set out to do.

So, after discussing everything BUT music-making, perhaps I should share a bit about how we actually make music. I don't tend to engage in warm-up games as, in my experience, these are seen as stupid or silly by teenagers (with children and adults however, we always have fun being silly together before embarking on the 'serious' work). The exception to this is anything with drumsticks – they seem to be the epitome of cool for some reason, but are not always safe or practical to use depending on the environment. Usually, I start off with a very common song that people tend to know. For example, with the Moving On project, I used 'Lean On Me'. Initially I'll play the chords in an extremely simple one-handed voicing on the piano and invite participants to sing along. But after one or two attempts, I ask if anyone would like to learn to play the chords on piano. I have yet to experience a project where a participant doesn't volunteer and in most cases there's someone who can play far better than I do. Depending on what instrumentation is available on site, I may also teach someone to play the bass line and guitar chords. By first learning a well known three or four chord song the starting point is familiar to the participants and they quickly recognise when they have managed to play and sing the song correctly. This quick sense of success leads them to believing that they CAN be musical.

At this point, it becomes clear who is reticent and who is willing to jump in. Of course, neither way is wrong, it's just a reflection of each participant's approach to the project, how they make music and how they engage. It helps me to gain some initial insight into each person I'm working with, but it's still only touching the surface. In my experience, there can be a strong reaction to being asked or expected do something. Taking a much more relaxed approach is often the only way to ensure that people engage. I do this by making suggestions quite passively, without distilling a sense of expectation and not making their choice the centre of attention but continuing to focus on what else is happening in the room. Many times, I'll turn around to find that the participant has chosen to do the task/join in, when they don't feel that if they choose *not* to, they will have 'failed' or disappointed me. Once it's clear how quickly it's possible to play a song, we very quickly turn to composing a new tune. This is done by simply asking the group to put the three or four chords they just learned into a new order. The beginnings of a new song are born! The group then decides what kind of song they want to write. I often start by giving them the simple choice of a happy song or a sad song after which we'll go into more detail. With lyrics, sometimes someone will already have an idea for them, other times we have to go through a process to explore what the group wants to write about. When writing from scratch, I employ two songwriting approaches in combination. One involves eliciting images relating to a theme, e.g. if the theme is 'goodbyes' I might ask them to imagine a train station, a hug goodbye or hanging up a telephone etc. The other is creating a list of rhyming words that relate to the topic, expanding them into rhyming sentences and finally stanzas. The group will also choose tempo, time signature (mostly 4/4) and feel. Melodies can be challenging, but mostly come as we speak the lyrics or play the chords round and round. In a recent workshop, one extremely shy participant said she heard a melody in her head, but didn't want to hum it out loud. She and a fellow participant went to another room so that she could hum it to her privately. The fellow participant then relayed it to the rest of the group.

Bearing in mind that there may be different levels of literacy in the group, I try to work with a series of letters and colours for chords and arrangement indicators. I do not use musical notation. With input from participants, we will discuss what symbols they would like to reflect an action. For example if the melody goes 'up' they may want an upward arrow. Different instruments often get highlighted in different colours.

Once we get to the point of chords, melody, lyrics and feel, we keep practising. We will fine tune, change, discuss and debate the way it will start and end, etc. If the group has decided that they want to record, if at all possible, I will try to do so in a professional recording studio or an extremely well-equipped college studio. Recording in a college is often a very unintimidating way for participants to have an experience of a college, e.g. a possible 'back door' into further education.

I try never to let the height of our work be the last thing we do together. I aim for there to be one or two sessions after any recording or performance to allow time for the group to reflect, review and celebrate our work together as well as say goodbye. Closure is important, as is exploring what next steps might be available to those who want to continue with music-making. Discovering they're good at playing an instrument can be empowering, but without support they may not continue. Sometimes, there is a next step, but more often than not, there is nowhere for them to continue to play music in a way that is not too formal or intimidating. I find this one of the more challenging parts of my work – ending a project without being able to offer concrete next steps for the participants. Again, being up front with the group, not promising anything I cannot deliver, is key.

For me, underlying all the work I do is a sense of 'duty of care'. Although a term often associated with liability in law, I associate it with the responsibility we have as music practitioners towards our participant groups, especially if they are vulnerable groups. We must know our strengths *and* our limitations. Although I am a firm believer that we cannot standardise the field of Community Music, or any other arts practice, I do believe we must work with a very high set of standards. This can be isolated work with little support, so we must ensure that we have a network of peers with whom we reflect, share and develop as practitioners.

Recently, in a workshop, a 15 year old participant asked, 'Why do you always answer a question with a question?' to which I replied (with a question), 'Why, does it bother you?' He replied that it can get a little annoying, but he understands why I do it and that I wasn't just 'giving them the answers'.

I am transparent and he is smart.

I love my work.

References

MacDonald, R., Kreutz, G. & Mitchell, L. (eds.). (2012). *Music, Health & Wellbeing*. Oxford: Oxford University Press.

Juslin, P.N. & Sloboda, J.A. (eds.). (2003). *Music and Emotion: Theory and research*. Oxford: Oxford University Press.

Music and looked after children

Helen Chambers

Introduction

This chapter will focus on music making with looked after children and young people, a 'group' often considered 'hard to reach', 'vulnerable', or 'living in challenging circumstances'. They are over-represented in the groups who are 'not in education, employment and training' (NEET) or in contact with child and adolescent mental health services (CAMHS) or youth justice.

Most school-aged looked after children will be part of the usual class or youth group, and may not attract additional consideration. Some may be taking part in targeted programmes in out-of-school settings, working with community musicians and youth arts workers. I hope the information and observations in this chapter will be of interest to musicians working with children, whatever the setting.

I will consider who the children and young people are, and why they may be looked after, and hard to reach. I will draw on research and practical examples of good, creative practice with children cared for by 'corporate parents'. I use the term 'children' particularly to draw attention to the pre-teens, and because many older young people have been denied a nurturing childhood.

> Before I didn't want to sing because my heart was hurting. I was really angry but I really wanted to sing. When you sing you can show how you feel. I didn't feel shy anymore about singing at the end.
>
> (Girl, Myrtle Theatre Company, quoted in Petrie & Knight, 2011)

Who are looked after children?

Children are a great deal more than a set of statistics, so it may be helpful to get these out of the way.

There are 67,050 children in England looked after at 31 March 2012 (DfE, 2012); 75% of all these children were cared for by foster carers. Approximately another 8% were cared for by family and friends. Many people think of teenagers in residential care homes as the majority of those 'in care', yet children in residential care are approximately 11% of the total population of looked after children and young people. Most children who are in the care of the local authority live in a family, just like any other child.

Children enter care at any time throughout their life if circumstances raise concerns with health, care, education and other services, as well as at a parent's request. In 2011, 24% were under five years of age at entry to care, 18% aged 5-9 years and 58% over the age of ten years.

Like any other child they need a 'good enough' parent who looks out for them, speaks out on their behalf and responds to their needs. For children in care this is a statutory role for local authorities – all councillors and council officers share the corporate responsibility, and this must be shared by everyone including health bodies, education services, police and youth justice, as well as private and third sector organisations (DCSF, 2008).

Services aim to support children living with relatives, friends and foster families, or sometimes – especially for older young people – in children's residential care homes, special boarding schools and secure units.

Section 20 of the Children Act 1989 – Voluntary Care
Under Section 20 of the Act, the local authority has a duty to provide accommodation for 'children in need'. This accommodation – either in foster care, residential care or a kinship placement – can be long or short-term, and does not involve the courts. The parent retains full parental responsibility.
Section 31 of the Children Act 1989 – Care Order
The court can create a care order under Section 31(1) (a) of the Children Act, placing a child in the care of a designated local authority, with parental responsibility being shared between the parents and the local authority. It can only be made if the court is satisfied that 'the harm, or likelihood of harm, is attributable to … the care given to the child, or likely to be given … if the order were not made, not being what it would be reasonable to expect a parent to give … or the child being beyond parental control'. The court may make an interim care order (for up to eight weeks in the first instance) to investigate a child's home circumstances.
(Social Care Institute for Excellence (SCIE), 2012)

Many people believe that children come into care because of their behaviour – they are out of control. In fact only 2% come into care for 'socially unacceptable behaviour'. Abuse and neglect account for 62% of children coming into care, and family dysfunction a further 14% (DCSF, 2008). The longer term consequences of this pre-care experience may affect a child throughout their life.

A child or young person's experience in care varies. Frequent placement moves and consequent instability of home and education are significant problems for many children. More than 10% of children in care had three or more placements in the year ending March 2011; 44% of children had only one care placement in one year (DfE, 2012).

This means that a sense of belonging and attachment to people and place may be severely disrupted, resulting in anxiety, depression and a poor sense of security and trust in others. This is in addition to the difficulties they may have experienced before coming into care, and is reflected in their having significantly higher levels of mental health and emotional well-being problems. Additionally, looked after children are nine times more likely to have a Special Education Needs statement and their achievements are significantly less than their peers.

Why are looked after children hard to reach?

Looked after children are individuals with differing interests and personalities, they are not a homogenous group. Children have ordinary busy lives, and also have additional calls on their time and sometimes additional needs and difficulties that need to take priority for them and their carers.

As music educators you may already work with looked after children in an early years group with their carers, in an after school primary choir, or in a youth band or project. How might you recognise them as 'looked after'? Hopefully you won't, unless you are working on a project set up to work with 'looked after young people', 'Children in Challenging Circumstances', or perhaps when you are with NEET young people, where they may be over-represented. You become one of the additional people in their lives.

Figure 1 indicates some of the other people who may be part of their lives, and it will depend on individual circumstances who is important to them, and how they spend their time.

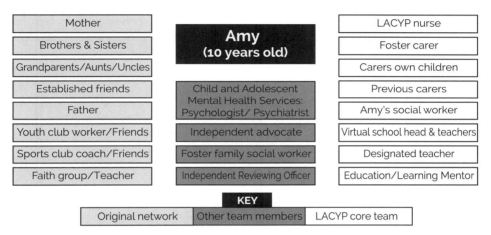

'Contact visits' with parents, siblings and other family members can occupy much or little weekend and out-of-school time. This is generally a high priority and greatly affects their emotional worlds. Reaching children and young people usually means reaching the carer and children's services managers first. Experience indicates that the arts and creative sector are not well understood within children's services, especially in their contribution to emotional well-being, resilience and placement stability (Chambers, 2009). This lack of understanding of each other's worlds, priorities and potential often provides significant barriers, especially in times of diminishing resources.

Should we target a group?

There can be concern that 'targeting' a particular group labels and discriminates and this should be avoided. Some children and their carers welcome the additional understanding, support and time that can provide a stepping stone to general provision, or simply an opportunity to meet others in similar circumstances. The comments below were made by a carer and a young person involved in the Sing Up National Children's Bureau (NCB) Looked after Children Programme, 2009-2011.

> You can't take them everywhere because of some of the behaviour problems. But here it didn't matter, no one took any notice and it was good for them to let off steam. (Foster Carer)

A girl, speaking about the older young leaders said:

> *I like to meet new people in the care system – I know what they're about. I look up to them because they have their future – it's inspiration for me* (Girl, age 15)

The Customs House in South Shields is building on its work with NCB and Creativity, Culture and Education (CCE) (Sheikh, 2013) to provide a Families who Foster programme, that includes activities and Arts Award support for carers' own children and grandchildren, as well as their foster children. The model is popular with carers and local care services as it 'normalises' the care experience and helps build attachment and placement stability, key concerns for children's services.

When targeted projects are developed it is important that enough planning time is given to effective partnership work between cultural and children's services partners to build confidence and professional relationships. Musicians and others often find it difficult to find the right person to speak to, one who has the time, seniority and commitment to attend meetings and ensure communication within their service. Partnership work is essential if work is to have lasting benefit and be sustainable.

The day-to-day care for the children is placed with foster carers or residential care workers, supported by social workers. This includes their travel to any activities. Even when young people are able to travel independently it may be the carer or social worker who ensures they remember and turn up!

In their evaluation of the Sing UP NCB Programme with looked after children Petrie and Knight (2011) commented:

> *Foster carers manage a busy and complex workload. If they are to maintain children's engagement with the singing sessions, the foster carers' own needs require consideration, for example regarding the timing of sessions, traffic and parking issues.*

Good practice with looked after children and young people

All musicians must contribute to safeguarding and promoting the welfare of children in the community and adhere to correct procedures and policies. I hope that we can take as a given that good practice with looked after children is underpinned by the Music Leader & Sound Sense Music Education Code of Practice (Sound Sense, n.d.) as well as any additional professional training in youth arts, teaching or care practice. The Sing Up Training Programme for musicians and others working with looked after children and young people (figure 2) contains a helpful indication of good practice.

Figure 2
The following pointers are based on leaders' experiences of working with all children, as well as those looked after. They build on the Young Leaders 'How-to' guide. • Ensure that equality and accessibility of all young people is considered. • Pay attention to the inclusion needs of children with physical disabilities – including sensory – when using instruments or equipment, and those with special education needs.

- Share appropriately and sensitively information gained about the participant across the workforce. Try to keep to facts rather than conjecture/hearsay.
- Keep in place consistent structures that the young people have had a part in designing, including group agreements.
- As a delivery team plan more work than you will need and be flexible according to the group dynamics of the day.
- There may be a wide spectrum of needs and behaviours in mixed groups. Try to use fully inclusive techniques and styles of games and processes to include all. This may mean some work has to be individually tailored to a child.
- Be aware of including different learning levels and styles.
- Be aware of the subject matter occurring in things like lyric writing and the impact this may have on individuals.
- Participants' moods or attitudes may vary from week to week – try not to make assumptions and allow opportunity for changes and development.
- Try to be affirming of all contributions even if they are not what you intended or required.
- Think about issues that can have unintended consequences that may cause trouble e.g. leaving instruments lying around so their unsupervised use causes a problem. This can introduce negativity into the relationship.
- Avoid 'spotlighting' children and young people (e.g. assigning solos etc) until you are sure they are ready. Use indirect exercises to build leading and turn taking.
- Be aware of things like loud noise, darkness, photography etc that can be a cause of concern for some young people.
- Music and emotions are very closely linked. Using games to explore this safely needs full planning, considering what outcomes may occur and what is in place to support the unexpected.
- Involve participants in your evaluation from the beginning.

One of the frequently mentioned worries for practitioners is that of safeguarding and child protection. Pie Factory Music, an organisation based in East Kent, has a set of safeguarding policies and enhanced procedures to ensure safe care of participants and practitioners, which advise practitioners to provide:

- a clear line of accountability for musicians
- enhanced CRB process
- awareness of legal guidance
- principles of Good Practice for Community Musicians
- promoting good practice with children guidance
- enhanced permissions and safeguarding requirements

- recognition and indicators of abuse and bullying
- information on responding to a young person making a disclosure or allegation
- reporting procedures for the above
- key contacts
- clear drop-off and pick-up arrangements

I make a plea that you work with others and not in isolation. This may be as part of a larger music organisation, or as a sole practitioner within a wider partnership. Building good partnership relationships with strategic partners and funders is a vital stepping stone to sustainable, safe practice.

Petrie and Knight (2011) commented that much of a project's success was dependent on the strength of the partnerships formed between the music organisation and their main partners in the local authority. A weak partnership could have a negative impact, while a strong partnership was mutually beneficial.

As a project leader from Sound It Out (ibid) said:

> We have a very good partnership with the local authority – they know the young people and the carers trust them. It wouldn't have been possible without their support.

Many artists find that as trust is developed between care staff, carers and practitioners, it provides better understanding of needs and difficulties that arise. This does not mean the sharing of confidential information or loss of a child/young person's privacy, but rather that as a professional practitioner you are making a contribution to the life experience of the young person and are valued accordingly.

Whatever the music you make it is important to keep the enjoyable, fun, participation of children and young people with whom you are working at the centre of your practice. Sheikh (2013) used a Theory of Change Model to evaluate how art and cultural activities promote resilience and wellbeing of looked after children. One finding was that high levels of planning and preparation, as well as flexibility of practice to meet needs and adapt to venue, are essential. It is not so much about providing music classes as about providing fun places in which to make music.

Towards a pedagogy with looked after children

For those who mistrust theories it may be helpful to reflect on Deane, Hunter & Mullen (2011) in their introduction to the review of Singing Beyond the Mainstream:

> The intention of using theoretical frameworks is not to demonstrate academic links. Kurt Lewin himself, both an academic and CEO of a major US company, used the memorable phrase: 'there is nothing so practical as a good theory.' We take this to mean both helping make sense of experience and also guiding future action.

Work with three multi-arts organisations and their local authority partners (Chambers, 2009) demonstrated that arts practitioners working with social pedagogic values can engage in work that is supportive of emotional wellbeing, as well as building the arts skills of the child. Much high quality arts practice involves creative practitioners working in partnership with the care system based on the principles of social pedagogic practice, and this will be the focus of the rest of the chapter.

The term social pedagogy can be off-putting - it is hard to pronounce! Move beyond that and think of it as where education and care meet. It is education in its broadest sense, concerned with bringing up children and supporting their development overall:

> ..a physical thinking, feeling creative human being in relationship with other people and already contributing to our society. (Petrie, 2011)

The pedagogue helps sustain the child's overall development, by means of a relationship built on trust and active encouragement for the child. Building children's resilience and confidence, opening their eyes to new possibilities, and offering activities that are challenging – but not too challenging – are all part of pedagogic practice. In Denmark, the training of social pedagogues includes pedagogy and psychology, social and health studies, communication and management, as well as arts and creative practice known as 'the common third' (Chambers & Petrie, 2009b).

Social pedagogy provides a theoretical, ethical and practical understanding for working with children and vulnerable adults. Pedagogues reflect using their heads, hearts and hands. They think about what is happening in a situation and the part their actions, and those of others, may have played. They consider how they feel about the situation, colleagues and participants; and how this may affect them. Finally, they reflect on what they and others do, and might do differently. All these elements advise their future practice individually and as a team of people supporting each other and those in their care.

Music educators are not social pedagogues, but these principles can inform their work and help to build better understanding of the team of people who surround the child/young person. It was with this in mind that Professor Pat Petrie and I worked with arts practitioners to develop the 'artist pedagogue' role (Chambers & Petrie, 2009b). This is based on a set of social pedagogic principles and values (figure 3) and a reflective learning framework for practice (figure 4). The generic term artist can be read as 'music educator' or 'musician'. When helping develop the framework, Myrtle Theatre Company said:

> *Artist Pedagogues understand that working with children in care, especially artistic work that taps into emotions, can be extremely challenging emotionally for the adults working with them, they need to be prepared for this. (Chambers & Petrie, 2009b)*

Figure 3: Principles and values for artists and creative practitioners working with looked after children

- Aspire to provide the best for all children, to build confidence and open doors to opportunity.
- Ensure safe boundaries of confidentiality for the exchange of information and the building of mutual relationships.
- Work with their head, hands and heart to support children's wellbeing and to make sure that the approach to creative practice is flexible. This is to accommodate the variety of situations that may arise for looked after children and the children's responses to these.

- Aim high with regard to artistic achievement and at the same time be realistic about what is achievable - ensuring the child's wellbeing must be given priority over other considerations.
- Work in partnership with carers and members of children's services to ensure children's participation is adequately supported and resourced.
- Keep children and workers safe from harm, by putting child protection procedures, appropriate risk assessments and enhanced Criminal Records Bureau (CRB) checks in place.
- Reflect on their practice based on the values and principles of social pedagogy, below.

Figure 4: Reflections on principles and practice for artist pedagogues

Area for reflection	In practice
Children as whole persons	There is a focus on children as whole persons and support and consideration for their wellbeing, physically, emotionally, socially and creatively.
	There is place for the expression of fun and joy, as well as more difficult emotions.
Relationship with children	The artist pedagogue sees her/himself not only as an artist who inspires children's creativity, but also as someone whose relationship with the children can have a wider effect.
	The relationship between the artist pedagogue and the children should be based on respecting the children and building their trust.
	The children need to experience a sense of security as a basis for developing confidence and a feeling of worth in themselves and in their creative practice.
Relevant theories and self-knowledge	The artist pedagogue is open to learning opportunities such as finding out about relevant theories, such as attachment theory.
	Artist pedagogues are also observant of their own emotional reactions to the work. They need to reflect on the feelings that arise in the sometimes challenging demands they may meet when working with children.
	The artist pedagogue applies both theory and self knowledge to their practice.
Everyday activities, as well as creative work	Artist pedagogues are practical. They pay attention to the everyday activities that their work involves, alongside those that relate more directly to creativity. This may include, for example, arranging and giving consideration to mealtimes and snacks, settling-in times at the beginning of work; and transport arrangements.

Being and working together	The artist pedagogue fosters the importance of working together as a group. This applies to all the children and adults who are involved in a piece of work including, for example, carers.
There is no feeling of 'us and them' among the different professionals who may be participating, or between adults and children. This understanding can be demonstrated, for example, by everyone sharing mealtimes or snacks, or clearing up.
The artist pedagogue acts to ensure that the group values all its members. The whole group contributes to the creative work, to the emotional climate and can be an important source of mutual support.
The rights of children to be heard	Artist pedagogues do not limit their understanding of children's rights to procedures and legislation. They believe that children have a right to contribute their experience and ideas to the activities in which they participate – creative and otherwise.
A strength of creative practice is that it is a means by which children's voices may be heard about matters that concern them deeply. However, creative activity with looked after children should not necessarily be 'issue led'. Play and fun can be just as appropriate.
Team around the child	Artist pedagogues value teamwork and respect the contributions of others in bringing up children. They form good working relationships with other professionals, members of the local community, and especially with parents and carers. This is for the wellbeing of the children concerned and to underpin the success of the creative activities undertaken.
Positive role models	Artist pedagogues should be aware of themselves as role models for the adults and children with whom they work.
This should be reflected in the respect they show to others and the importance they attach to attentive listening and responding supportively to other group members.

When discussing practice in the light of the reflection framework, I will draw on examples cited in two reports, Give them the Best (Chambers & Petrie, 2009a) and I want to Sing (Petrie & Knight, 2011).

Considering the reflection framework

The child as a whole person is the essence of child-centred practice. We move beyond labels such as 'SEN' or 'hard to reach' to ensure a child experiences music as part of their life. In the Sing Up NCB evaluation of seven different music organisations, working with children holistically rather than seeing music activities as separate from the children's other experiences, or as a solution to a problem, was seen by almost all of the leaders involved as essential for good practice.

> *Everywhere, the intention was that the children should enjoy creativity and have fun, rather than produce a polished performance and this approach was successful.* (Petrie & Knight, 2011)

> *We are community musicians and we have to work with well-being in a holistic way, about feeling good, positive engagement and finding out what the children are like and are good at.* (Singing leader, Music Pool ibid)

Building relationships and sustaining them appropriately with children whose lives have already been affected by loss and separation, and often neglect and abuse, can be complex. It is not the place of this author to write about attachment difficulties often experienced by looked after children, as well as others. A simple overview can be found in *Understanding Why* (Ryan, 2006), and more detailed information from other authors (e.g. Schofield & Beek, 2006; Cairns & Stanway, 2004; Golding, 2007). Consistent, safe and boundaried relationships between practitioners and children are essential to build trust and enable a child or young person to express themselves. It is important that there is a clear entry and exit strategy for the work, so that children know that this relationship is time limited and expectations of something more sustained are not formed. Expect good things from children, give appropriate responsibilities and boundaries and remain the responsible adult with other team members. Tim Fleming of community music organisation Whitewood and Fleming commented:

> *Attention to detail is crucial – always go the extra mile for them, maintain a commitment to this. Give them the best you can in all respects – the best artists, equipment, and work environment.* (Chambers & Petrie, 2009a)

Relevant theories and self-knowledge - for the purpose of this discussion I am taking social pedagogy theory, described earlier, as a base for practice. The work of social pedagogues and artist pedagogues builds on relationships that are both personal and professional. The 'personal' self is that which our friends and family know, but we share more sparingly in our professional lives. The artist pedagogue is encouraged to relate with others, share appropriately, and not be afraid to reveal themselves as thinking, feeling people with their own experiences, sense of fun, compassion etc. We meet as fellow human beings. The professional self is developed through theory and practice and is informed by ethics, values, knowledge and experience. Artist pedagogues also support children's well-being and self esteem. This is reflected in their approach to the children, as well as how they cooperate with social workers and carers. The 'private' self consists of the personal matters that we may decide not to reveal, depending on the context of the people we are with, (although this private self is at the core of the creative self, performer or composer). Self-knowledge may be acquired over time and through honest personal reflection, allowing us to think how our own feelings and history may affect a situation, and allowing us to behave in the best interests of the child.

Everyday activities that are shared help to bring a commonality between participants and practitioners, build trust and make music and music-making a part of common life events. Conversations in the minibus are often prized in youth work. Many artist pedagogues value conversations when making food and eating together with children.

Being and working together - experienced, effective arts organisations, bring together, train and support artists that work with looked after children. They provide space after each session for reflection, where they use head, heart and hands to consider how things have gone, and plan for the next one. This team approach has been essential in building trust between team members, and in developing the skills of practitioners. Arts practitioners often benefit from involving care staff and carers as equal partners in activities, involved in planning and reflection. It is important to be clear about the expectation placed on each practitioner. If the carers and education staff can trust the artists to provide a safe space, and keep it open for expression, then all benefit. It is important to clarify expectations with all who are present, rather than be disappointed that carers do or don't intervene. In the Sing UP NCB programme Pie Factory Music, singing leaders identified the positive effects when foster carers were present in the sessions:

> *It was really effective having the foster carers in the workshop with the children. For some children it gave them enough confidence to take part and once they were engaged the foster carers stepped back and let the child work independently. For those young people with more severe needs, it was helpful to have another voice of encouragement and practically another pair of hands to help with the workshop. On the whole I observed that having the foster carers in the workshop gave a feeling of safety to the children.* (Reflective Journal – singing leader, Pie Factory Music, in Petrie & Knight, 2011)

The right of the child to be heard is both a right for participation in family and school life and a necessary part of creative expression. There may be many reasons why looked after children feel not heard, despite many consultation exercises. Foster carers and social workers may wish to act, but be prevented by resource or local and national policy, especially if there are safeguarding concerns.

When children and young people write song lyrics, or devise work, they can express wishes and experiences that are hard to hear, but have a right to be heard. If safeguarding concerns arise then it is essential to talk with the child's social worker, not simply with the foster carer or residential care worker.

> *The quality of the singing was wonderful, some of the looked after children had written songs – both words and music. They were very prepared and committed and the singing was very confident. It was moving to see the relationships that they had with the musicians and with each other.* (Petrie & Knight, 2011)

Team around the child may be a misnomer for the experience of how effectively the many people who affect looked after children (figure 1) actually join up. Information may not travel between a child's carer and social worker, or the foster carer's social worker. Petrie and Knight considered reflective learning conversations between partners as major vehicles for professional development as part of good quality practice.

Being a positive role model – a positive adult in the life of a young person - is a discipline and affects how practitioners think, feel and behave with children, young people and each other. Social media can sometimes place what was personal into the public domain – sometimes inadvertently and inappropriately.

I think it's remembering that everything you say has an impact on them and that training on social pedagogy really helped us understand that a lot more. It was definitely worth doing. The fact that you're playing a part in how they all develop – I know we should be aware of that anyway but sometimes it's difficult.
(Support worker, Sound it Out, in Petrie & Knight, 2011)

Evaluating your work

At the beginning of any work you are doing it is important to think how you will evaluate, so be clear about the purpose of the work, who has decided this and why. I have outlined below some possible areas, and examples you may want to consider. Place children and young people at the centre and consider funders' requirements– the latter can be vital to sustainable practice. I suggest below some points to consider.

How are you evaluating?

- What resources do you have for the evaluation - people and money?
- When should it be done?
- How can you collect the relevant information for the evaluation?

What are you evaluating?

- The quality of the music/art achieved at the end of the project e.g. performance quality, publication (e.g. Dillon, 2010).
- Quality of the inclusive process and engagement of children (e.g. Chambers, 2009).
- Development or improvement of communication skills (e.g. Sempik & Munro, 2010).
- Identifying defined qualities of resilience and well-being (e.g. Sheikh, 2013).
- Participation in service development (e.g. Chambers & Ryan, 2007).
- The quality of the artists' practices (e.g. Petrie & Knight, 2010).
- Action research to understand how the process has worked (e.g. Chambers & Petrie, 2009).

How can best practice be achieved?

There is need for consistent funded provision of work with trained and supported musicians who are confident that their work is valued by children, carers and the corporate parent.

There is need for better understanding of the value of music and the arts by children's services, not purely for the talented, but rather as a part of a fun and ordinary life.

There is need for a greater awareness of how artists working with carers can enhance communication skills, personal expression and resilience.

There is a need for nurturing consistent care for some of our most vulnerable children who are in the care of the corporate parent.

I hope the foregoing chapter provided some ideas of how best practice can be achieved. It may be summarised by an acronym 'PASTE'.

Partnerships, policies and procedures

Artist pedagogues

Sustained funding and relationships

Training and support for artists who work with looked after children

Evaluation that informs practice and funders

References

Cairns, K. & Stanway, C. (2004) *Learn the Child: Helping looked after children to learn - a good practice guide for social workers, carers and teachers.* London: British Association for Adoption and Fostering (BAAF).

Chambers, H. & Ryan, M. (2007) *How to use Creative Methods for Participation.* London: NCB.

Chambers, H. (2009) *People with Passion: Getting the right people around the table.* London: NCB.

Chambers, H. & Petrie, P (2009a) *Give them the Best: A final report about the development of a learning framework for artists who work with looked after children and young people.* (Unpublished).

Chambers, H. & Petrie, P. (2009b) *Artist Pedagogue Learning Framework.* London: CCE/NCB.

Children in Care in England (2012) SN/SG/4470 House of Commons Library.

DCSF (2008) *Care Matters: A time to deliver for children in care.* London: DCSF.

Deane, K., Hunter, R. & Mullen, P. (2011) *Sing Up Beyond the Mainstream: Towards a learning programme.* http://www.singup.org/fileadmin/singupfiles/previous_uploads/Sing_Up_BTM_towards_a_learning_programme.pdf (accessed 01.08.2013).

DfE (2012) *Children looked after in England (including adoption and care leavers) year ending 31 March 2012* (SFR 20/2012). London: DfE.

Dillon, L. (2010) *Looked After Children and Music Making: An evidence review.* London: Youth Music.

Golding, K. (2007) *Nurturing Attachments: Supporting children who are fostered or adopted.* London: Jessica Kingsley.

Petrie, P. (2011) *Communication skills for working with children and young people: Introducing Social Pedagogy.* London: Jessica Kingsley.

Petrie, P. & Knight, A. (2011) *'I Want to Sing': Sing Up National Children's Bureau Looked After Children Programme Evaluation.* London: Institute of Education, University of London.

Ryan, M. (2006) *Understanding Why: Understanding attachment and how this can affect education with special reference to adopted children and young people and those looked after by local authorities.* London: NCB.

Schofield, G. & Beek, M. (2006), *Attachment Handbook for Foster Care and Adoption.* London: BAAF.

SCIE (2012) *Introduction to Social Care.* http://www.scie.org.uk/publications/introductionto/childrenssocialcare/ (accessed 01.08.2013).

Sempik, J. & Munro, E. (2010) *Relationships Matter: An evaluation of a communication skills course for young people.* Loughborough: Centre for Child and Family Research.

Sheikh, S. (2013) *Evaluation of CCE/NCB Arts and Cultural Activities Project with Looked After Children.* Creativity, Culture and Education.

Sound Sense (n.d.) *Music Education Code of Practice.* http://www.soundsense.org/metadot/index.pl?id=25842&isa=Category&op=show (accessed 01.08.2013).

Beyond access – towards equality of outcome: the challenge for instrumental music educators.

Evelyn Grant

> *Musicians and educators are engaged in a fundamentally social, political and cultural enterprise.* (Jorgensen, 2003)

Is there a music educator anywhere who is not aware of the debate over the last three decades around issues of social inclusion? Is there an instrumental music teacher anywhere who would not approve of the concept of providing education outreach programmes to people in disadvantaged communities? Many initiatives prioritise access and initial engagement in musical endeavour. However, less consideration is given as to how best to facilitate and support students through progression and development to high levels of musical skills and achievement. Against the background of standardised frameworks for educational qualification in so-called 'first-world' countries, it is timely to examine the interfaces between access level and further engagement in music education, and the value systems that underpin progression. Grappling with these evolving issues demands a commitment to democracy in our own practice and perspectives; engaging with and learning from those involved in so-called 'outreach' or access programmes. Can equality of musical access lead to greater equality of musical outcome? Equality of outcome could be recognised or defined in at least two ways; firstly, through successful progression through the formal education system to professional level; secondly, through significant social engagement at an amateur, participatory level.

As social inclusion has become an important issue in music education, instrumental music educators from a classical music background have been particularly challenged.

Internationally, it is argued that existing and emerging music schools need to dismantle the social exclusivity that has arisen around traditional instrumental training in classical music (Small, 1977; Hallam, 1998; Philpott & Plummeridge, 2001; Carruthers, 2005; Allsup, 2011). On the issue of responsibility for moving 'beyond access' towards greater equality of musical outcome, and towards achieving fairness in music education, Wayne Bowman's assessment of how instructional methods in music education have evolved - and are perpetuated - is provocative:

> The formula, as one might call it, seems to be something like this: (1) Start with an understanding of music derived from and well-suited to one particular mode of musical engagement and practice. (2) Craft a definition of musicianship derived from its basic tenets and demonstrable primarily on instruments that have evolved in its service. (3) Privilege curricula and pedagogies that serve to nurture that kind of musicianship. (4) Select students for advanced study on the basis of criteria well-suited to these modes of practice. (5) Hire faculty to serve the needs and interests of such students. And (6) assess success in terms of the extent to which the norms and values of that tradition and its conventions are preserved. (Bowman, 2007: 116)

Broader approaches

Some further and higher education institutions have responded to the debate on the democratisation of music education by offering courses in different musical genres and by providing community music training. (Gaunt & Papageorgi, 2010). Some teachers have embraced the principles of community music in support of widening access. Community music programmes are acknowledged as providing participants with 'access to and education in a wide range of musics and musical experiences' (Price, 1996). The extent to which community music can 'complement, interface with, and extend formal music education structures' (ibid.) is particularly relevant in relation to equality of musical access, opportunity, progression and outcome.

Veblen and Olsson (2002) describe the characteristics of community music as privileging creativity and participation, wherein the diversity of learners' cultural backgrounds and individual abilities both informs and enriches their musical and personal development. This work demands that teachers use approaches to teaching that are flexible, inclusive and person-centred, and assessment procedures that are dynamic and holistic. Of particular note in this context is the emphasis on the lifelong musical learning of the individual and the community.

In its broadest sense 'community music predates institutionalised school music education by thousands of years' (Elliott, 2012). Elliott's philosophy of 'praxial' music education has greatly influenced the alignment of community music principles and instrumental teaching since the publication of his Music Matters in 1995. Moreover, Higgins refers to the community musician as a 'boundary-walker', and acknowledges that community music's initial venture:

> offered an active resistance toward institutionalised structures and was particularly evident in the critiques toward the various gatekeepers of cultural monies and the education establishment, both seen as custodians of "high" art and therefore continuing the oppression of working-class musical vernaculars. (Higgins, 2012: 7)

Multi-culturalism and an ever-evolving view of what counts as music education have highlighted the need for musicians to develop a more flexible range of skills (Jorgensen, 2003; Cole, 1999). Studies in ethnomusicology have brought a new respect for music from cultures other than the Western European art music tradition, and, indeed, have challenged the dominance of Western art music in education (Blacking, 1973; Nettl, 2005). Hence, new opportunities to engage in creative music-making have arisen which are founded on emerging thinking on social inclusion, a broader view of education, and an emphasis on addressing disadvantage, life-long learning and cultural diversity.

Many formal education institutions and arts organisations have developed outreach programmes, and include modules on 'community music' or 'music in the community' in their courses (Rogers, 2002; Grant, 2006). In recent years, jazz and traditional music have been added at undergraduate level at some conservatoires which, heretofore, had concentrated on the transmission of Western art music.

Disadvantaged or underserved?

Outreach programmes target communities that are designated 'disadvantaged' in relation to access to music education opportunities, for reasons that might be economic, geographic, and/or cultural. Much attention has been paid in recent years to how diverse musical styles, pedagogical approaches, and flexible modes of teaching, learning and assessment, might be employed to engage the interest of young people in 'disadvantaged' communities. There has been considerable focus on the importance of placing a value on the social outcomes of such programmes, on the use of music as a tool for social inclusion, or social change. (Walker, 2007; Tunstall, 2013; Minguella & Buchanan, 2009; Seymour *et al.*, 2012.)

To ensure musical progression routes, supportive conditions need to prevail, which not only identify and counteract the barriers to inclusion, but also facilitate the deeper engagement that may lead to the further development of musical and personal skills and knowledge. However, changing long-held views as to what counts as music education is not a simple matter in instrumental tuition. Sloboda (2011) posits the concept of 'paradigm reflection' in response to social and cultural changes – institutional examination of what is taught and for what purpose. In promoting such reflection, musicians have sometimes been relatively slow to translate their skills to other contexts. This, in turn, can limit their understanding of musical practices that are outside their own discipline

In an examination of musical childhoods in 20th-century Britain, Pitts' research

> has shown the value of a supportive, responsive, and coherent musical environment for young people, which is at its most effective when the musical opportunities of school, home, and the wider world coincide in clear and purposeful ways. (Pitts, 2012: 195)

The term 'underserved' is used frequently in the USA in relation to disadvantaged communities and educational disadvantage. The concept of serving the community or, perhaps, acknowledging a deficit in service provision, places a sharper focus on the responsibility of the music educator to better serve young people who experience disadvantage and lack of opportunity. How can the music teacher facilitate the advancement of a young musician who has had the opportunity to access music education or training through a community-based project, and wishes to progress through the formal/institutional system or develop their musical skills and knowledge elsewhere? Who assumes the responsibility for the facilitation of appropriate progression opportunities?

These are challenging questions, particularly for music teachers in the classical music tradition who, themselves, have most likely received a 'master-apprentice' music education, with a major emphasis on skills training, alongside musicianship development. Bowman (2002) asserts that

> the master-apprentice mode of applied musical instruction too often focuses on the imitative repetition to the detriment of education ideals like independence, or the refinement of technical skills at the expense of curiosity, flexibility and experimental-mindedness. (Bowman, 2002: 75)

The teaching system with which classically trained teachers are involved can often assume a certain socio-economic profile, with its concomitant learning behaviours, and may not take cognisance of the 'otherness' of more diverse cultural and learning backgrounds. This contrasts with the 'context-specific' nature of outreach projects, which have been especially designed to serve the community in which they are delivered (Grant, 2006). Formal music education institutions have been slow to commit to bridging the gap between these two modes of delivery, which is fundamental to levelling the playing-pitch between those who are underserved and the significant minority for whom it is acknowledged that formal instrumental music education has been constructed (Sloboda, 2001).

Clearly, most young people will not become professionally involved in music (Hallam & Creech, 2010), but why should it not be a viable option for all? The Further Education sector has made a significant contribution to the ambitions of those from a non-classical music background who do wish to pursue a career in music (Conlon & Rogers, 2010.) However, even where government policy supports educational rights for disadvantaged students, there are significant barriers to progression to higher levels of education and achievement in relation to instrumental music. This is demonstrated in an excerpt from a Association of European Conservatoires Handbook (2010), which highlights the need for a more effective interface between the various levels of educational attainment:

> Without a system of support and encouragement reaching back to the earliest years of children's education, it is hard for young people from less privileged backgrounds to acquire the necessary preliminary skills to audition successfully for entry to conservatoires.

Advances in the training of 'classical' musicians

There has for many years been a tradition of support from classical music composers and educators for more collaborative and participatory methods of music-making. Music educationalists like R. Murray Schafer in Canada, George Self and John Paynter in England pioneered creative group work in the classroom, as well as ideas on composition and improvisation in the school music curriculum. Richard McNicol stresses the social value of working in groups in classroom composition, developing skills that will be essential in later life:

- developing ideas
- working as a team
- discussing and negotiating
- leading and being led
- presenting oneself in front of people

(McNicol, 1992: 6)

These considerations occur in present-day community music projects, which frequently draw on pedagogic principles pioneered by Paynter, Schafer, McNicol and others. Paynter's ideas on classroom composition, explored in *Sound and Silence* (Paynter & Aston, 1970), are similar to the workshop practices in many community music projects. These classroom pedagogies have presented interesting ways in which to bridge between different forms of musical notation. Similarly, the work of Green (2002, 2008), Allsup (2004, 2008) addressed the issues of bridging between popular and classical music pedagogies.

However, many musicians who have trained in the 'master-apprentice' model, lack the confidence and skills to work in this way.

One possible solution is the provision of appropriate continuing professional development opportunities. In this respect, the U.K. Music Manifesto report found that:

> Some research suggests that barriers to those who want to train or engage in further professional development are less to do with the training opportunities available and more to do with money, time and lack of information about what is available... There is also debate about the skills that musicians and the music industry, including education, need for the 21st century. (DfES/DCMS, 2005: 79)

Drawing on research from the Guildhall School of Music and Drama Connect Project, the report summarises the qualities the music teacher or leader needs for the future:

- Be comfortable with improvisation and composition with the ability to play by ear;
- Be aware of the fundamental qualities of music and flexible in applying them across genres;
- Be comfortable expressing musical ideas away from their instrument;
- Be able to lead and facilitate;
- Be excited by possibilities beyond their own discipline.

(ibid: 80)

Guildhall Connect developed from the groundbreaking Performance and Communications Skills course, established in 1984, as a progressive training for classical musicians. The participants on the programme engage with neighbouring communities from disadvantaged areas of London. Many of the approaches used in the Guildhall Connect projects involve improvisational forms of music-making, alongside aural and non-notational practices. These ideas have fed into the development of pedagogy at the Guildhall (Gregory, 2005).

Formal, non-formal, informal learning

In contrast to the more formal learning experiences of Western art musicians, most pop and rock musicians are self-taught and self-motivated (Green, 2002). Green's work on informal music learning led her to developing a new pedagogy for the school context (Green, 2008). This has become a cornerstone of the Musical Futures project, which defines 'formal' as that which is taught by adults in schools, college, etc; 'non-formal' as led by adults in community contexts; and informal as led by young people working alone without the constant presence of adults. Allsup (2008) further notes the rapid growth of research interest in this area, and how:

> the paradigm has shifted from descriptive research on what popular musicians are actually doing....to heuristic investigations in the whys and hows of popular music and informal learning, especially as these domains intersect with schools, schools of education, methods of instruction, and our profession's efforts to diversify curricula.

This research has major implications for the delivery of programmes in contexts of educational disadvantage, in that it has done substantial work around finding ways to engage teenagers in practical music making that is relevant to their age and circumstances, and that connects their in-school and out-of-school interests and experiences, motivating them to provide their own stimulus rather than being dependent on the support of parents.

El Sistema

For many classically trained musicians, the success of the El Sistema project in Venezuela has resulted in increased confidence that classical music can, indeed, be a vehicle through which disadvantaged communities can be engaged in music education and training. Or, looked at from another perspective, El Sistema gave classical musicians the confidence that their training could be adapted to serve 'underserved' communities.

The El Sistema project, which involves 400,000 young people in orchestral and choral training in Venezuela, now has 125 youth orchestras, 30 professional adult orchestras, and dozens of choirs. The model has influenced projects in over 25 countries all over the world. Its founder, José Antonio Abreu (2009), refers to El Sistema as a project of 'social rescue'. In the context of classical music education in so-called 'first-world' countries, it may be wiser to advocate for the model from the perspective of social justice rather than social rescue. The latter is a concept that may, unwittingly, help perpetuate the status quo, with such projects happening 'in the margins' - outside of the 'real work' of formal institutions.

There has been a certain scepticism as to how the model would translate to locations outside of Latin-America, and challenges are certainly emerging. For it to be successful, it is important that the key elements of the model are properly understood and valued. 'Immersion' is key – intensive engagement in after-school activity (notably a feature of successful musicians in other genres). El Sistema teachers believe in both the social and musical mission of the programme; a network of support for the family is developed, which spreads into the community; a value is placed on the development of social capital. Perhaps the least mentioned principle of the model is 'love'. 'To speak of love in relation to teaching is already to engage in a dialogue that is taboo' (hooks, 2003). hooks (the pseudonym of the American feminist author, Gloria Jean Watkins) defines love as a combination of care, commitment, knowledge, responsibility, respect, and trust. 'When these basic principles of love form the basis of teacher-pupil interaction the mutual pursuit of knowledge creates the conditions for optimal learning.' This is central to Abreu's philosophy and to the success of El Sistema. Tunstall (2013) quotes Eric Booth's essay 'El Sistema's Open Secret'

> The single most challenging statement about El Sistema's success is that they have learned now to love their neediest children well into the twenty-first century. In the U.S., we must pause and admit that we do not know how to do this.
> (Tunstall, 2013: 271)

It remains to be seen if the success of the Venezuelan model can be both replicated and sustained elsewhere; and whether further and higher education institutions can attract students from the programmes and enable them to progress to the highest levels.

Summary

An appreciation of the social and cultural barriers experienced by young people from disadvantaged backgrounds is necessary for music educators and music education institutions at all levels, if a meaningful dialogue is to happen, whereby the gaps in progression routes can be addressed. Starting from the suggestions in the Music Manifesto Report (cited above), the skill set required by instrumental teachers to facilitate this progression needs to be debated and defined. The whole issue of progression needs to be approached as an issue of social justice, not as a gesture of social rescue. It will only succeed where there is a mutual respect between those working in the traditional sphere of the 'academy' and those working with a community music approach.

Resonating with Higgins' (2012) image of the community musician as 'boundary walker', Bowman decries the fact that:

> we have created border stations and staked out territory in ways that have resulted in wilful ignorance of problems beyond the range they demarcate and defend. We have created and patrolled boundaries with scant attention to the socio-political and ethical concerns that were also kept out. (Bowman 2007: 122)

Teachers must honestly address their own stance on the issue of the democratisation of music by responding to Bowman's provocation and articulating how they might 'operationalise democracy' (Allsup, 2008) in their own practice.

Government departments and formal educational institutions must be more pro-active in bringing the rhetoric of policy on equality to committed action:

> …and when pressed to put their visionary ideas into practice, advocates of educational transformation such as Freire and Parker Palmer may start with a cellular "grassroots" approach but inevitably wind up calling for concerted political and institutional action. And music teachers seeking to transform music, education and society require institutional as well as individual change. (Jorgensen, 2003: 92)

References

Abreu, J. A. (2009) The El Sistema Music Revolution. www.ted.com/talks/jose_abreu_on_kids_transformed_by_music.html [accessed 30th July, 2013].

Allsup, R. E. (2004) Imagining Possibilities in a Global World; Music, Learning and Rapid Change. *Music Education Research*. Vol.6. No.2.

Allsup. R. E. (2008) Creating an Educational Framework for Popular Music in Public Schools: Anticipating the Second-Wave. *Visions of Research in Music Education,* 12.

Allsup, R. E. (2011) Popular music and classical musicians: strategies and perspectives. *Music Educators Journal* 97(3): 30-34.

Association of European Conservatoires (2010) *National Music Education Systems.* http://aec.cramgo.net/Beheer/DynamicMedia/PolifoniaotherPublications/Publication_NationalMusicEducationSystems-EN.pdf [accessed 2nd August, 2013].

Blacking, J. (1973) *How Musical is Man?* Washington: Washington University Press.

Bowman, W. (2007) Who is the 'We'? Rethinking professionalism in music education. *Action, Criticism, and Theory for Music Education.* 6 (4) Online publication. http://act.maydaygroup.org/articles/Bowman6_4.pdf [accessed 10th July 2013].

Bowman, W. (2002) Educating Musically. In R. Colwell & C. Richardson (eds.) *The New Handbook of Research on Music Teaching and Learning.* New York: MENC/Oxford University Press.

Carruthers, G. (2005). Community music and "the musical community": Beyond conventional synergies. *The International Journal of Community Music*, 3. [Retrieved July 25th, 2013 from http://www.intellectbooks.co.uk].

Cole, B. (1999) *Community Music and Higher Education – A Marriage of Convenience.* London: Royal College of Music / Professional Integration Project.

Conlon, J. & Rogers, L. (2010) Music in Further Education Colleges. In S. Hallam & A. Creech (eds.) *Music Education in the 21st Century in the United Kingdom.* London: Institute of Education.

DfES/DCMS (2005) *Music Manifesto Report No.1* London: Department for Education and Skills/Department for Culture, Media and Sport.

Elliott, D. J (1995) *Music Matters.* New York: Oxford University Press.

Elliott, D. J. (2012) Commentary: Music in the Community. In G. E. McPherson & G. F. Welch (eds.) *The Oxford Handbook of Music Education* (Vol 2) Oxford: Oxford University Press.

Gaunt, H. & Papageorgi, I. (2010) Music in Universities and Conservatoires. In S. Hallam & A. Creech (eds.) *Music Education in the 21st Century in the United Kingdom.* London: Institute of Education.

Grant, E. (2006) *A community music approach to social inclusion in music education in Ireland.* (Unpublished PhD Dissertation) University College, Cork.

Green, L. (2002) *How Popular Musicians Learn: a way ahead for music education.* Aldershot: Ashgate.

Green, L. (2008) *Music, informal learning and the classroom.* Aldershot: Ashgate.

Gregory, S. (2005) Creativity and Conservatoires: The agenda and the issues. In G. Odam & N. Bannon (eds.) *The Reflective Conservatoire.* London/Aldershot: Guildhall School of Music and Drama/Ashgate Publications.

Hallam, S. (1998) *Instrumental Teaching: A practical guide to better teaching and learning.* Oxford: Heinemann .

Hallam, S. & Creech, A. (eds.) (2010) *Music Education in the 21st Century in the United Kingdom* London: Institute of Education.

Higgins, L. (2012) *Community Music: In theory and in practice* Oxford: Oxford University Press.

hooks, bell (2003) *Teaching Community.* New York: Routledge.

Jorgensen, E. R. (2003) *Transforming Music Education.* Bloomington & Indianapolis: Indiana University Press.

McNicol, Richard (1992) *Sound Inventions* Oxford: Oxford University Press.

Minguella, M & Buchanan, C. (2009) *Music as a Tool for Social Inclusion.* Cork: Cork City Council.

Nettl, B. (2005) *The Study of Ethnomusicology: 31 Issues and Concepts.* Illinois: University of Illinois.

Paynter, J. & Aston, P. (1970) *Sound and Silence: Classroom projects in creative music.* Cambridge: Cambridge University Press.

Philpott, C. & Plummeridge, C. (2001) *Issues in Music Teaching.* London: Routledge Falmer.

Pitts, S. (2012) *Chance and Choices: Exploring the Impact of Music Education* Oxford : Oxford University Press

Price, D. (1996) *The Challenges to Future Community Musicians.* Paper delivered at the ISME CMA Seminar 'Here Comes the 21st Century - The Challenges to the Future'.

Rogers, R. (2002) *Creating a Land with Music.* London: Youth Music.

Seymour, C. et al. (2012) *Knocknaheeny Youth Music Initiative – An Evaluation.* Cork: Cork City Council Social Inclusion Unit.

Sloboda, J. (2001) Emotion, functionality, and the everyday experience of music: Where does music education fit? *Music Education Research*, 3: 243- 255.

Sloboda, J (2011) Challenges facing the Contemporary Conservatoire : A Psychologist's Perspective. *Article for the Incorporated Society of Musicians.* http://www.ism.org/ [accessed 25th July 2013].

Small, C. (1977) *Music, Society, Education.* Hanover: Wesleyan University Press.

Tunstall, T. (2013) *Changing Lives: Gustavo Dudamel, El Sistema, and the Trasformative Power of Music.* New York: Norton & Co.

Veblen, K. & Olsson, B. (2002) Community Music: Towards an international perspective. In R. Colwell & C. Richardson (eds.) *The New Handbook of Research on Music Teaching and Learning.* New York: MENC/Oxford University Press.

Walker, R. (2007) *Music Education: Cultural values, social change and innovation.* Illinois: University of Illinois

Websites:
Musical Futures - www.musicalfutures.org

Debussy and/or dubstep: non-discriminatory approaches to choosing musical repertoire within a broad and balanced curriculum

Robert Legg

A short time ago I accepted an invitation from a friend to help judge the annual talent contest at a local comprehensive school. Over the course of a long evening we saw many excellent performers, but a fourteen-year-old singer called Taylor, whom we named the overall winner, outshone the rest. Taylor's performance was fluent, rhythmically immaculate and perfectly in tune. But what really marked her out was her self-assured ability to communicate with the audience; that, and the way in which she subtly embellished her repertoire, showing a faultless understanding of its musical style. She was, one of the other judges remarked, 'the real thing'. At the end of the night, I asked her whether she planned to take music as one of her GCSE choices. 'Nah,' Taylor replied, outsized trophy in hand, 'I don't like *that kind* of music.'

This exchange, I thought, demonstrated one of our profession's most entrenched problems. Taylor's reference to *'that kind* of music' was a salutary reminder that, as much as musical taste can bring people together, it can also be a powerfully divisive force. The meaning communicated in those few words seemed plain. *That kind* of music referred to a culture that was not Taylor's own, a culture quite different from *her kind* of music, the kind she knew intimately, the kind she performed with sophistication, the kind which evidently contributed to her very identity. It was obvious from the refinement of her winning performance that *her kind* of music was something Taylor completely embodied; by contrast, *that kind* of music was something she considered from a distance. It was something alien, perhaps inoffensive, but nevertheless foreign. Taking GCSE music, she thought, meant studying *that kind* of music, and consequently she had pushed the subject aside. It was disappointing to think that Taylor, so clearly a very able musician, had ruled herself out of the formal music curriculum.

We can foresee various negative consequences of her decision: those affecting the wider music education community, which will lose a promising student, and those affecting Taylor herself. It is impossible to know whether doors will be closed against her permanently, but it is conceivable that, by electing not to study music at Key Stage 4, Taylor will limit the range of formal musical opportunities available to her at Key Stage 5 and beyond. Meanwhile, of course, peers whose prior musical experience fits better with the curricular repertoire will progress more readily to GCSE music, perhaps never giving a thought to the fact that what Taylor calls *that kind* of music is also *their kind*. And herein lies the problem for music education: musical taste is neither neutral nor inconsequential, nor is it the product of rational decision-making alone; rather, it is, in part at least, an inescapable cultural inheritance that works actively to shape and reshape our lives and our academic opportunities.

What we call a person's 'taste' is not necessarily freely chosen; and, as the above anecdote illustrates, distinctions drawn between the music of popular taste, on the one hand, and music which constitutes the 'legitimate' object of academic study, on the other, can act to exclude or disenfranchise individuals and groups within society. It is even more important to recognise that just as individual learners' tastes can be of great consequence, the decisions that educators make about the musical repertoire studied and performed within formal curricula can play an important role, albeit an often-unacknowledged one, in promoting or preventing fair access. Whether we like it or not, such choices are powerful. With that in mind, the remainder of this chapter considers the ways in which we can use what we know about cultural reproduction to inform the selection of repertoire that we, as professional music educators, make every day in the service of a broad and balanced curriculum.

Musical preference and cultural capital

The relationship between music and social stratification has a long and by no means uncomplicated history. Various well-rehearsed examples amply demonstrate the fact that music has often been a socially-segregated activity. The jealous guarding of Allegri's *Miserere* by the privileged inner circle of the seventeenth-century Papal Court (Arnold & Carter, 2002) serves to illustrate the musical exclusivity of Italian high society, while bawdy and satirical songs known to have been popular amongst audiences of more modest means (D'Urfey, 1991, for example) exemplify practices prevalent at the other end of the social spectrum. Conversely, it is often suggested that eighteenth-century Venetian opera was enjoyed by citizens of all social backgrounds (Storey, 2002).

In modern times, the link between social class and cultural practice has been more robustly demonstrated and better understood. Pierre Bourdieu's (2010) detailed and wide-ranging account of cultural life in 1960s' France, for example, shows how cultural tastes, and musical tastes in particular, were routinely structured along class lines. Bourdieu's analysis of his own empirical research demonstrates that, of all cultural markers, musical taste in adulthood is amongst the strongest predictors of a person's educational level and social class. He showed that a musical preference for high-brow or 'legitimate' works, exemplified at the time by Bach's *Wohltemperierte Klavier*, was most likely to be found amongst highly-educated, professional people, whilst a taste for what he called 'popular' music – 'light' classical pieces like Johann Strauss II's *Blue Danube* – was expressed more often by those who had limited formal education and who were employed in poorly-remunerated manual, clerical and minor commercial jobs (2010: 8-9). A recent replication of Bourdieu's study within a contemporary British context found that, whilst other markers of social class had succumbed to greater levels of cultural 'omnivorousness', music, alongside theatre-going, remains as much a marker of social gradation in twenty-first-century Britain as it had been in France during the sixties (Bennett *et al.*, 2009).

The 'cultural capital' which inhabits differing tastes, Bourdieu argues, is by no means inconsequential or 'disinterested'; rather, it is an accrual of skills, knowledge and educational advantage which, like other forms of accrued capital, has a realisable exchange value in the real world. This notion moves us away from purely descriptive analyses in which we might observe, for example, that consultant surgeons have a taste for Italian opera, towards more significant claims in which, to continue the example, these medics' taste for, and familiarity with, the music of Puccini and Verdi – their investment in this particular form of cultural capital – plays an active role, however small, in their academic, professional and social success. In what Bourdieu calls a 'cycle of reproduction' (2010; Bourdieu & Passeron, 1990) such musical preferences play a part in sustaining and perpetuating divisive social structures. So our highly-paid surgeons' knowledge of *verismo* should not be seen as a mere incidental *product* of their general cultural education but rather as something that has itself *contributed* to their socio-economic standing and professional achievements.

For music teachers concerned with social justice the implications of this way of thinking are profound and troubling. On the one hand, familiarity with 'legitimate' musical genres and repertoire seems to be a possible prerequisite to the attainment of privileged positions with our social hierarchy, placing an apparent burden on us to spread knowledge of these cultural artefacts as widely as possible. On the other hand, as Taylor's example has shown, achieving the musical acculturation that this would require is incredibly difficult given how alienating the music of one social group can be to someone well versed in that of another. Perhaps more importantly, we must ask ourselves whether our responsibility as teacher is not only to identify and operate within these existing social structures but also, where we observe that such structures are divisive, to seek to change them.

It might be persuasively argued that out of this problem emerges one of the fundamental contradictions of modern music education. Whilst it might be supposed that the majority of music teachers are keen to espouse progressive and egalitarian principles – that music is for all, and that everyone is a musician – we cannot ignore the apparently divisive results of the large-scale cycle of reproduction in which we are implicated. At present, certain kinds of music are evidently *not* for all, and the effects of this fact may be wide-reaching. This contradiction is made all the more complicated because, as Bourdieu points out, the selection of works for the school curriculum is part of the establishment 'sanctification' (Wacquant, 2004) or 'academic consecration' (Bourdieu, 2010, p. 58) that defines 'legitimate' taste in the first place. So not only is 'legitimate' taste something of a moving target, it is also one which, in some small way, we are responsible for moving.

The current iteration of the compulsory curriculum (QCA, 2007) allows a great deal of freedom where repertoire choice is concerned, and this obliges the teacher to make deliberate decisions about the kinds of music to which his or her students are exposed. What music should students listen to in lessons? What music should they perform? What (if any) music should be the stimulus for their composing activities? In responding to these questions, teachers weigh the merits and demerits of various approaches. Does it benefit students overall for the curriculum to pursue an in-depth and exclusive focus on 'legitimate' works? Or should an attempt be made to achieve comprehensive coverage of a wide range of genres and traditions? Should society's dominant culture be prioritised? Or, where these differ, should the students' own music cultures take precedence?

Approaches to curriculum design
Cultural literacy

One answer to these questions, much admired by the United Kingdom's current Secretary of State for Education (see, for example, Gove, 2013), is offered by E. D.

Hirsch's cultural literacy model (1988). Hirsch, an American educationalist and literary critic, advocates a curriculum built on the identification and teaching of core knowledge. His straightforward prescription is as follows. Within each subject domain, of which music is one, the community of educators should distil the 'core facts' and then prioritise these as essential knowledge to be taught in the compulsory curriculum. Hirsch argues that by applying this approach uniformly, regardless of students' own backgrounds, a level playing field for learning can be created. It is, he suggests, 'the only sure avenue of opportunity for disadvantaged children, the only reliable way of combating the social determinism that now condemns them to remain in the same social and educational condition as their parents' (1988, p. xiii).

In an appendix to his text, Hirsch presents a list of words, phrases and concepts which he suggests should constitute the 'core facts' that 'every American needs to know' (pp. 152-215). Amongst the four thousand or so entries are approximately 128 which relate to music. These include the names of fifteen of the most celebrated classical composers – from Bach and Beethoven to Verdi and Wagner – as well as the names of the mainstream orchestral instruments, a collection of Italian musical terms, and the titles of songs from the Anglo-American folk repertory. Popular cultures are represented by references to the Beatles and a small handful of American singers from the 1950s and '60s. Hirsch's list is not, in itself, a curriculum. But establishing a compulsory programme of performing, composing and listening activities based on this list would certainly be possible, despite the fact that various sub-questions – which of Bach's works should we teach? How is 'the symphony' best exemplified? – would still require the teacher's consideration.

In practical terms, advocates of cultural literacy construct their curricula using repertoire from mainstream western classical music. The current draft of the UK's new national curriculum (DfE, 2013), itself strongly informed by Gove's veneration of Hirsch's ideas, provides no list of approved names, directing teachers' and students' attention instead to the works of 'great musicians and composers' (pp. 3-5). Since *greatness* and *composer* are terms with strongly cultural ties to the western classical canon, however, this phrase introduces – whether intentionally or not – an implicit bias towards European music of exactly the kind that is advocated and practised by Hirsch. Another example of a curriculum which reflects the aims of the cultural literacy movement – albeit somewhat before that movement's time – is the A-level music syllabuses of the 1950s, which, as I have discussed elsewhere (Legg, 2012), prescribed the study of works from a surprisingly narrow range of sources: the big 'names' of European classical music alongside a number of more recent British composers. The similarity between Gove's current rhetoric around 'the sublime genius' of 'the best' works for musical study (2011) and the A-level syllabus of this pre-Bourdieusian era is certainly striking.

On paper, it is an idea that appears to carry certain advantages. The prospect of a shared vocabulary and a common frame of reference for discussing music might be considered appealing, whilst the idea of widening access to the cultural capital of the dominant group has an obvious allure. Closer analysis, however, reveals a range of problems with the practicability of the scheme's implementation and, more importantly, with the desirability of its ultimate aims. Who gets to choose the core knowledge, might be a critical first question. Even if agreement could be reached about the core facts that populate the final list, the practice of working through this catalogue of musical artefacts, personalities and phenomena in the classroom is very likely to result in a curriculum far less participative than the one to which we aspire. Thus cultural literacy risks breaking with a central tenet of modern music education.

Hirsch's promise of greater equality of opportunity is worth probing, too. It is counterintuitive to suggest that a curriculum contained within the dominant group's cultural space will provide a truly level playing field. In fact, the reverse seems likely: as we have seen already, the alignment of middle-class students' cultural inheritance with a Hirschian curriculum will be greater than that experienced by those from other social classes, surely giving such students a head start in the race to gain familiarity with the cultural practices officially sanctified by their appearance on the list. At best, a drab academic monoculture would emerge; at worst, the culture capital of the dominant group would be promoted, to the detriment of other social groups and of any cultural variety within the school curriculum.

It is worth considering Taylor's likely response to this Hirschian prospectus. A consummate musician, she is nevertheless unlikely to be familiar with the composers on Hirsch's list, since her own musical background is firmly rooted in popular styles. The first probable consequence of Hirsch's plan is that, given the opportunity, Taylor will drop his musical offering just as quickly as she rejected the current GCSE offer. Even had she experienced a classroom diet of 'the classics' throughout her primary education, the dissonance she perceived between school music and *her* music would be too grating. In an alternative scenario, Taylor might elect to continue her musical studies but, with limited opportunity to use the skills, knowledge and understanding that derive from her experiences of popular music, we could expect her to do less well than similarly able peers whose experiences are aligned with the classical music tradition. In either case, it seems likely that social divisions will be strengthened.

Critical social theory

An alternative perspective, from the standpoint of critical social theory (for example Bernstein, 1975; Freire, 2000), leads us to consider these questions very differently. Through this lens, the construction of a curriculum using materials predominantly from the classical tradition is problematic in two ways: first, as already suggested, it unfairly disadvantages students whose familiarity with this repertoire is not already well developed; second, and perhaps more importantly, it advances yet further the cultural capital of the dominant group by lending it a form of establishment validation. This second process is a good example of Bourdieu's claim that in 'complex societies … the school has taken over [the] work of sanctification of social divisions' (Wacquant, 1996, p. 154) since it demonstrates how teachers, motivated by the immediate needs of the students in front of them, can contribute significantly to the cycles of reproduction which maintain large-scale cultural divisions. From this perspective, Hirsch's cultural literacy approach can be construed as collaboration in a discriminatory power dynamic or even, as Bourdieu himself puts it, as an act of 'symbolic violence' (Moore, 2008, p. 104).

The logical result of these ideas is the employment of materials from a wide range of non-dominant musical cultures. In applying this approach, popular music, world music, indigenous folk music and other academically disenfranchised musical traditions can be the object of listening activities as well as valid starting points for performing and composing.

A major benefit of this approach is that the musical cultures of many more students can be integrated into the learning experience, and built upon, in the way the advocates of informal learning approaches have suggested (D'Amore, 2009; Green, 2001, 2008).

Repertoire possibilities within a curriculum informed by critical social theory are virtually limitless. Pop and rock music, from both the mainstream and specialist ends of the spectrum, provide a particularly rich range of options, including everything from the most contemporary tracks to music more than a century old. Similarly, a focus on music of the socially disadvantaged paves the way for the inclusion of everything from modern protest song to the work songs of historically oppressed and enslaved peoples. Turning to the music of women composers, so often written out of music history (Bowers & Tick, 1986), offers an alternative perspective on the narratives of the western art music tradition, whilst the exploration of non-European musical cultures provides a fascinating range of opportunities: from the well known – djembe drumming and gamelan, for example – to the more obscure (Sharma, 1998; Stock, 1996).

For Taylor, the hypothetical implications of this approach are profound. A curriculum based, at least in part, on music from her own tradition is likely to be a far more appealing prospect than one based on music she regards as irrelevant: this makes it probable that she would continue her musical development within, rather than exclusively outside, the formal school setting. Meanwhile, the opportunity to bring her prior musical experiences into the classroom, and to benefit from the experiences of her peers, means that Taylor's performance in formal assessments will better reflect the skills she demonstrates in other quarters. Nor is the benefit of this approach limited to Taylor. The breadth of a curriculum based on these musical traditions has the potential to widen the musical purview of all students who encounter it.

E. D. Hirsch's response to such a proposition is easy to imagine. What, he might ask, will happen next? What hope is there of integration into other parts of the education system for students whose musical learning is so removed from the dominant tradition and, moreover, so piecemeal? Would Taylor's musical learning allow her access to prestigious HE institutions or to a career as a well paid professional, perhaps even – to return to an earlier example – as a consultant surgeon? What common ground could she expect to find when discussing music with those educated elsewhere? The Hirschian view, in summary, might be that on the altar of wider social advancement is sacrificed a promising individual's future success.

Ways forward

As we have seen, ideas from cultural literacy and critical social theory provide very different perspectives on the question of choosing musical repertoire for the classroom. The differences are both practical and political. This chapter does not seek to synthesise or reconcile these positions; rather, it offers three practical principles with which the thorny problems of repertoire choice, engagement and equality of opportunity can be negotiated. These partial solutions will no doubt be familiar to many practitioners of music education. Nevertheless, they bear repeating here not only because it is always beneficial to think and re-think one's practice but also because, as suggested earlier, external pressure from legislators and commentators in support of a curriculum model based on 'high' cultural forms is increasingly in evidence. These suggestions, then, are ways in which music educators might seek to achieve a degree of breadth and balance in their curricula whilst striving to meet the needs of as many prospective students as possible.

Acknowledging students' musical preferences

Failure to acknowledge students' own musical practices and preferences within the curriculum has been widely identified as the cause of a problem with student engagement. Evans summarises this well when he writes that students 'feel an underlying mismatch between their interest in popular culture and the messages they perceive they are getting from their teacher about the superiority of western art music' (Evans, 2012, p. 198). It follows that bringing students' own musics into the classroom helps significantly to address low levels of engagement. There are various ways in which this can be done, including the formula suggested by Green in which 'learning begins with music chosen by the learners themselves' (Green, 2008, p. 9). This approach requires a level of flexibility not normally associated with a purely teacher-led curriculum, and, for this reason, a degree of courage on the part of the teacher. Pursuing an informal pedagogical model of this kind necessitates a willingness to become the facilitator of learning rather than its director, and demands that the teacher accept a greater element of unpredictability with the classroom experience.

The opportunity to play – and imaginatively *play with* – their own music is one that students evidently enjoy, notwithstanding the fact that, in order for it to be successful, support and mediation from a teacher is often required. This technical support may take a variety of forms – advice on decoding notation; help with transposing or adapting a piece; instrument-specific guidance – depending on the demands of the repertoire and on the needs of the particular students.

Drawing on musical commonalities to broaden students' horizons

Another form of support a teacher can usefully provide is to direct students toward previous unexplored areas of musical repertoire. Focusing on musical phenomena common across styles and genres creates opportunities to introduce students to new areas of music – from all kinds of traditions including those typically identified as 'high' or 'low' – as well as to dismantle hierarchical ideas of musical categorisation which they may have developed, inherited or been taught. Demonstrating how a particular feature or device is used in chart music, for example, as well as in venerated classical works helps students to see these not as discrete categories but as part of a wider continuing tradition of tonal music. It might be argued, in turn, that the perceived palatability of all kinds of music is enhanced as a consequence.

Opportunities for these pedagogical side-steps offer themselves up surprisingly frequently. Students exploring prominent bass riffs in rock music, for example, can be introduced to music structured by a ground bass. Similarly, a focus on a ubiquitous chord progression like I-vi-IV-V allows the teacher to segue between eighteenth-century piano sonatas, 1950s American pop music and a variety of musical theatre traditions. Meanwhile, exploiting deliberate parodies and reworkings can lead from Bach's *Air on the G String* to Procol Harum's *A Whiter Shade of Pale* or from Coolio's *C U When U Get There* to Pachelbel's Canon in D major. Alternatively, links can be constructed by drawing upon a common function of music from different styles, whether that function be to accompany dance, for example, or to demonstrate instrumental virtuosity. We might expect this practice, too, to help students to perceive musical categories less hierarchically.

In spite of these advantages, however, one potential pitfall associated with this approach must be acknowledged. By choosing to link repertoire items by their musical features, devices or functions, care must be taken not to sacrifice participative and generative processes like composing and performing in favour of the abstract learning of music theory's 'rules' or the 'facts' of music history. An effort must be made, therefore, to ensure that active pedagogical strategies like *playing* and *playing around with* take precedence over tools like *showing* and *telling* in which the students' role is predominantly a passive one.

Avoiding 'cool' vs. 'uncool'

The preceding principles identify ways in which students can be drawn away from problematic characterisations of music as 'cool' and 'uncool', 'boring' or 'exciting'. By dignifying students' own music with a place in the curriculum and by emphasising commonalities across contrasting styles and traditions we can attempt to foster in ourselves and in our students more inclusive and culturally omnivorous attitudes to music. A third principle, however, is to include in the curriculum a range of music repertoire which falls outside the binary classification of 'cool' and 'uncool' that some students may have established. Whereas singing an English folksong or a contemporary pop hit may well register respectively as 'uncool' or 'cool' activities amongst students in some British schools, for example, singing a South African song (see, for example, l'Estrange, 2004), by contrast, may carry fewer negative or positive connotations.

The strategy of choosing repertoire laden with fewer cultural markers of 'cool' or 'uncool' is a well-tested one. It is also one that invites the teacher to look further afield to musical traditions beyond Europe and North America when looking for repertoire ideas and, consequently, offer the possibility of a more plural and diverse culture of school music.

Toward conclusions

These three tentative suggestions notwithstanding, making a clear prescription for action in this area is difficult. In part, this is because the answers at which each of us arrives will depend on the questions we have asked and, in turn, upon the values, beliefs and purposes that underlie the music education which we hope to deliver. One further point, however, can usefully be made. That is that we should not allow a shift towards – or *back* towards – curricula based on dominant-group cultures to be undertaken unthinkingly or by default. The consequences of such a move – a move already detected by some – would be significant and long lasting.

As for Taylor, of course, she remains outside the formal music curriculum. Whether *her kind* of music will win a more significant place in the classroom of tomorrow, or whether the resurgence of dominant-group cultures will drive it out altogether, is yet to be seen. It is satisfying to imagine a context in which her pursuit of music at school is a natural and integral part of her development as a talented and engaged musician. How realistic is this vision, however? On this question, I suggest, rests the success, perhaps even the survival, of music education as a key component of a universal educational entitlement.

References

Arnold, D. & Carter, T. (2002) Allegri, Gregorio. In A.Latham (ed.) *The Oxford Companion to Music*. Oxford: Oxford University Press.

Bennett, T., Savage, M., Silva, E., Warde, A., Gayo-Cal, M. & Wright, D. (2009) *Culture, class, distinction*. Abingdon: Routledge.

Bernstein, B. B. (1975) *Class, codes, and control: theoretical studies towards a sociology of language* (2nd rev. ed.). New York: Schocken Books.

Bourdieu, P. (2010). *Distinction: a social critique of the judgement of taste*. London: Routledge.

Bourdieu, P. & Passeron, J.-C. (1990) *Reproduction in education, society and culture* (rev. ed.). London: Sage.

Bowers, J. M. & Tick, J. (1986) *Women making music: the western art tradition, 1150-1950*. Urbana: University of Illinois Press.

D'Urfey, T. (1991) *Lewd songs and low ballads of the eighteenth century: bawdy songs from Thomas D'Urfey's "Pills to Purge Melancholy" (1719)*. Boulder, Colorado: Bartholomew Press.

DfE. (2013) Music: Programmes of Study for Key Stages 1-3. London: Department for Education.

D'Amore, A. (2009) Musical futures: an approach to teaching and learning (2nd ed.). London: Paul Hamlyn.

Evans, K. (2012) Music 14-19: choices, challenges, and opportunities. In C. Philpott & G. Spruce (eds.), *Debates in music teaching* (pp. 197-208). Abingdon: Routledge.

Freire, P. (2000) Pedagogy of the oppressed (30th anniversary ed.). New York: Continuum.

Gove, M. (2011) The need to reform the education system. Speech made at University of Cambridge on 24 November 2011.

Gove, M. (2013) The progressive betrayal. Speech made at the Social Market Foundation on 5 February 2013.

Green, L. (2001) *How popular musicians learn: a way ahead for music education*. Aldershot: Ashgate.

Green, L. (2008) *Music, informal learning and the school: a new classroom pedagogy*. Aldershot: Ashgate.

Hirsch, E. D. (1988) *Cultural literacy: what every American needs to know*. New York: Vintage.

l'Estrange, A. (2004) *Songs of a rainbow nation: four songs from South Africa*. London: Faber Music.

Legg, R. (2012) Bach, Beethoven, Bourdieu: 'cultural capital' and the scholastic canon in England's A-level examinations. *Curriculum Journal*, 23(2): 157-172.

Moore, R. (2008) Capital. In M. Grenfell (ed.) *Pierre Bourdieu: key concepts* (pp. 101-117). Durham: Acumen.

QCA. (2007) *The National Curriculum*. London: Qualifications and Curriculum Authority.

Sharma, E. (1998) *Music worldwide*. Cambridge: Cambridge University Press.

Stock, J. (1996) *World sound matters*. London: Schott.

Storey, J. (2002) Expecting rain: opera as popular culture? In J. Collins (ed.), *High-pop: making culture into popular entertainment* (pp. 32-55). Malden, MA: Blackwell.

Wacquant, L. (1996) Reading Bourdieu's "Capital". *International Journal of Contemporary Sociology*, 33(2): 151-170.

Wacquant, L. (2004) Lire 'Le Capital' de Pierre Bourdieu. In L. Pinto, G. Sapiro & P. Champagne (eds.), *Pierre Bourdieu sociologue* (pp. 211-230). Paris: Fayard.

Music Mentoring
– Notes from a seaside project

Phil Mullen

These are notes and stories from work I did this year (2013) in primary schools in Clacton-on-Sea. Clacton is part of that very peculiar English phenomenon, the sink resort. Butlin's has long gone and with it the summer money. The town contains many signs of poverty, both material and spiritual[1]. Clacton itself is now the second most deprived seaside town in the country[2] and one ward, Jaywick, has been named the most deprived place in England[3].

This kind of economic depression can have a profound impact on how families and children are, how they think about themselves, how they imagine their futures. I was asked to work in mainstream schools with the most vulnerable kids, helping them to engage, see themselves as learners, get on with each other, sometimes just to have fun and enjoy themselves. Oh, and to make music also.

We called the programme Music Mentoring because it had that aspect of being immersed in music while still having a close eye on the children's needs for warmth, nurture, affirmation, creative expression and being in a positive, high functioning group that was so crucial to the success of the Youth Music Programme of the same name[4].

I worked with a range of students, two schools a day, a couple of days a week, over 150 kids in all. Sometimes it would be one-to-one, sometimes a pair, maybe a trio. The maximum group size was six. I worked quite closely with the SENCO (Special Educational Needs Coordinator) in most of the schools, getting a good 'need to know' briefing. I would be told about conditions such as Autism or Asperger's syndrome, anything that might trigger challenging behaviour, any major incidents and things such as bereavement. I didn't want and didn't get family histories but I knew that most of the kids' backgrounds were troubled.

Chime bars and Songwriting

I did a lot of work using chime bars with the children in Clacton. I really like chime bars, as they are a truly democratic, inclusive instrument - everyone plays one note each. They are very good for making up melodies. Just ask the children what order the notes should go in and if they want repeats. Oh, and later where we should put some spaces. If you have a C scale and leave out F and B this gives you a pentatonic (five-note) scale, which is very useful for playing around with. Singing along with chime bars helps strengthen a sense of vocal pitching and they are also very useful for songwriting.

When we are songwriting I tend to start by handing out Cs, Fs and Gs to kids so that each one has a chime bar. If there are six children then that is 2 per note. I then ask them for an order for four plays. Then they play one of the notes once every four beats and we have a structure. Some good ones are CFGC, GFGC, and CGFG.

We then add some words, which they speak rhythmically across the structure. These could be a list of things we like, or a feeling someone has, or something that happened during the week. There is an infinite number of topics for songwriting. I find it best to pick things the kids are interested in.

After they have spoken the words rhythmically a few times, some of the kids usually start to sing them and the others join in. It doesn't happen every time, but almost every time.

One Clacton song with a group of Year 4 children was called 'The Most Summer Fun'. I asked them what they liked to do over the summer and in about five minutes we had the following lyric:

> It's the most summer fun x 2
>
> Being a majorette
> Going paintballing
> Going on holiday with my family
> Going bowling, going bowling
>
> It's the most summer fun x 2
>
> Going to the war museum
> Cheerleading
> Having a water fight
> Going swimming, going swimming
>
> It's the most summer fun x 2.

Collectively the group had written a piece about something that interests them, they were proud of it and happily performed it to the rest of their class, something the type of kids I work with rarely do.

Sometimes I get them to write about what is happening in the room. For instance one day my glasses fell off and one of the children caught them. This quickly led to this surrealistic lyric:

> We've just caught a pair of flying glasses
> It's pretty cool getting time off classes
> Now we can't stop ourselves laughing – Hahahahaha
> It's a cuckoo it's a lion it's our weekly music classes

My favourite song from the work in Clacton was with a Year 3 group, who wrote on the theme of cowboys. We all played our instruments sparsely as they conjured up the atmosphere of a dust storm in the desert;

> Yee-ha – and the cowboys swing their hats around x 2
>
> Spiky cactus
> Horses gallop
> Sand winds
> Tumbleweed
> Whips whipping
> The horse's side
> Leaves are whooshing
> On a tree
>
> Yee-ha – and the cowboys swing their hats around x 2

It took up most of one half-hour session to put it together and I was very impressed. It evokes a sense of place, conjures up visions of action and even has some onomatopoeia. In the large class most of these kids are disengaged and getting into trouble. The music (and the class size) helped motivate them to use their creativity and to work dynamically together.

Jim

Music can have a very great power over children's emotions and ability to engage. One student I had for one-to-ones, Jim, from Year 6, was pretty regularly in a troubled state during the lunch hour just before our session. He got into fights with the other kids, sometimes had to leave his classroom before break, and often needed one-to-one time with the SENCO. He would sometimes come in to my session and just slump with his head on the table. Occasionally there would be tears in his eyes and he would breathe and sigh for a few minutes, trying to get control of his emotions.

When we did get started on the music, usually writing on GarageBand, he was almost always able to do productive, good quality, compositional work. This tended to get better every week and he became, in a very positive way, a real tech geek (tech-based musicians see this as a good thing).

Initially there was a lot of bravado from Jim, saying he could play this instrument and that and that he knew all about recording. I decided not to challenge that but made sure to model everything we were doing and talk about it in a matter of fact way, as if he knew it but also letting him pick it up if he didn't. This worked well and he got used to experimenting with different sounds, styles and structures. Importantly, in terms of musical progression, he got into the minutiae of editing, working some fine detail into his breakdowns, combining opera, dance rhythms, sound effects and well-found hooks. Editing computer music puts the lie to the idea that young people have short attention spans. The fact is, like most of us, they can give in-depth attention to anything once they are interested in it.

As we came to the last term and Jim prepared to move to secondary school, we would spend about a third of each session talking about his musical ambitions (mostly about becoming independent in making his tracks) and how music was a help when things were difficult in life. This was very much the mentoring side of music mentoring and I was pleased that Jim had found a safe haven and secure place within his own music making.

This is a song about rules

I really like rules. Let me rephrase that. I REALLY LIKE RULES. Music workers I know tend to talk more about boundaries than rules but I have a confession to make. I don't really (i.e. fully) understand boundaries. I suspect most of the kids don't either. I do understand rules. You decide what is and is not appropriate behaviour to make the group work well and agree to stick to that behaviour.

With rules I need a couple of things in place, like respecting each other and the instruments, but otherwise it is totally what the kids decide. In the first session I will suggest we need some rules, turn it over to them and wait a while (that is very important). Then they always (so far) come out with some fairly sensible ideas. What is really important to me is that the children understand that by doing certain things and stopping yourself from doing others, you can help make a group perform better.

Once the group makes their own rules, they don't really want to break them. They will, because they forget, and also because sometimes the rules they make are too tough for that group at that time, so you might need to modify them. But usually a group is much less likely to kick against a set of rules they have made themselves than a set of rules imposed on them by an outsider.

Once the rules are agreed it can be useful to remind the group of them from time to time. This could be by writing them out and putting them up on the wall. I prefer to rearrange the words of the ground rules into lyrics for a freshly composed song. This might sound daunting but is actually pretty easy. I play some backing chords on guitar as a framework and then the kids choose which line and then say or sing the line rhythmically against the chords. Pretty soon we arrive at a full song.

One of my favourites of these was with a group of six lively and very talented Year 4 kids in Clacton. I used the G Em C D sequence (the fifties doo-wop thing) and they wrote and sang the following lyrics:

> This is a list, a list about rules x2
> Don't play instruments really really loud x 2
> Don't push people, push people off the chairs x 2
> This is a list, a list about rules x2
> Don't, don't, don't, don't, don't, don't, don't, don't, don't, don't, don't, bully each other x 2
> Treat the instruments with respect x 2
> This is a list, a list about rules x 2

Moving away from the strict words of the rules to add in repetitions and a more musical flow really helped the song.

We all really liked this song, and that pride got everyone to practise it for performance, tightening pitch, entries, exits and dynamics. The group then performed it both for the class and for the headmaster separately. It was great to see this small group of kids, who are usually at the 'naughty' end of the spectrum, singing out loud and clear about how to behave to make the group better.

An unfortunate remark

In one session a child made a remark that affected me profoundly. It was our last day together, myself and a group of four Year 3 kids. One of the boys, Mark, was autistic and needed quite a lot of attention. The other, Joe, was always getting into trouble. There were also two girls, Penny and Lena, and Mark's TA (Teaching Assistant).

From session one we had hit the ground running, learning fun movement songs like *Pick a bale of cotton*[5], *Tony Chestnut*[6] and Toots and the Maytal's *Monkey Man*[7]. As well as this, they recorded a funky GarageBand track where they all had equal roles and got to write their own solos. I managed to keep the pace pretty 'up' and the emphasis was on making learning fun.

We did some chime bar and songwriting work and I was surprised when I asked them what they wanted to sing about. They said they wanted to write a lullaby for a baby. They came up with the chime bar pattern CGFG and I accompanied them on guitar using a 6/8 feel to help set the mood while they wrote the lyrics. Within a few minutes they sang the following:

> Don't cry oh baby
> Don't cry oh baby
> I will look after you
> I will rock you
> I will feed you
> I will calm you down

So on the last day when I handed out the CDs it was no surprise that the feedback was positive and everybody left feeling good about the group. Then Joe turned around and made this remark as he was leaving, "I wish my Dad was like you". To be honest it hit me deep in the gut. On one level I was very pleased that these sessions had such a meaning for him, but I was completely wiped out by how 'wrong' the comment was. All I found I could do was 'professionally ignore it'. I pretended I hadn't heard anything, kept my head above everyone's eye level, thanked all the kids and said goodbye.

Facing fears

When I say I work with vulnerable kids, people assume they are those who don't do well academically. Frequently this is true. Sometimes, though, kids who do well at their studies have other problems to face - life situations such as bullying, bereavement or not fitting in. I find they can sometimes be a bit closed up, afraid of failing, scared of spontaneity.

I had one group of six Year 5s, who were about the quietest kids I had ever come across. Nothing I could do would make these kids smile. I would ask them what they liked, what they wanted to do (write about), what was fun for them. No response. I really floundered for weeks with them and then realised during a rhythm warm-up that they listened really carefully and tried very hard to get things right. In fact the harder the exercise the harder they would try. So, instead of my usual creative approach, I switched to teaching them basic djembe rhythms, moving on to several interlocking parts at the same time while I also made the piece structure increasingly complex and shifting.

They rose to the occasion and became a tight little rhythm group, taking care to match the right tone (drum stroke) to the right rhythm. Things started to relax; they smiled and said they enjoyed it during our feedback sessions. I even got them to take two-bar solos while accompanied by the others and they started, with encouragement, to take chances and play loud enough to be heard above the rest. They were working hard and knew it.

Towards the end of the term I told them we were doing a performance for their class. They became absolutely terrified again and I almost said we don't have to. But for some reason I didn't (I usually am against any coercion especially with vulnerable groups). I coached them through it, rehearsing entry and exit from the space, order of the pieces, each solo (they set the solos rather than improvised at this stage). Most importantly, I went through what could go wrong, how we would deal with it, what could go right and how that would make us all feel and how, after our hard work, we deserved the applause we might get.

The day came and the performance went super well, better than all the rehearsals. In the feedback afterward I asked them what they had most learned from the programme. Clare, the girl who had been most nervous all the way through, said, "I have learned how to face my fears".

Trio

One of the most interesting teaching experiences I have ever had was with three Year 4 children in a school in Clacton. We worked for about 40 minutes every week for two terms in what could best be described as a cupboard. It was a tiny room where staff stored things but it had a full view window and video camera for children's protection, so it was the best place for one-to-ones and small group work.

We did some drum and guitar work but spent most of our time writing tracks on GarageBand on computer. GarageBand, in my opinion, is the most useful tool for working with so called 'hard to reach' kids, especially at primary age. It teaches them about music - especially motifs, structure, balancing volume levels, space, timbre, contrast, arrangement and orchestration - in a way that they can quickly understand, both intellectually and in practice. GarageBand can very easily produce high quality sounding pieces, so for primary-age children this can boost their self-esteem and make them proud to take CDs/ MP3s home to play to family members or carers.

What was fascinating about working with these three kids was that they had to work on the tracks together and find a way to give everyone their space. This was made more of a tricky task through the make up of this group. The two boys, Frankie and Sean, had Asperger's syndrome and Autism respectively, and the girl, Jemma, was a selective mute, which meant that although she had no physical damage to her voice she was unable to speak.

I made a decision from the start that the group would work completely inclusively at all times and stressed with them the need for us to function really well as a group. Jemma used thumbs up or down to communicate as well as nodding her head or shaking. Everybody starting using the thumbs up or down (or sideways for neutral) signs and we recorded by letting everyone lay down one instrument track at a time. This is done by either selecting from loops or playing in parts. Everyone was fine with this and I was also able to let each child mix the volume balance of the instruments and play in their own (virtual) keyboard or guitar solos. We produced 14 tracks together and each of the kids had at least one track where they had been the main composer.

It wasn't all smooth sailing. The boys had more of a natural rapport with each other and made similar musical choices so I had to work hard to stop Jemma from being sidelined. It was, I have to confess, more difficult for me to help her progression than theirs, because of her lack of spoken language. What was particularly hard was when the boys would be pulling a track in a certain direction and then Jemma's contribution would tear a hole in that and leave it less stylistically unified than it had been before. Frankie started to voice his frustration in our feedback sessions. This was interesting because I realized that I was working with him on how to feel and express frustration without melting down.

This was difficult for him, and in a number of sessions the final feedback included one or two thumbs down from him and also sometimes from one of the other two. When it came to the end of the first term all of the children wanted the group recordings and their own solo efforts but not the recordings of the other two to take home. The music was something they enjoyed very much but for all of them it was hard to be in a creative AND democratic group.

We stuck with it into the next term and the entire group started to get noticeably better. They took more control of what they were doing and seemed to be learning how to structure. In the feedback sessions, Sean started to make positive and insightful remarks about how the session had been and how the group was and how they needed to cooperate. This had an impact on the others and the group became slowly more cooperative.

I was delighted when I was pressing CDs at the end of the term to hear Frankie ask for the others' solo efforts to be included on his, something that seemed light years away a couple of months before. Both the others followed suit and the sessions ended with fine recordings and also a sense of being a good working group.

Coda

The work I have done in Clacton has proved very successful. The children have enjoyed it, learned new skills, discovered new sides to their creativity and, most of the time, got on with the rest of their groups.

The schools have seen an improvement in the children's behaviour outside the music sessions and some increase in focus as well as marked increases in motivation and being more settled at school.

For me, the big thing, apart from being proud of the work and my own learning, has been meeting such wonderful people, smart, creative, funny, rebellious, cheeky and highly capable. Many of these children have life stories that children shouldn't have and many of them get excluded from classes very regularly. Most just can't cope with being in a class of thirty, struggling with subjects they find distant and difficult. For them, music gives them a space to be at their best, creative, in control and respected by those around them.

The names of all the students have been changed.

[1] Centre for Social Justice (2013) *Turning the Tide: Social justice in five seaside towns.* http://www.centreforsocialjustice.org.uk/UserStorage/pdf/Pdf%20reports/Turning-the-Tide.pdf(accessed 08.09.2013).

[2] http://www.gazette-news.co.uk/news/local/clacton/10626416.New_figures_reveal_Clacton_as_second_most_deprived_seaside_town/

[3] (http://www.theguardian.com/society/2011/mar/29 /jaywick-essex-resort-most-deprived)

[4] Deane, K. Hunter, R. & Mullen, P. (2011) *Move On Up: an evaluation of Youth Music Mentors.* Youth Music http://network.youthmusic.org.uk/resources/research/move (accessed 08.09.2013).

[5] http://www.singup.org/songbank/song-bank/song-detail/view/249-pick-a-bale-o/

[6] http://www.singup.org/songbank/song-bank/song-detail/view/520-tony-chestnut/

[7] http://www.youtube.com/watch?v=XQ6mQnx7OIc

Why Technology with hard to reach kids?

Gawain Hewitt

'Alfie' is ten years old. He is a wheelchair user and somewhere on the papers at his school would be the words 'Profound and Multiple Learning Difficulties.' He is non-verbal and has limited movement. But Alfie plays the electric guitar. Alfie has experienced the rush of hearing sounds he has created flow and mix together. When he plays he has a light in his eyes and, like every musician, he knows that in order to improve he must practise, and that hard work lies ahead.

This is what music technology can do: lift a child who is, in so many ways, 'hard to reach' to a place where new possibilities open up for them. Music-making is a unique and profound activity that somehow gets right to the heart of what it is to be human, and appropriate use of technology can give children and young adults better access to this very human - and humanising - place.

Anyone who has listened to Mozart or Moby and then picked up a violin or sat at a keyboard will understand that achieving a level of 'success' with traditional instruments can take huge amounts of time and dedication. I began learning the cello aged just four, yet years later I was still working hard on achieving a polished sound. With technology we can get round some of these problems of delayed gratification and give students who may struggle to maintain interest more instant rewards for their effort, encouraging them to participate further and engage more fully. My musical education ran from fundamentals and core techniques to high-quality performance; for hard to reach children technology allows this to run in reverse - beginning with fantastic sounds and eventually leading them back, should they wish to, to the craft and knowledge.

Traditionalists might baulk at this topsy-turvy idea of music first and theory later but, as in Alfie's case, 'backwards' was the only way forwards. We should not only celebrate his participation in music, but work actively to promote access to music from whichever direction it comes, believing that the humanity of the student, of the class, and of society as a whole will be enhanced by this access. This view is inline with that of the disability charity Scope, who say that:

> The social model of disability says that disability is caused by the way society is organised, rather than by a person's impairment or difference. It looks at ways of removing barriers that restrict life choices for disabled people. When barriers are removed, disabled people can be independent and equal in society, with choice and control over their own lives[1].

Reorganisation, choice and control were all important for Alfie. Before I had worked with him, he had not had any musical experiences that were even close to what a boy of his age could expect. He had listened to music and had percussion instruments strapped to him with Velcro, and well-meaning support staff had clapped his hands for him in time to music. Other 10-year-olds were exploring exciting bands across loads of genres; why should Alfie's tastes be any different? By using an iPad and experimenting with different positions so that he could create sounds by touch, we began to give Alfie control over his musical world. Connecting this to a device called 'Soundbeam' - which can be calibrated to control sounds with anything from large limb gestures or small eyelid movements – we enabled Alfie to choose from an almost limitless palette of sounds. Slowly, carefully, we were able to work with him to discover which instruments he wanted to play. And finally, with the Soundbeam controlling an electric guitar, Alfie was there in that place: independent, equal, creating music, making sounds, being human.

Technology has smashed down the barriers to accessing music - music that is technically complex and rewarding. And it is for that reason that it works so well with hard to reach children, whether they are in Pupil Referral Units (PRUs) or facing disabilities. Given this, I want to explore and share what my experience working in this area has taught me, from pedagogical issues to details of different technologies and applications, finishing with a number of other case studies to outline the different ways that these have worked in practice.

Pedagogy and Process

As many parents and carers soon discover, children find technology intuitive and often operate it with confidence. Consequently, the use of technology in music significantly narrows the gap between beginner and expert. For me as a teacher this means that I can be more of a guide, working alongside the children and young people as they learn and discover. This change to the teacher/student dynamic can be helpful when working with hard to reach children. Because technology allows music to be introduced to them in an accessible way they are able to get more immediate rewards, while working alongside a teacher means there is nothing preventing them from taking music to the highest level. The flexibility that the technology affords also allows a student to personalise the curriculum. Within set boundaries they have the choice to take the elements that interest them to create a unique learning experience.

Sound creation and sound choice

The broad sound choice and sound quality that music technology offers help a learner to create music that sounds good and can be completed quickly. This is important as it gives a real sense of achievement. Musical taste is highly personal, and the huge palette of sounds - from traditional musical instruments to loops to synthetic and electronic sounds - means that young people are able to express their individuality. Ownership of their musical creations improves commitment to lessons and engagement in learning. Choosing what sounds to use for a piece of music is in itself a creative act, with a young person demonstrating curation as well as creation.

My experience working in inner city PRUs and Youth Clubs has been that niche sub genres of music can be extremely important to a young person's sense of identity. The diversity of sounds that music technology offers can help to bring cultural authenticity at a street level to the 'hard to reach' classroom.

In the 'hard to reach' classroom, as in any situation, it is vital to appreciate that you will encounter a range of musical preferences; not all children and young people listen to Grime or Hip Hop! Music technology allows you to cater for plurality and diversity within the classroom, giving each young person different sounds and allowing each learner to have an experience that is tailored to them.

Accessibility

As already discussed, technology is all about music-making becoming accessible: accessible for those with what I would describe as extreme learning styles, accessible culturally and accessible to those who face disabilities. In a busy classroom, with students working with a wide range of musical styles, it is important to manage the audio environment carefully. Using headphones means that a student can work independently and privately. This can be effective in the 'hard to reach' classroom as a child or young person can disappear into their own world and make mistakes without fear of peer judgement.

Group dynamics are a challenge in any classroom, and this is accentuated in a PRU. By using headphones some of these challenges can be attenuated. However, inviting young people to work in their own world can be both a positive and a negative: the security of their own world can create issues for the teacher making sure that time is being well-used. I try to make sure that there is time within sessions to encourage the class to work together and develop group-work skills.

Technology can also be used to navigate the transition between private and shared space. I ran a series of sessions in North London with a class of year 11 children who are on the Autistic Spectrum. Working in small groups of four, each child had their own iPad running Garageband, with both headphones and small speakers available to them. During the session I allowed the class to have distinct times where they were working privately on headphones, and at other times they used the speakers and the electronic instruments to jam and compose together as a group. The appropriate selection of technology allowed this class to move quickly from being in their own world to being supported to work together, addressing social cohesion and group dynamics.

Multiple entry, development and exit points

Children and young people can come in to music and progress in a whole range of ways and technology allows for multiple entry, development and exit points. A young person can enter music making creatively as an arranger, a singer, a songwriter, a producer or an instrumentalist. They can also enter technically through an interest in IT, electronics or DJ-ing. The flexibility of entry points allows children and young people to explore the subject from different angles, which in turn suit different learning styles and interests. The same is true for the development of skills. Due to the breadth and diversity of the subject, a child can choose to learn a new skill, build on an existing skill or complete a creative task with skills already learnt. There are also rich possibilities for peer learning and the opportunity for young people to develop expertise in the classroom, whether in a particular technical process or in the artistic understanding necessary to make music in a specific genre. This can impact the group dynamic in turn by giving the child an opportunity to gain acceptance through this growing expertise. The exit points are as numerous as the entries, and include record production, record engineering, live sounds, songwriting and being an artist.

Creativity

While music technology is a craft with a logical sequence of events, skills don't have to be learned in a specific order, and so music technology is a subject where a student can both be creative and have measured learning outcomes. It offers the potential for very clear musical and technological progression, but also the freedom to follow your own creative pathway. A teacher can set very clear boundaries for assessment but also leave freedom for children and young people to achieve in their own way, allowing for radically different outcomes. Using headphones, a young person can work on their own and have total control of all the parameters.

For someone with low self-esteem, being able to say "I did all this myself" is not the same as being creative as part of a group. This ownership through creativity means they have responsibility for their own work and, in my experience, when given creative responsibility children and young people rarely mess up their own pieces, instead making positive choices, displaying improvement towards vision and demonstrating musical excellence.

This is useful and important in the 'hard to reach' classroom because creativity, unlike knowledge, is a completely level playing field. Most children can access their imagination with support and one child's imagination is as rich as the next child's. So, regardless of their technological knowledge, all children in a music technology class have the opportunity to succeed through creativity.

Pedagogy in Practice

Having given a pedagogical overview of why music technology can be so important, I want now to focus on what this work looks like in practice, with some examples from my own work.

Recording

When working with hard to reach young people I will often begin by demonstrating and teaching them how to record audio into a computer. Being able to record and manipulate the sound immediately can open the lesson with a light touch as the sounds can be really funny. Changing pitch and timbre and playing back the sound to everyone is engaging and silly while introducing a key fundamental skill of music technology. When working with children who are non-verbal, learning how to record and edit their own or a friend's voice becomes a way to give the child a voice, and on occasion has even encouraged a normally reticent child to speak or sing.

Arranging and creating

Using blocks of sound, or loops, children and young people can learn the basics of arrangement and musical structure. This works in the 'hard to reach' classroom because children and young people are immediately using very high quality sounds, which is affirming and engaging. From here children and young people can gradually move to using music technology as a tool for composition, constructing original melodies and recording them into the software, while retaining the loops as a musical scaffold. In time students can construct multi-instrument compositions with the technology allowing them to combine composition, arrangement and instrumentation in one experience.

Processing and editing

Technology allows children to manipulate and process sound using effects, filters and editing. Sound can be manipulated live or in the computer using effects such as echo, reverb or phaser, which change voices or instruments, making them sound electronic or 'spacey' by adding a produced sound. This can really encourage a reluctant vocalist to sing or speak, which can be helpful in the 'hard to reach' classroom as children and young people can practise a creative discipline without feeling too exposed. Sounds can also be cut up, reversed and distorted in editing programmes, allowing the young person to practise the skills of production. Equalisation, pan and volume, while simple and easy to understand, are the 'trade skills' of a professional recording engineer, typically used on a mixing desk.

By beginning to edit sounds in these ways young people are starting to listen critically, making decisions about what they do and don't like. Thus, editing sounds is not just a craft, but also a context for learning reflective practice. Through editing it is possible to begin to develop a critical faculty and practise positive self-criticism and the development of a creative vision.

Sampling

Sampling is a technique where a recorded sound is made into a new instrument for use live or as part of a musical production. It allows a young person to experience sound creation and understand where electronic sounds come from. It also allows them to begin to create sounds which are unique to them, which gives creative ownership. A task that I have found works well in PRUs is giving a class audio that has been sampled (edited) from a well known piece of music and asking them to re-work it into a track themselves. An example is Mozart's 'Queen of the Night' aria from The Magic Flute as sampled on the track 'Like You' by Kelis. If you compare the tracks you will notice that Kelis has taken one vocal line and repeated it as a physically impossible vocal hook, which gives the track an ostinato or loop, as well as being full of tension (as the singer appears to never breathe). I begin by playing the class the Kelis track. Then, immediately and without comment, I play 'Queen of the Night'. I ask the class what they have in common and use this as a way to begin a discussion about Kelis and also Mozart, opera, the singer on the recording, theatre and genre. The opportunity for extra learning here is rich and I may choose to give the class a handout to complete, with the name of the composer, the name of track and dates.

Mixing and balancing

The connecting and plugging in of wires, the routing of sound through a music technology system and the balancing and mixing of sound are other great ways to engage students for whom mainstream school can be difficult, and are techniques that I have found work well in PRUs. Engineering - the craft of sound management, recording and balancing - is a subject in itself, with a separate career path. Being inherently physical and concerned with problem solving, it suits some learning styles well while also giving a student status in the classroom.

Equipment

Beyond the pedagogical issues, what are the core pieces of technology that can be put to use? I will now give an overview of some different types of music technology and their use in the 'hard to reach' classroom.

Software

GarageBand is a piece of software for Apple computers and iPad which is extremely easy to use and allows you to record using real sounds with a microphone or with sounds generated by the computer, such as a realistic emulation of a piano or drums. You can arrange and manipulate loops or blocks of pre-recorded audio to create new pieces of music. It is a fantastic entry point to music-making and it is possible to create very sophisticated music with it. Sequel and Mixcraft offer similar experiences on PC.

Soundplant and Audacity are free and easy to use software that work on PCs and Macs. Audacity allows recording and editing of sound and Soundplant allows samples to be edited and played back live. Both are extremely easy to use and can be used in broad settings.

Cubase, Logic and Pro Tools are among the most well known audio and sound programmes for computers, and are found in most top recording studios. These are complex and therefore they can be difficult to use in the 'hard to reach' classroom, but they do represent a more advanced progression route.

Tablet computers including iPads

Tablets and iPads have made music technology very easy to use. iPads have apps which allow you to record, edit, manipulate and create music that can cover most angles of music technology in some way. They also provide an extremely easy, intuitive and fun way to play software instruments, allowing a pupil to play a realistic emulation of a trombone, flute, piano, drums or pretty much any other instrument that you can think of. The closeness to the technology means that the gap between the creative mind and the physical mind diminishes – it is very close to playing an actual instrument. This is also true of their use in the classroom. Because you can hold an iPad, and use it with a small portable speaker, you can use an iPad as you would use any instrument in the classroom. Standout apps on the iPad include GarageBand, which allows you to play many instruments and to sequence, and Thumbjam, which gives a completely new interface to use for playing back sounds. Also apps such as Bloom give a completely new and different experience, being part musical instrument and part composing tool.

Mobile Phones

While phones are normally banned from the classroom, I have at times found it useful to allow their use in the 'hard to reach' classroom. The modern phone has apps that allow it to double up as a sophisticated piece of music technology and as a storage place for a young person's music collection. Finding a way to plug a phone's output into a mixing desk is an engaging and relevant way to introduce audio engineering, while using music they choose as a backing track for rapping, singing or improvisation gives the task cultural authenticity and also opens conversations around music choice, reflective listening and genre.

Hardware

Switches are a very simple interface that make triggering sounds in class very easy. You can get switches that play sounds on their own and ones that play sounds off a computer. They can be used to allow children or young people to have different sounds for a prepared lesson, much as you would use chime bars or percussion. Adaptations exist that allow switches to be triggered with almost any movement, including head and breath, making them very accessible to disabled children and young people.

Guitar pedal effects are simple, you connect an instrument to an effect on the way to an amplifier, which allows manipulation of sounds in a very easy way. You can also get similar units for microphones, which allow easy manipulation of voice.

Microphones in themselves are excellent technology. Just presenting a child with a microphone can sometimes be all you need to persuade them to sing or rap.

Synthesisers and drum machines are individual instruments that generate drum and electronic sounds and can be extremely useful as robust and simple machines, allowing a student to pursue one discipline on their own or in the group context.

The Skoog is an instrument that has been designed specifically to be accessible to disabled children and is proving to be popular in some special schools. It interfaces with a computer and allows a child to trigger sounds using different coloured buttons.

Soundbeam is an instrument that converts movement to sound. You can set it to be sensitive from 30cm to 6m and anything in between.

Leapmotion is a new interface that converts movement to sound for the computer. Very affordable, it will run on any modern Mac or PC computer and has its own easy to use software.

Recently there have been products coming onto the market which allow a more experimental approach to music and technology. An example that I have been using a lot has been Makey Makey. This is a circuit board that connects to a computer. You attach two wires to the board, and when you complete the circuit the computer can be set up to trigger a sound. The brilliant part is that you can complete the circuit using plasticine, water, fruit, flowers, people – in fact anything capable of conducting a very tiny (and very safe) amount of electricity. Combined with Soundplant you can create an intuitive and fun musical trigger, as well as making interesting accessible instruments for disabled children.

Case Studies

I want to end with a few case studies showing how I have worked with various children, all of whom presented different challenges to accessing music.

Tommy attended a PRU in London in 2011. He had been expelled from school, and was also a looked after child. When I first worked with him, his response to music was "I can't do it" or more specifically "this is shit". Learning that Tommy was into Garage music, I showed him on Logic how to make a beat, add a bass line, and then vocals with effects. Music Technology proved to Tommy that he was in fact able to make music. The sounds available to him gave the session a cultural authenticity, with the piece we made fitting into his musical world. Playing the track to his class gave Tommy status, as well as the role of a peer mentor and role model, others praised his work and aspired to making something as good themselves. Later in the term Tommy's carer came in to hear his work. Music technology changed not only his opinion of the subject, but also, I would argue, his opinion of himself. With support, Tommy remained engaged throughout the term. This is an example of music technology's ability to provide a different entry point to the subject for a child who considered that music was not for them.

Raquel is 15, a victim of sexual abuse and had been expelled from school. I worked with Racquel at a PRU and she was not at all engaged in my music lessons. In trying to engage with her I asked her what music she liked and she said she listened to Sneakbo (a London based Grime artist) among others and named three tracks in particular. For the next lesson I prepared 8 sounds that sounded like Sneakbo. Just presenting her with this as a limited palette persuaded her to use the equipment, explore manipulation of the software and therefore the sounds.

Paul was 12, small for his age and fitted some of the stereotypes you would expect of a child in a PRU. He had a very short temper and had recently smashed a door in the school, causing more than £4000 worth of damage. When discussing my work I am frequently told "oh, they'll love music technology" or "you've got it easy, as you have all the toys". It is assumed that music technology or the opportunity to rap would be a great incentive for children in PRUs and/or with Social, Emotional and Behavioural Difficulties (SEBD) and that they will naturally enjoy it and excel. Paul wouldn't even come into the class. I sat down with him for more than an hour, just to gently discuss why he was so against even coming into the lesson. Eventually, in tears, and with the support of a learning mentor, Paul told me that he hadn't been allowed to play the flute at his Primary school. Wow, that wasn't what I was expecting to hear. And he still wanted to play the flute. I can't teach flute, and I didn't have a flute to offer him, but I could offer him flute sounds on a keyboard, and together we found a way for him to learn some piano repertoire on a keyboard using flute sounds. Over the years I have taught in PRUs, nothing has been more popular than learning to play well known melodies on the keyboard, even when technology, decks or the microphone has been the initial hook to get the child engaged. Therefore we must be very careful not to make assumptions about our learners, and I have found having a broad offer has been a good approach.

I recently ran a session in a PRU where I set up one computer with 6 pairs of wires coming from a Makey Makey. The pupils' task was to make a musical sculpture out of play dough and metal cutlery and use it to trigger a sound. We would then extend this by playing a piece together at the end. Each instrument was wired to my computer and the sounds I was able to select from my workstation. So with one computer and one Makey Makey up to 11 instruments can be made. This session worked well because of the combination of a physical making task with music programming. By using the music technology to circumnavigate their own perceptions of what a music lesson was, they engaged, enjoyed the making and were able to perform a piece at the end. It also added a cross-curricular element as we discussed how it worked, touching on electronics and design and technology in the process.

Again using Makey Makey, but this time in a school for children on the Autistic Spectrum, I worked with a group of young people who were making music to the theme of water. I made three music switches out of buckets of water, so the sound was triggered when they put their hands in the buckets. This served to give a musical context that was extremely tactile, encouraging exploration. It was also very close to the subject matter. And of course a lot of fun and messy!

It isn't just the physical aspects of music technology that can make the difference. The conceptual possibilities can also be very useful when working to engage students who have been expelled or for whom mainstream school is a difficult environment.

Music technology can present music in a new way, literally and metaphorically. Its impact is difficult to pin down, precisely because it is so flexible. What I do know is that music is made more accessible when using technology, allowing children and young people who are outside of mainstream music teaching to circumnavigate barriers to achievement, whether these be a physical or psychological disability, attitudinal barriers, a learning disability or extreme learning style. I do not see a difference between musicality on traditional instruments or musicality on technology. These are merely different tools to express and share musical ideas.

The names of the students have been changed

[1] http://www.scope.org.uk/about-us/our-brand/talking-about-disability/social-model-disability (accessed 30.08.2013)

Singing and the body

Beth Allen

I think it is taken for granted that it is more challenging to work with hard-to-reach children than mainstream children. That I will have to work harder. That my tool bag will have to be deeper. That I will need more patience. That I will have to be more observant, more careful, more delicate and more precise with my interventions. That I will need to think more before I move.

What I want to add to that list are some ideas I explored while studying for my MA in Voice. The MA involved a term of detailed body work looking at resonance, breath and articulation in small, slow detail. This was followed by a term on language and our sensory learning method; our connection to words and the meaning of self-expression; and expressing other people's words and thoughts. In the third term I studied my own passion, which is the relationship between speaking and singing, and thinking about what speaking has to offer singing and what singing offers speech. So here are my most useful discoveries for working with hard-to-reach children though voice.

Speaking versus singing

There is a wide spectrum of voice usage, from whispered conversation through to operatic aria, and there is no simple line between singing and speaking. There is a large area of crossover where one can support and help the other. For example, it is possible to find spoken word pieces that are so musical – poems, choral speaking and Shakespeare – where the language is in long musical phrases, the rhythm is strong and the musical use of sounds, alliteration and onomatopoeia is as much about what we hear as what we feel. The music of some of Shakespeare's sonnets resonates perfectly with hip-hop. The work of the Hip Hop Shakespeare Company brings these connections alive[1]. These spoken pieces are creative pieces, so close to music the only thing missing is sustained pitch[2]. Teenage children will appreciate the work of dub poets such as Linton Kwesi Johnson[3]. By repeating some of these works out loud and examining and savouring the words, children can come to see the links between poetry, reggae and also rap. They can also move beyond the story and the potential bravado of rap to an understanding and appreciation of some of the sonic skills involved.

Rap itself can frequently be highly poetic and it is difficult to single out any one from the many examples of high quality work. A good starting place is the documentary 'Something from Nothing: The Art of Rap'[4]. It is also possible to find songs that appeal to our logical self, which are not about sustained pitch but about the pleasure and fun in word play and language tricks. *Back of the Bus*[5] and scouting songs such as *You'll never go to heaven*[6] are full of communal joke-making and shared joy in language.

Singing and heightened language can use interesting vocabulary and auditory tricks that bamboozle, as in some rounds. For example *Black Socks*[7] is a round that can work very simply and the lyrics are fun and cheeky, especially for use with boys. It is possible to sing it with any number of entries. They can come in after only one note and create a really interesting sound. Onomatopoeia, alliteration, rhythm and rhyme are auditory tricks that please and stimulate the ears. The limerick *There was an old woman of Ryde*[8] springs to mind.

It is also possible to use sound effects, such as beatboxing or the sounds used in comics and cartoon films, to create incredibly complex rhythmic patterns and place them carefully to tell a story or simply to express a mood. These sounds are as far from operatic aria as possible, as aria relies heavily on the extended vowel for emotion and self-expression. And, let's face it, all kids love making sounds! Some sound pieces using market trader cries or train sounds can be found in the two Voiceworks collections[9]. You could compose your own soundscape using car horns to make a street scene, or machine sounds to make a cotton mill. Try writing a ghost story with the kids and get them to add in vocal sound effects like creaky doors, howling (were)wolves and wobbly ghosts. The Sing Up website contains a lot of good material that is very accessible for hard-to-reach children. Two good examples are *Button Factory*[10] and *Boom-chicka-boom*[11], while tongue twisters can be found on the Indian Child website[12].

So there are lots of ways of exploring musical and vocal activities without having 'in tune' or 'harmony' at the top of a list of skills. It is possible to approach singing from a different angle and use all the other benefits it can offer. For instance, one second-language English speaker at a nursery school had had three of his front teeth removed by the dentist, so we wrote a little chant as a caution. We had a lot of fun adding actions and the boy himself became the leader of his own chant. It is really a song but there is no pitch requirement. We found we could split into groups and make a chorus of the last line.

> Chocolate, chocolate, I'd eat it every day
> But chocolate makes the dentist take my teeth away
> Chocolate sticks and chocolate eggs a----------re
> Just for a treat or I'll lose my pegs!

Whether this is a mantra or propaganda is up for discussion but the boy was happy with his reminder.

Exercise and energy

After a long sing I am very happy and physically exhausted. I feel I have run a marathon. I am using muscles internally that I don't engage in speaking every day. Singing is an aerobic activity. The extreme internal muscle workings required for singing a long phrase – engaging diaphragm, pelvic floor, intercostals (between the ribs) and the vocal folds, all in conjunction – provide a kind of internal Pilates class. Combined with the effects of a supercharged carbon dioxide/oxygen exchange, singing makes for a potentially serious mood enhancer. It is also excellent exercise for its own sake and is ideal for anyone unable to use their limbs. The SEN school I work at, on the Fylde, is interested in singing as exercise for all its wheelchair-bound children.

So singing is exercise and can be used to punctuate other activities and change energy. Rhythm can create energy and help sustain a weary child. I would recommend a strong rhythmic song when a class or child is flagging. However, it is worth noting here that a strong rhythmic song can also send an already giddy group of kids into uncontrollable glee. It is very easy to lose control of a class with the wrong song choice. Simply put, a fast, rhythmic song will speed up the bodily systems by creating energy.

Breath and relaxation

Singing can promote a balanced exchange of oxygen and carbon dioxide where the oxygen stimulates or wakes up the system, while the expelling of carbon dioxide slows and calms the system. The above section talked about fast and energetic songs where lots of oxygen is taken in. However, there are other songs and heightened speech pieces which involve the slowing down of the exhale with longer phrases. If we want to calm down the bodily system (e.g. for panic attacks or hyperventilation) we sometimes use blowing out into a paper bag. This slows down the exchange and forces the diaphragm to slow down. Many relaxation and mood management techniques rely on breath, on counting ins and outs (Buddhist meditation) or using nose breathing (Yoga meditation), which is slower than mouth breathing.

It is important to have some songs that either employ slow singing or a long phrase with nowhere to inhale. There is an American cowboy song, *I'm going to leave old Texas now*[13], which always works to calm a class down as they have to imagine a cowboy in the blazing heat crossing the plains on a tired horse.

Similarly, with eight-year-old twins with autism whom I teach, we create a train soundscape and enjoy the speeding up and slowing down of the rhythm, but finish with them making a long, slow *tshhhhhhh*. As the steam is let out of the pistons with a wail of a whistle, we imagine the train disappearing into the distance, and they settle and relax a little further.

Repetition

Singing allows you to repeat ideas without getting bored. This is great not only for lesson learning and times tables, etc., but also for positive language and mantras. In all the short stay schools and PRUs I have worked in, there has been a policy of voicing and reflecting good behaviour, so an endless stream of "Well done", "Good sitting", "Great listening", "Good lad", etc. is used as a way of encouraging and reprogramming good behaviour. Singing can do something like this, too, if you choose your songs carefully and make sure the language gets the message across in a way the children can get behind.

Words that are cheesey are the worst for repeating, but playful is good, or you write your own with a pleasing rhyme or cheeky rhythmic cluster of words so it can be sung again and again. Singing can also be used to develop group mantras – not airy-fairy hippy ones, but mantras that are practical and useful. An example of a useful mantra that is in our everyday language is 'I am my own boss'. A great one for kids is in the theme song from 'Malcolm in the Middle': *Boss of me* by They Might Be Giants[14].

There is a great song called *Good To Be Me*[15], which has a psychedelic 60s feel to it and a Fosse-style dance. It is hugely popular in mainstream schools, as it ties into their PSHE curriculum work. However, I find children sometimes perceive it as a bit too cheesy and it can feel wrong with a small group or individual, so *Three Little Birds*[16] by Bob Marley or *Don't Worry, Be Happy*[17] by Bobby McFerrin might do a better job. There is another good PSHE song on the Sing Up website called *Ain't Gonna Let Nobody*[18] which can be easily adapted to let children vent their frustrations around bullying or other issues.

Listening and focus

Using different methods of meditating has been a real eye-opener for me. Just sitting still and silent is considered to be the height of a well-trained body and mind. There are a few simple methods that lead up to this that help you slow down with more support. Listening to your environment is one way. Use your ears to collect all the sounds and hear the world as a piece of music. Creating soundscapes for either your own real environment or an imagined one starts engaging the ear (e.g. using sounds of nature at a beach or in a wood). Listening is a slow sense – much slower than your eyes. It takes longer to process the information and involves some thinking, but lots of kids will really respond to dealing with this kind of stimulus especially if they are auditory learners. Using a stimulating sound world and making a sound world that is worth listening to, and being quiet for, also encourages children to employ nose breathing, slowing down their oxygen exchange. Teachers sometimes complain to me about the quality of listening in the classroom and I always reply, 'If you want children to listen, you have to provide something worth listening to!'

Conclusion

Working with hard-to-reach children through voice is a very creative process. It has to be more playful and more fun for the child than may be necessary in mainstream education. There is so much more to learn about human nature and what stimulates and what calms a child that is hard to reach, and the results, when you discover those keys, provide a rich reward for the practitioner.

[1] http://www.hiphopshakespeare.com/site/ and at http://www.youtube.com/watch?v=DSbtkLA3GrY (accessed 09.09.2013).

[2] More examples in Patten, B. (ed.) (1998) *The Puffin Book of Utterly Brilliant Poetry*. London: Puffin Books.

[3] examples at http://www.youtube.com/watch?v=Zq9OpJYck7Y and http://www.youtube.com/watch?v=9BKN8C9taZg (accessed 09.09.2013).

[4] Directed by Ice-T. DVD released by Kaleidoscope Home Entertainment (2012).

[5] http://www.maxilyrics.com/pete-seeger-if-you-miss-me-at-the-back-of-the-bus-lyrics-89d4.html for lyrics and video link (accessed 09.09.2013).

[6] http://www.campfire.pwp.blueyonder.co.uk/Story/heaven.htm (accessed 09.09.2013).

[7] www.youtube.com/watch?v=0hNybeSt3TM and http://www.singup.org/songbank/song-bank/song-detail/view/501-black-socks/ (accessed 09.09.2013).

[8] In Hunt, P. (ed.) (2003) *Voiceworks 2*. Oxford: Oxford University Press.

[9] Hunt, P. (ed.) (2001) Voiceworks. Oxford: Oxford University Press, and see above.

[10] http://www.singup.org/songbank/song-bank/song-detail/view/7/ (accessed 09.09.2013); also in Voiceworks 2 (see note 8).

[11] http://www.singup.org/songbank/song-bank/song-detail/view/162-hey-my-name-is-joe-button-factory/ (accessed 09.09.2013).

[12] http://www.indianchild.com/tongue_twisters.htm (accessed 05.09.2013).

[13] http://www.singup.org/songbank/song-bank/song-detail/view/499-cowboy-song/ (accessed 05.09.2013).

[14] http://www.youtube.com/watch?v=x5Za8HggalY (accessed 09.09.2013) .

[15] Lyrics by Melanie Barber Music by Geraldine Grant and Phil Needham. Taken from *Seal Songs Keystage 1*. Wakefield District Council.

[16] http://www.youtube.com/watch?v=zaGUr6wzyT8 (accessed 09.09.2013).

[17] http://www.youtube.com/watch?v=d-diB65scQU (accessed 09.09.2013).

[18] http://www.singup.org/songbank/song-bank/song-detail/view/444-aint-gonna-let-nobody/ (accessed 05.09.2013).

Music Group Work with LGBT Youth

Catherine Pestano

This chapter looks at how person centred music group work can help a young person to self-actualise. Perhaps for each of us human beings at any age this 'becoming a person' (Rogers, 1961) is our artistic pinnacle; the most deeply creative act. Creative group work is explored in this article through reflections on an out-of-school music activity with a particular group experiencing social exclusion: Lesbian Gay Bisexual and Transgender youth and those questioning their sexuality or gender (LGBTQ). The wider principles relating to inclusive group work, applicable beyond this minority group, are also noted. Discussion includes some practical detail, some thoughts on working with oppressed groups in isolation and how to promote later integration and general wellbeing.

> Will you join my cause and save me? 'cos I'm falling and there's no one here to hold me.... (song lyrics, LGBTQ project, 2009)

Young people contemplating issues of sexual orientation and gender identity can have a hard time in our society, despite many improvements to civil rights over the last 20 years. Perpetrators of homophobia and discrimination continue to hurt young people and adults at many levels, affecting their wellbeing. Young lesbian, gay bisexual and transgender youth are identified as being at risk due to their external and internalised experiences of societal hatred and discrimination, sometimes called 'minority stress' (Meyer, 2003). A report commissioned by Stonewall, in partnership with YouGov (Guasp, 2012), found that 55% of young LGBT pupils experience homophobic bullying at school, over half of whom report that teacher witnesses did nothing to intervene. Consequently they have higher rates of maladaptive coping mechanisms such as substance misuse, self-harm and suicide attempts, with higher levels of mental health needs, counselling and support needs.

A useful concept in working with young people is that of resilience (Grotberg, 1997), referring to those qualities that protect a young person from the worst impacts of their challenging circumstances. Research from the Social Care Institute for Excellence (SCIE), looking into what fosters resilience in young people, suggests that self-esteem and self-efficacy are key, along with feeling happy at school (Bostock, 2004). This literature suggests that strategies which promote resilience include enhancing communication and self-expression, through participating in valued enjoyable activities (ibid). This can include a creative music group, where young people can learn to explore ideas, build trust and work together with others, share their feelings and find acceptance, and succeed in producing something they can feel proud of. As acceptance both by society and also within the self are key issues, promoting resilience is an ideal youth-centred approach that I recommend be applied to initiatives supporting young people who are LGBTQ. In my work with local organisations, I choose to do this through the provision of creative music groups, an overview and an example of which follow.

Creative Croydon, a small voluntary community music organisation, has secured several small innovation oriented grants to do short term, out-of-school music projects with young people (aged 15 – 22) who either identify as part of the queer community or are questioning their sexuality or gender identity (LGBTQ). In order to reach relevant young people we liaise with other small specialist organisations in the Croydon or Bromley areas who have contact with them as part of their niche youth work provision. LGBTQ youth tend to absent themselves from local services for fear of meeting someone they know, and also move around services a lot due to relationship issues. It can be hard to reach and retain them in a service. Similarly, the services meeting their needs are under much pressure and staff have little spare time for liaison even when a project is freely offered. This means that a fair amount of development time is needed even for a short project.

We tend to staff the projects with LGBT community members. This is not essential, as many other workers with empathy and imagination could also do great work with these LGBTQ young people. However on a short project we find that it is beneficial to have live role models. These workers have an in-depth lived experience of surviving and being LGBT in a hostile world. Rather than being private about their lives, workers are encouraged to answer questions from the young people, where they feel the questions are not too intrusive. This provides an additional resource for the young people as they explore issues around being LGBT in a world not always comfortable with this.

We need to navigate the pressures on our partner organisations as they seek to satisfy their multiple funding streams and fit that with our need for an open agenda in the music project. Choice is an important principle in the creative music session and so sometimes we have had to resist requests from partner agencies to focus on themes such as safe sex or bullying, in order to preserve a focus on the young people's preferences, while also seeing how we can make some room to meet the needs of the partner agencies. An example of one project is the Bromley 'SNAP' group run by the Metro Centre and some more detail is offered here as an illustration of our work.

Project overview

We provided 10 sessions of 2-3 hrs music–making across 10 weeks, during the regular youth group slots. Staff input was two youth workers and two LGBT music facilitators for a group of up to twenty young people, not all of whom might be in the room at any one time (chill out space provided).

Activities and session structure varied depending on the groups and their needs. Each session usually included a mix of whole group and small group activities, and a mix of existing repertoire and creation of new work. We also aimed to include a little community culture and history, partly to assist the partners in meeting external policy and funding requirements but mainly because our particular community has a fractured history and the culture is easily lost over time. For example, our project leaders were a generation older than the youth workers, two generations older than the group members and the different generations knew very little of each others' history and culture. Learning songs important to others in diverse LGBT communities, hearing music and seeing artefacts from these generations enriched the sense of community and connection between participants and other staff in the LGBT projects. For example, songs of historic importance such as *Glad to be Gay* and *Somewhere over the Rainbow* (popular as an emotional plea for a better, freer existence, sung by gay icon Judy Garland) were surprising hits. This allowed for the beginnings of shared dialogue in which ideas and values in other areas could be reflected on, questioned and re-evaluated in relation to the young people's experiences, enabling a climate in which critical thinking and Freire's critical consciousness (Spruce, 2012) might begin to develop.

This group included young people with a wide range of additional needs, including those using Child and Adolescent Mental Health Services (CAMHS), Looked After Child (LAC) status, and several with Autistic Spectrum Disorders (ASD). A number of others made use of other LGBT specialist counselling and support services. Their ethnic profile was a mix of black, Asian, white and mixed heritage. At the youth club their needs for a safe space to socialise were well met but activities tended to be single-session with little focus on ongoing collaboration, so it seemed we might contribute something new here.

We met with the young people and listened to what they might like in a music project, which included space to try new things and opportunities for those with music experience to use existing skills. A wide range of musical tastes were shared, providing the young people with a chance to be the expert in their chosen form and teach us about it, playing it on their phones to illustrate. They were very interested in their own chosen topic of love and also open to ideas from the youth workers about issues to do with bullying. We established the group contract or groundrules for working supportively together, building on their existing group codes. We asked whether they would like accreditation and most said not. We brought most of the kit and encouraged young people to bring any instruments they had whether or not they could play. We brought a mix of folk instruments from diverse cultures, rock instruments and music technology, to appeal to a wide range of tastes. In our experience LGBTQ youth tended to be less tribal in their music tastes than those in our mainstream groups – playlists included death metal, country and opera together.

Structure

A session would typically begin with socialising, then moving into some whole group creative music-making using improvisation techniques on the instruments and encouraging people to swap and try different sounds. This was developed using exercises which encouraged listening and responding across the group. Instruments such as the didgeridoo and drum pads encouraged a spirit of playful exploration. Next, we would look at LGBT cultural history and then share a song. We would then do some brainstorming leading to collaborative whole group songwriting or move into our smaller groups to develop pieces. At this point we would offer ourselves as a resource if needed but also give participants space to work out something for themselves. Developing this aspect further we all visited the spaces where the different small groups were working to hear how things were going. This meant that people had to try to pull something together, however small, to share. We ended sessions with celebratory singing of one of the group songs we had learned or written. Something similar would occur each week in a kind of familiar routine.

The young people's voices

The materials the young people generated enabled them to explore a range of feelings and experiences. Themes included their fear and alienation, in a world so often negative about LGBT issues, which at times could turn in on itself as self-harm. Some examples of their lyrics follow:

> *Cruelty's on heat and pain ran away,*
> *life in clockwork motion and pain with lightening speed....*
> *a controversial love story with a power crazy feel*
> *maybe they can bribe you to believe their lies someday*

Another nightmarish werewolf song with themes of destruction and transformation allowed feelings of confusion, fear and a sense of otherness to find expression.

Determination to join together to stand up for their right to exist was another powerful focus:

> *We'll fight the fight, we'll stand our ground*
> *We'll pay the price, we're not backing down*
> *It's not gonna be easy but we're not standing alone*
> *but standing as one*

Other material included lots of love songs:

> *You've kept me strong, so strong, for so long*
> *You give me love, ecstatic love*

and 'surviving a breakup' songs:

> *I'm on my way to a brighter day,*
> *I'm stronger than I've ever been before*
> *I ain't breakin' no more*
> *There just no way I'm ever coming back to you.....*

A musically edgy electronic track, a song about love in adversity, hesitant but brave, revisiting an experience of school lunch room bullying, became something of an anthem for the group:

> *What we feel inside is love, passion and desire,*
> *Don't stare us down, or make a sound*
> *We're only human, we're all the same*
> *We're only human, we're all the same*

At times we used pastiche to promote playfulness and self affirmation. *O Happy Day* allowed the group to flirt with terms from LGBT life that are often used as abuse by those outside the LGBT community but which need to be reclaimed in order to use them comfortably. And so we had, '*Oh happy gay, Oh tranny gay, Oh dykey gay, oh fairy gay*' as a blithe and blissful outro to a fairly outrageous pastiche version celebrating our shared LGBT diversities.

One young LGBTQ man shared, "If not doing this music group I would have been attending and hanging out at the project but would not have made so many links with other people. I really loved this, music brings people together. What I liked best was getting to write songs with my friends" (Pestano, 2011).

Why a separate group?

A colleague who is starting up a LGBT choir by invitation has recently been challenged - Why do you have to have a separate group for LGBT singing? This is a common concern as some people feel that integration should be the focus of any work but if people lack social connections or capital this can be difficult. Jonathan Porritt (2007) summarised the two kinds of social capital that people need: *bonding and bridging,* both neutral terms, which need to exist in balance. People who have experience of displacement or oppression need to feel safe and strong within their own community first (bonding) before moving outward to connect with others different from themselves (bridging). What looks like isolationism is merely a basic expression of the hierarchy of needs identified by Maslow (1943), where feeing safe comes before reaching out. LGBTQ youth benefit enormously from having a group just for them in which to build their emotional and social skills and feel validated. They can then feel strong enough later to go into wider society with these skills in place. One of our project leaders, Myrtala Thomas, commented, "I feel that for them the benefit of the project came from being able to express themselves creatively, amongst their peers, in a situation where their sexuality was not the issue." (Pestano, 2012). A young woman participant shared that "the lyrics I wrote with my group helped me to deal with a certain situation I found myself in which was related to homophobia".

The youth workers commented on their considerable surprise at the degree of cooperation displayed on the music project. In their experience young people were much more "...held back and dysfunctional" in regular sessions and noting that the activity "...created a shared experience and brought the group closer together" (Pestano, 2011). They valued the contribution that the collaborative creative process added to youth group experience as it took participants "out of their comfort zones which allowed them to express themselves openly". Social capital was enhanced by individual feedback processes between group members as part of the closing activities. A permanent record was then available to participants as a treasured memento that would also boost self-esteem and reinforce the personal learning experience.

> *We're really cool and rather fab,*
> *If you don't like us then you are sad*
> (Group lyrics, 2010)

Broader issues

Fostering a climate for creativity

Rogers and Freiberg (1994) set out principles of the creative classroom and facilitative teaching relationships, offering this perspective afresh to counter the rise in educational conservatism prevalent in the late 80s/early 90s. Creative work needs an atmosphere conducive to participants lowering their customary defences and relaxing enough to take up their own autonomy and agency in the activity. For creativity to thrive, people need to feel comfortable to make mistakes (Holt, 1962), so showing that any errors or unexpected sounds are enjoyable and potentially fun or creative is valuable. As project leader, in order to achieve a climate where risk taking is welcome (Henry, 2001), I must reflect these principles myself while maintaining overall authority and responsibility for the sessions. In any music workshop activity there is a need to maintain a balance between order, enough for the session to function without descending into chaos, and freedom, which releases the powerful playful inner child and its accompanying energy. This is particularly important in LGBTQ sessions where the sense of self has been devalued by society and this then internalised in many cases.

Higgins (2012) writes about the essential nature of the welcome as helping create this climate. This welcome can be established through both verbal and nonverbal means, including aspects such as how the seating is arranged, employing more egalitarian circles than hierarchical classroom settings. Open body language and non-threatening stance, warm tones of voice, refreshments as well as materials of quality can all communicate: 'you are welcome and equal here; we are on an adventure together and I am a resource for you'. Having specific activities to offer together with a willingness to share control and ownership of proceedings stimulates deeper engagement with the learning possibilities. The LGBT element of the welcome was easy as the leaders were all out as LGBT themselves, which helped add to a sense of safety. For those not of the community but wanting to communicate an inclusive welcome this needs to be clearly stated. When I trained as a social worker there was nothing explicitly stated by my teachers or the college at any time that LGBT students were welcome and so I spent a year wondering about the tutors' attitudes and not feeling safe to be 'out'. Don't assume that your students will feel safe if you do not explicitly say they are. (This probably goes for your LGBT colleagues as well).

As well as musical skills, many other qualities can be developed. Capacities to question, explore, challenge and to be emotionally congruent are all life skills for both teachers and students. These attributes can be fostered, in the music education classroom or workshop session, through creative and improvisatory play. Skills can be built in relation to communication, flexing of the wonder muscles, collaboration and the spirit (or perhaps *sprite?*) of making mischief and enjoying rather than being disturbed by the unexpected. The youth workers were surprised to see the levels of cooperation generated by the creative music sessions, especially given the additional challenging circumstances many faced. A young LGBTQ woman with autistic spectrum needs said that she liked best "collaboratively creating a musical piece. I've never been in any kind of independent music group before".

The search for identity

'We are perhaps all of us engaged in a struggle to discover our identity, the person who we are and chose to be' (Rogers & Freiberg, 1994: 52). For many of the young people with whom we work, and possibly ourselves as well, some aspects of our LGBT identities are not respected by society. Religious condemnation is an important distress factor for many. Active homophobic ideas in society are compounded by ignorance, for example the conflation of the completely separate issues of homosexuality and paedophilia. Young people and adults can take this negative evaluation on board and it causes great conflict and distress as they struggle with making sense of their own minority experience. There are similar issues for many other children and young people who are perceived as different but for some of these differences society now holds a more enlightened view than others – disability is protected to some degree and children are no longer devalued for being who they are. The impact on self-esteem when who you are is deemed unacceptable cannot be overestimated.

The benefits when we feel accepted show in project leader Myrtala's recollection of one LGBTQ young participant's experience:

> One young LGBTQ man began the sessions as a shy, quiet individual. I worked closely with him during the first session as he had literacy issues. In later sessions I noticed that although he did not join in so much with the song writing he would happily bang along on available percussion instruments whenever possible. I was later told by one of the staff members that it was the first time he had actively participated in group activities. By the end of the project he was one of the strongest and most vocal singers and would excitedly express any new discoveries he made to other group members. (Pestano, 2012).

Finding your voice in a music project can translate outwards into being able to stand your ground and find a voice in the wider world. One young man who was a former looked after child, still supported, grew in confidence across the project, moving from tentative speaking to taking lead singing positions and being able to encourage his colleague with Aspergers syndrome to keep trying to sing until she delivered in a way that she was happy with. It was moving to see his emerging sense of self.

Challenging behaviour

Where life circumstances have been difficult for a young person, this can show up as challenging behaviour and certainly our LGBTQ projects had their share of this. Youth services tend to have a more inclusive approach than the schools and mainstream classrooms I have worked in, with non-escalatory engagement being standard. Sometimes the difficulties of trying to work together in a music group, with freedom and less directive input, can get to young people in our groups and someone becomes aggressive. As a social worker I know that an essential survival skill is energy and the capacity to challenge. This certainly applies to LGBTQ youth who have a hidden difference and so must continually judge whether and how to 'come out' about their sexuality or have it ignored. When facing an aggressive youth who has experienced oppression or emotional hurt it can be helpful to remember how much worse is the passivity of those who have retreated and given up hope. If this behaviour can be reframed in the worker's mind as the indication of a feisty sense of self-worth, it can be celebrated and channelled rather than punished. Society's messages to suppress sexuality and not speak of it can lead to an over-emphasis on the part of the young LGBTQ person, once permitted, to be loud and proud and a bit aggressive. This needs gentle handling and kind acceptance to enable the young person to integrate this new identity within an atmosphere of safety and welcome. The challenge for those of us working in settings where there is zero tolerance of aggression is to learn a broader range of ways to respond to such behaviours so that children retain access to this group source of growth. Responding as a human rather than an authority figure is a valuable tool and not necessarily weakness. De-escalation is a valuable skill for managing these behaviours in LGBTQ youth and others who have experienced marginalisation or rejection. Training emphasises managing our own fears so that we can contain the unpredictability of others. Key qualities needed in this work are being open-minded and tolerant, kind, calm, empathetic and patient (Cartwright, 2013).

Age and safeguarding

Many people get very worried about addressing the topic of sexual orientation with those under 16. If in any doubt get permission from your manager or specialist teacher. Two examples of good projects for the 11-15 age bracket are mentioned in the resources below and the fundamental issue is that it is perfectly legal to raise issues with those under 16, especially if just giving a message of acceptance. Stonewall found that only half of gay pupils report that their schools say homophobic bullying is wrong, even fewer in faith schools (Guasp, 2012). It is damaging for young people to have no acknowledgement that their sexuality is normal. The Equality Act 2010 means we all have a duty to ensure that they have that acknowledgement.

Reflections

How can we apply this learning to our own practice? If you identify as LGBT or have students who do, then the applications may be easy to make without further guidance. These may relate more to exploring issues around creative participatory music work through membership of an organisation such as Sound Sense, and resources such as the further reading below.

If you are new to thinking about issues of inclusion for this group, either relating to staff or students, then you may find the following questions helpful:

- Is it possible that one of my colleagues or students may be LGBT or questioning their sexuality?
- In what ways do my words and actions show acceptance of choices different from my own?
- What do I need to work on in order to be comfortable with greater levels of dissent and diversity of lifestyle?
- Are there existing festivals that our institution celebrates where projects, workshops, performances may appropriately expand our understanding of inclusion, freedom and civil rights? (Some ideas are provided below.)

I know how excited and relieved I was to teach in a school in the Isle of Dogs during LGBT History month, when I saw a 40-foot wall display validating LGBT lives.

One simple example of how the general curriculum can be used in an inclusive way involves the song *(Something inside) so strong* by Labi Siffre, a patron of LGBT History Month. Many schools and choirs sing this song, with its powerful anti-racist message. But how many also use the opportunity to honour the audacity of Siffre's life, and the early courageous choices that he made in relation to his sexuality? He was 18 when he got together with his partner Peter Lloyd who was 21. At that time it was illegal for them to be together, in contrast to their heterosexual peers. They are currently in their 50th year together. Freelance community musician Roshi Nasehi comments "I like to take the opportunity to tell students that Siffre was concerned about allowing Eminem to sample him because Siffre saw Eminem as attacking gay people in some of his work" (conversation with the author, 2013). In this way, a music educator can help students to stop and think about language and its impact while attending to a different music task.

What next

Sadly some of the projects that we have worked with are threatened due to funding cuts, so the support infrastructures that enabled us to reach these young people are reducing. This trend makes it even more important that both within school and outside of it that all of our young people feel safe. It is hoped that this chapter offers some ideas and resources that might be taken into mainstream practice in schools and youth services. Creative Croydon will continue to seek funding and sponsors for further projects.

Summary/Conclusions

Music group work with an excluded minority such as LGBTQ youth can be emancipatory and life-affirming, strengthening resilience. It can provide relief, connection and fun, which in turn can allow for an acceptance of self and an increasing sense of inclusion and entitlement. These benefits also apply to other groups facing challenges and to mainstream children and young people, all of whom can benefit from the practices and approach outlined here. LGBTQ youth need our schools to be safe spaces and now the law requires this unequivocally. A safe space for LGBTQ youth is a safe space for anyone experiencing difference and is a goal worth striving for.

Utilising creative approaches to music work with young people offers immense scope for the refreshment and whole person connection of both student and teacher. This article aimed to offer ideas as to how, in group music activities, we can forge an atmosphere where all aspects of the individual feel welcome. A second aim was a chance to reflect on wider issues of inclusion in readers' own workplace settings. The learning arising from these LGBTQ projects can be far more broadly applicable. I hope that something from this discussion may be of interest to music educators who hope to free themselves, their institutional environment and their students from the prevailing 'don't see, don't tell' culture, and move together into a place of creative celebration and self-acceptance.

> You and me we can be free, for I can see reality
> I want to fly into the sky and scream and yell You cannot make me conform you see, for I can see reality

(Song lyrics LGBTQ project, 2010)

Acknowledgements

Thank you to the wonderful young people with whom we worked; our funders Sound Connections, Youth Music and London Councils; our partner agencies, Metro Centre and Croydon Youth Development Trust; the other project workers: Myrtala Thomas, Anne Crump, Maria Sewell and Andre Oldfield and other team members. And thank you to the other colleagues who took time to contribute their thoughts and practice. Participants' names kept confidential.

References

Bostock, L. (2004) *Promoting resilience in fostered children and young people.* London: Social Care Institute for Excellence (SCIE).

Cartwright, J. (2013) *Working with Children in Challenging Circumstances.* London: Sound Connections.

Grotberg, E. (1997) *A guide to Promoting Resilience in Children: strengthening the human spirit.* The Hague: Bernard van Leer Foundation.

Guasp, A. (2012) *The School Report: the experiences of gay young people in Britain's schools in 2012.* London: Stonewall.

Henry, J. (2001) *Creative Management.* London: Sage.

Higgins, L. (2012) *Community Music In Theory and In Practice.* New York: Oxford University Press.

Holt, J. (1962) *How children fail.* New York: Penguin Education.

Maslow, A. H. (1943) A theory of human motivation. *Psychological Review* 50(4): 370–96. Retrieved from http://psychclassics.yorku.ca/Maslow/motivation.htm (accessed 02.07.2013).

Meyer, I. H. (2003) Prejudice, social stress, and mental health in lesbian, gay, and bisexual populations: conceptual issues and research evidence. *Psychological Bulletin,* 129: 674-697.

Pestano, C., (2011), LGBT SNAP Project Evaluation Report (unpublished).

Pestano, C., (2012), LGBT Bridge Project Evaluation Report (unpublished).

Porritt, J. (2007) *Capitalism as if the world matters,* London and Sterling: Earthscan,

Rogers, C. (1961) *On Becoming a Person: A Therapist's View of Psychotherapy.* London: Constable.

Rogers, C. & Freiberg, J. (1994) *Freedom to Learn.* New York: Merrill.

Spruce, G. (2012) Musical knowledge, critical consciousness and critical thinking. In G. Spruce & C. Philpott (eds.) *Debates in Music Teaching.* London: Routledge.

LGBT Calendar

Other possible times of the year when LGBT issues can be highlighted include:

January 27 - Holocaust Memorial Day (our pink and black triangles were symbols from the Nazi era)

February - LGBT History Month http://lgbthistorymonth.org.uk/

March 8 - International Women's day

May 17 - International Day Against Homophobia (IDAHO)

June/July (varies) - LGBT Pride – regional variations

October - Black History month (can highlight Black LGBT icons)

November/December - UK Disability month http://ukdisabilityhistorymonth.com/ (can highlight LGBT disabled figures such as Alan Turing)

Resources and Further Reading

The Equality Act http://www.legislation.gov.uk/ukpga/2010/15/contents

Stonewall:

School Report - http://www.stonewall.org.uk/at_school/education_resources/7957.asp

Videos: http://www.stonewall.org.uk/what_you_can_do/campaigning_opportunities/it_gets_better_today/default.asp

Schools OUT:

Classroom online resources http://www.schools-out.org.uk/

Music lessons http://the-classroom.org.uk/category/the-materials-to-use/by-subject/music/schools-out-music-lessons/

Equality Act briefing http://www.schools-out.org.uk/?resources=the-equality-act-2010-and-public-duty-powerpoint-presentation

Ten ways to support LGBT youth in education (leaflet) http://www.galyic.org.uk/docs/10ways.pdf

Best Practice: LGBT Work in Schools, LGBT Youth NorthWest– Policy framework, key messages, good practice examples and FAQ sheet make this an accessible and valuable reference. http://www.lgbtyouthnorthwest.org.uk/wp-content/uploads/2012/09/BestPracticeGuide_LowRes1.pdf

Sound Sense, the professional association for community musicians. www.Soundsense.org

Educate and Celebrate (INSET provider) http://www.ellybarnes.com/

Under 16 service example https://www.metrocentreonline.org/youth-services/under-16/

Developing a grassroots international community music network serving people with disabilities

Donald DeVito

The Sidney Lanier Center is a state-funded school for 200 children with intellectual and physical disabilities between the ages of 3 and 22 in Gainesville, Florida. Centers provide the least restrictive environment and small class sizes to accommodate students with the most profound of behavioral and intellectual disabilities. Student participants have needs that occur from autism, cerebral palsy, Prader-Willi Syndrome, Williams Syndrome, or traumatic brain injury, in addition to speech language, intellectual and/or physical impairments. I chose to teach at this school because I wanted to give the students an opportunity to receive the many benefits of music education and demonstrate the abilities that others perceived they lacked. This chapter will highlight the life-changing experiences of the students in the arts, from receiving their first music experiences, to Skyping with universities, performing in Carnegie Hall and engaging through collaborative education for underserved populations around the world.

My first work at Lanier was adapting the music education curriculum to accommodate the individual needs of the students. One approach was adapting communication devices called Go Talks, which allow the teacher to record multiple cells to create an audio recording matched with visual aids to help students who cannot speak, write or sign to communicate their preferences and to answer questions during instruction. For example, if a student desired an apple during lunch, the Go Talk would be programmed with several choices, each with a corresponding visual aid (apple, orange, milk, juice and more). The teacher would record a cell in the Go Talk to state "I want an apple" when the apple picture is pressed by the student (and provides a voice for students who cannot speak). I adapted this equipment to record the melodies of several varieties of music taught in the lesson so the students could demonstrate their ability to differentiate between styles of music and identify their preferred music. This was especially helpful for my students with autism and profound intellectual and speech/language impairments who otherwise could not communicate, and it helped to quell some of the belief that children with autism do not respond affectively to music.

The Virtual Classroom: Sidney Lanier Center and Syracuse University, Universidade de Londrina, Weber State University.

Through my committee chair, Dr Timothy Brophy, I was put in touch with the International Society for Music Education (ISME) and their commission for Community Music Activity (CMA). The CMA is comprised of researchers, academics and practitioners who develop and engage with music education programmes for underserved populations internationally. At the 2006 ISME CMA seminar in Singapore, I gave a presentation on the community music programme at Sidney Lanier, a monthly evening drum circle that combined children with disabilities and their families and musicians in the community in an open and accommodating environment. Travelling to Singapore seemed a long way to go and I wondered how my students could directly benefit from my experiences at the CMA seminar. Seeing an article on Skyping, I typed a proposal for recruiting community music professors and practitioners to engage with my students online upon returning to our home countries. Several colleagues expressed interest: Dr. Emma Rodriguez Suarez of Syracuse University, Dr. Magali Kleber of the Universidade de Londrina in Brazil and later David Akombo, a Kenyan professor currently at Jackson State University. The nature of their engagement with my students varied.

Emma from Syracuse University wanted her students to learn how to engage with students with disabilities, getting to know them as people first and students second. Her university music education majors were paired one on one with my students in the first Skype session, which was used to get to know each other's interests and hobbies and gave the Syracuse students an opportunity to get to know how to adapt music lessons to meet the needs of their online students. In subsequent sessions the university students taught their lessons to their paired Sidney student and fine-tuned their initial adaptations.

Chante, a student with cerebral palsy and speech language impairments is self-conscious about her speaking voice. When seated in front of a computer with a large class of Syracuse students for the first time, she began the discussion with a simple hello. She had no prior knowledge of virtual classrooms or Internet conferencing and was eager to continue. Without stutters or nervousness, she began the first interaction between the two schools with a social conversation. Afterwards, Chante had a lesson in rhythm and continued her lessons in the next meeting (DeVito, Kleber, Suarez & Akombo, 2006: 194).

Celine had greater affective responses to music than any other student at Sidney Lanier. She suffered a traumatic brain injury when she was two and cognitively remains at this level with minimal ability to manipulate her hands or focus her eyes on a given person or item. She is unable to control a screaming sound when presented with new stimuli, not out of fear, but as a result of being unable to control her voice. In essence, she is a 17-year-old with the verbal communication of a two-year-old. Her primary goals were to maintain eye contact and to make choices between two objects by looking at the preferred item for as long as possible.

> Her most significant responses are through the affective responses to beautiful melodies, jazz, and Motown. Meredith, a Syracuse music education major, asked to develop a lesson that would assist Celine in: (1) recognizing Meredith's presence on the screen by focusing attention on her through instrumental performance and (2) perform with Meredith through hand over hand assistance by myself to help her keep a beat to the song presented in the lesson. (DeVito, Kleber, Suarez, & Akombo, 2006: 194).

One of Dr. Kleber's Brazilian students, composition major Rafael Rosa, composed Meu Balaio, a song describing the importance of the basket in Brazilian culture as a means of collecting things of 'value', in this case representing the shared musical experiences between these diverse populations. The pitch and rhythm of the song encapsulated traditional Brazil music and were arranged with the special needs of the students in mind. The lessons for her Brazilian students took place in Dr. Kleber's living room adding a social aspect to the atmosphere for her students and mine.

For Dr. Akombo, traditional Kenyan music was the order of the day with the song Jambo Bwana. This piece would become the signature song for the Sidney Lanier students in all of their major performances.

This first phase of the online programme developed at Sidney Lanier was presented at the 2008 ISME CMA seminar in Rome which led to more contacts and an ever expanding network of practitioners to engage with music.

Group Laiengee

Our next step was taking a local Gainesville connection and turning it into an outreach programme through international collaboration with children with disabilities in Guinea, West Africa. This would extend over the years to involve children with disabilities in Africa, Pakistan, England, Haiti and adults with disabilities in China. Lansana Camara is a community musician from Conakry, Guinea, whose family leads an ensemble in Conakry called Group Laiengee (Group Together) for homeless children and adults with disabilities. He was living in Gainesville on a green card (a visa that allows him to work in the U.S.) and sending funds from miscellaneous performances home to his family in Africa. He came to our local drum circle and brought a recording of the ensemble performing in Guinea. Camara's family comes from a long line of Griot musicians and they make their own instruments and sell them to support themselves and provide rice and assistance to the children who participate in the ensemble.

The approach taken in the online programme at Lanier was extended to Africa. In order to provide the funds and support needed, the Sidney Lanier Center nominated Lansana for the Jubilation Foundation Community Music Award, a $5,000 grant, which he was awarded. The funds were used to fly him back to Conakry where he organized performances, provided participants with rice and a sense of accomplishment and perhaps fostered a higher level of acceptance by the community for the children who participate. Their joy in participation has been evident on several video recordings of performances and community-based activities in Conakry. Thanks to a local music store, the band funds for Sidney Lanier were used to purchase the instruments from the teachers of Group Laiengee which provided the U.S. students with handmade authentic instruments to go along with the traditional music they learned from Lansana. Our students were able to share live performances with the children in Group Laiengee through the use of speaker phones since computers were not accessible for them in Conakry. Educational opportunities are difficult to come by for anyone in Conakry, and there were no direct links from Guinea to professional organizations besides Lansana. I wrote an article on our collaboration for the 2009 ISME Newsletter which goes to members in 70 countries. Javier Mendoza of the Chicago Arts Orchestra invited Lansana to perform with the children's orchestra and this provided several opportunities for support and funding that went back to the programme. The Group Laiengee programme and its collaboration with Sidney Lanier was included in the 2011 United Nations Compendium on Music as a Natural Resource, compiled by Dr. Patrick Schmidt and Dr. Cathy Benedict, which was designed to demonstrate the value of music as a means of self-sufficiency and support around the world.

DIScovering ABILITIES: NY and Carnegie Hall

It was always my goal to provide my students with the same life experiences as are enjoyed by non-disabled young adults. A local Gainesville high school music ensemble had recently performed in Carnegie Hall. This is one of the most prestigious activities that a music ensemble can strive for and one that I was eager to explore for my students. If you are a public school in the U.S. and you want to perform in Carnegie Hall, you generally have two options. The first is to audition to perform in 'festivals' which are typically organized by travel companies that rent the hall and then bring in the best (and largest) school ensembles who raise their own funds to pay the travel company for the hotel rooms and adjudication fees. The other is to rent the hall yourself which is rather unheard of for public schools. A head-on audition with non-disabled peers by a small school of students with disabilities was not in the cards. In fact, trying to have a call returned by many of the travel companies to begin the process was a difficult challenge when we mentioned our school size and special needs.

We would have to actually rent one of Carnegie's three halls ourselves, and we were told that Weill Hall, usually used for piano and quartet performances, was unbooked for one night in May. It would cost close to ten thousand dollars for three hours. A myriad of local music ensembles held benefit concerts to raise the money, including the Gay Men's Chorus of Manhattan, other fundraisers from our local Council for Exceptional Children (CEC) the professional organization for special education, Gainesville Chamber Orchestra, music education majors at the University of Florida, and a dozen African American Gospel Choirs from around Florida. Along with grants from the National Endowment for the Arts and Syracuse University we raised the nearly $28,000 to rent the hall and fly an ensemble of students with disabilities to New York.

The other important question was "What are we going to perform for three hours in Carnegie Hall?" The natural answer was to look at all the music we had learned on Skype through our international CMA contacts. As well as those already mentioned, these included Phil Mullen of ISME, Julie Tiernan from Ireland and her Traveller students in the NOMAD programme at Limerick University, and Andy Krikun of the Bergen Community College Popular Music Ensemble highlighted by Jimmy Vonderlinden, a college student with visual and physical impairments and a talented musician.

Locally we involved several Gainesville contacts that had provided our students with inclusive music settings, including the entire Santa Fe College Jazz Band under the direction of Dr. Steven Bingham. Our students were incorporated into the ensemble through a tiered level of participation on percussion involving maintaining a steady beat, performing a repeated rhythm pattern or improvising to the style of music. Dr. Bingham and his college students fund-raised to bring their jazz band to NY with my students performing the music of Duke Ellington and Benny Goodman in six songs with three Sidney Lanier students on percussion for each.

The students either sang or performed with our international music friends a repertoire ranging from Jambo Bwana to Sing Sing Sing to Meu Balaio. One of the many highlights was when Lyndon White II, one of my students with cerebral palsy who cannot speak, is profoundly deaf and can only sign about 10 single motion words, performed on the drum kit with members of the Santa Fe College Jazz Band. They accommodated him by improvising around his performance, giving him full access on one of the world's most famous stages to create his impressive rhythms on the drum kit. We decided to name our performance DIScovering ABILITIES. Dr. David Elliott made an entire floor of the music building at New York University available for us to practise before the event and the directors smiled as Kara, a student with Down's Syndrome, walked past a curious security guard at the front door of the building stating, "We have a rehearsal".

One of our most memorable moments came in the rehearsal session. We had thought that the guest musicians would perform separately the music of Ireland, Africa, Spain, and Brazil. At the rehearsal however, they all wanted to support and accompany the students as they improvised arrangements as a combined group. This meant African Kora (harp) being improvised into Irish traditional songs and Irish violin and flute performers into Brazilian traditional music. This combination of performers and instrumentation truly represented the international approach we have taken at the Sidney Lanier Center.

One of my favorite memories of the concert itself was near the end of the performance when Devala, a student who was usually shy and would not initiate long conversations, was so motivated by the event he came up to me between songs backstage and said he would like to sing with the jazz band sometime rather than play percussion. My response was, "Sure, we'll incorporate a song for you when they visit us at the school again". He replied, "No, I mean now. I'd like to go out and sing with the jazz band now". Here was Devala, having performed several songs on percussion, feeling so comfortable in his surroundings that he was confident enough to sing without rehearsal with Dr. Bingham and the jazz band on stage at Carnegie Hall. The whole concert came off beautifully and after a rousing performance the majority of musicians rode on a tour of the Hudson River the day after the performance

Collaboration and Connectivity in China and Pakistan

'Discovering Abilities through Harmony: An interdisciplinary music approach for students with disabilities with the Sidney Lanier Center, ISME CMA, and NACCM' was a project presentation about our New York performance which was shared with community musicians from around the world at the 2010 ISME CMA Seminar in Hangzhou, China (Suarez, E. *et al.*, 2010). At the main conference in Beijing I gave a presentation on music education for students with autism. This led to contacts with the Hui Ling Center for adults with learning disabilities and later collaboration with the Anhuali Community Center in a future trip (discussed fully in the next section).

Also in Beijing, Phil Mullen introduced me to Arthur Gill who teaches at a special education center for children with visual and physical impairments in Gujrat City, Pakistan. Arthur and I began Skyping and one of the first results was his students and mine singing to each other in our classrooms. Mine had to come to school early so his could finish in time to be back in their homes before nightfall. This was due to the unsafe environment at night. Arthur and I worked together to share music education ideas and experiences which we documented and shared with the Society for Education, Music and Psychological Research (SEMPRE) and published in ISME CMA's 2012 Seminar in Corfu (Gill & DeVito, 2012). In the U.S, Arthur presented with me through Skype at the National Association of State Directors of Special Education, where through my students' newfound Carnegie notoriety, they were invited to travel to Nashville to be the keynote presenters at the annual meeting. This organization develops special education policy in the U.S. and my students' keynote performance concluded with Arthur discussing our work together from Pakistan.

In the spring I was selected to receive the 2011 Clarissa Hug Award, the national teacher of the year for the Council for Exceptional Children (CEC). At the national conference to receive the award, I made contact with the Abilitations Company regarding the distribution of free Go Talk devices to the international programmes we have been collaborating with, which by then included Haiti, China and Pakistan. The idea was to adapt the technology for music education as previously described but in this case to fit with the different cultures and their own national curriculum. The understanding was that we would share the results with the company who could then market the technology in new regions and develop a varied curriculum which would benefit students with disabilities in more diverse regions. The Abilitations Company obliged and another door to my participation in community music would soon be opened.

ISME CMA Chair and the 1st Inclusive Performance at the China Conservatory in Beijing

I was honored with being selected to chair the ISME CMA 2012 seminar in Corfu, Greece. One of the activities that goes along with this is attending the ISME board meeting the year before. At the meeting, I had the opportunity to present the recent work of our online programme with our colleagues in Beijing and Pakistan. Professor Xie Jiaxing of the China conservatory (an ISME board member) saw the presentation and asked Phil Mullen and myself to give presentations at their 2011 Community Music Summit in Beijing. During this trip we visited the Anhuali Center for adults with disabilities and I brought Go Talks adapted with visual aids to play recorded examples of instruments. The students would select an instrument, listen to the example and then we would teach each other the English and Chinese names. One of the participants was a young adult with Down's syndrome who selected "guitar" and after hearing the music and listening to the English verbalization, after two tries smiled, stated "guitar" and looked to her Chinese teachers for approval. I was then told the Chinese word for guitar and the social music activity was educational and collaborative for everyone. We used another Go Talk slide programmed with a variety of jazz and Motown music. The Chinese participants selected a numbered cell and listened to the music, creating dances for everyone to follow.

Upon returning to Sidney Lanier, I had a Go Talk programmed with Chinese musical instruments and visual aids along with popular Chinese music so my students could have a similar encounter with the arts of a different culture.

Discussing the possibility of continuing our collaboration in 2012, Phil Mullen, Professor Xie and myself organized and led the first inclusive music performance in the China Conservatory of Music in Beijing between members of the Anhuali Center and students of the China Conservatory.

New efforts to raise awareness of international issues in the school and community

Through Catherine Pestano, whom I met at the ISME seminars, I had the pleasure of meeting teachers and members of Victoria House, which provides music and educational services to children with behavioural special needs in England. Our students completed a semester long project in which we composed music together online and performed together with the children in Victoria House. A report of the project (Rathbone & Pestano, 2013) was published in the April 2013 edition of Music Mark Magazine.

Our project with the Notre Maison Orphanage in Haiti utilizes Skype and highlights our Sidney Lanier student Lina's journey from being born with hydrocephalus in Haiti, where her mother passed away during childbirth, only to be left in the Abandonment Room (the actual name for it) at the hospital and rescued by Gertrude Azor, director of the Notre Maison Orphanage. She has since been adopted in the U.S. by the Cloutiers and is now a member of the Sidney Lanier music programme. We have weekly Skype sessions between our Center and the Notre Maison Orphanage including shared music education lessons. These include taking traditional children's songs such as "If You're Happy and you Know it" and performing them for each other in English and French Creole. Students sing the portions they are able to and those who are non-verbal can perform on percussion and replicate the appropriate movements to the songs. We have also improvised rhythms together as well as performing music for each other on special occasions such as Flag Day in Haiti. Lina's adopted mother Renee Cloutier summed it up by stating, "What the children experience brings great joy to them, especially in a world that does not always see their value through their disabilities" (Suarez, E. *et al.*, 2010).

The Gatorland Chapter of the CEC has sent $500 to the orphanage to purchase percussion instruments for our collaborative project. Lina travelled back to the Notre Maison orphanage at Christmas 2012 to talk to the people there about the importance of life and what people with hydrocephalus can accomplish.

After a year of shared lessons with Notre Maison, we are currently working on a plan to use online course technology offered by Blackboard as a central lesson base connecting all of the universities, schools, centers and community programmes and including academic lessons reinforced through music education themes, topics and activities for the children and training opportunities in community music and special education for the teachers. The technology used in online courses removes the real time requirement for every activity so students can enter comments and discussion topics with their teachers by typing them in for others to read at their convenience rather than having a set time to meet face to face for every engagement. The Live Classroom features allow face to face class activities and lessons in different countries similar to Skype but are enhanced so multiple classes and groups around the world can engage simultaneously. This real time interaction in the arts is obviously the heart and soul of our collaborations. The content will be determined by the curriculum in each location. A particular lesson concept (academic or musical) taught by a teacher at one location can be shared by all of the participating schools and centers with students sharing responses in the Discussion section of the online course. There is also a word wall that can build on related topics and concepts in another section of the online course. The teachers can assist with simple technology such as Google Translator to put the meaning of the words the students add to the word wall in each language represented by the participation locations (Pakistan, Haiti, China, USA/United Kingdom).

Conclusion

I had no idea that making one leap of faith in deciding to teach an underserved population would have such a profound effect on my life and the experiences that were to follow. The experiences I discussed in this chapter are at the heart of community music and have so much more to do with collaboration and empowerment than with charity or outreach. When we engage in the arts with people from other communities and backgrounds we all benefit from music education. Sending drums to Haiti is not charity, but the sharing of resources so we can all learn together. They are experts in Haitian music and culture and bring that as equals to our lessons and music making. The same is true for China, Guinea, Pakistan and all of the other people our students learn from and share their expertise with in return.

Replicating any aspect of this approach requires at its base level nothing more than a computer with a camera and an internet connection. Simply asking music educators at universities and community programmes in person or through email with a proposal to share music education experiences is what began the path the students in this programme have experienced. To a greater degree, it requires the heart to take the key element of music activity, shared affective responses, and developing that with all people regardless of their backgrounds or disabilities. As the title of the Carnegie performance announced, the purpose is to allow people with special needs to DIScover their ABILITIES.

At the 2014 CMA seminar in Salvador Brazil, Magali Kleber is already planning a Skype performance between Brazilian percussionists and the children in Notre Maison. Securing grants and taking part in fundraising events do not represent the heart of these experiences but simply facilitate a fair sharing of resources. The community and cultural development that comes from community music experiences and the collaborative engagement on a person to person level is the true heart of this field of music and has the power to transcend challenges for all, learning through cooperative and creative self expression in the arts.

References

DeVito, D., Kleber, M., Suarez, E & Akombo, D. (2006) *Projects, perspectives and conversations.* Paper presented at ISME CMA XI: 193-201.

Gill, A & DeVito, D (2012) *Collaboration and Connectivity: Developing community music programs for children with disabilities throughout Pakistan.* ISME CMA XIII: Transitioning from historical foundations to 21st century global initiatives: 96-98.

Rathbone, M., & Pestano, C. (2013) Border Crossing: A Skype creative music project with the USA at an EBD primary PRU. *Music Mark Magazine* (1): 26-29.

Suarez, E., DeVito, D., Kleber, M., Akombo D., Krikun, A., & Bingham, S. (2010) *Discovering Abilities through Harmony: An interdisciplinary music approach for students with disabilities with the Sidney Lanier Center.* ISME CMA, and NACCM. ISME CMA XII: Harmonizing the diversity that is community music activity: 87-92.

Developing inclusive instrumental musicking through a Primary School Orchestra

Andrew M Lindley

Introduction

Many schools have an orchestra. Sometimes a group of recorder players; sometimes there are a few violins, maybe a couple of cellos and classroom percussion. This is the story of how our orchestra developed at school, from humble beginnings to a large inclusive group that continues to grow and develop year by year.

The school is a large primary (around 420 pupils) in East Durham, an area of severe socio-economic deprivation. Around 20% of the children are on free school meals and other data present a similar picture. There is a physical disability resource base attached to the school. The children in the resource base are integrated into mainstream classes and are generally supported in their classes in the main school. The children mix well and social and educational inclusion is generally successful. Over recent years, music provision in the school has grown and the school is perceived in the community and the county as a 'musical school'.

Let's start an orchestra...

The situation I inherited when I began in the school was four violin pupils and an ad hoc choir for Christmas concerts. When I joined the school staff I added woodwind to the provision in school and the string teaching had risen to twelve violins and four violas. The music service provided a beginner strings orchestra once a fortnight in term time and a regional orchestra (Grade 4 and above) with the same frequency. Many of our players had no means of transport to get to the regional orchestra and so (unsurprisingly) gave up during their time in the beginner group.

I decided to fill the void by offering more activities in our school and with the support of the Head Teacher and Music Coordinator, discussed the idea with the rest of the staff and Governing Body. There were two guiding principles at this point;

- we must include as many of our children as possible, particularly those on free school meals (FSM) and those from the physical disability resource base
- we must start them off at the earliest possible point in their learning.

These principles are still at the heart of what we do today.

Unlike many more traditional ensembles, in our school orchestra there is no audition, no minimum level of ability (beyond the ability to play three notes), no restriction on instruments included, no age limit (except that imposed by the timetabling issues between key stages), which all results in children from across the whole Key Stage 2 age range working collaboratively, both with each other and with the two teachers involved. Currently, the orchestra includes a slightly higher proportion of children on free school meals than that in the school as a whole.

Crucial to achieving maximum possible inclusion is the running of the orchestra as part of our general curriculum *during curriculum time*. This removes many parental anxieties, raises the profile of music for all in school and, over time, has created a genuine expectation in school that all children will become 'musicians' as they progress through the Key Stages.

Overcoming barriers to involvement

There are many children who have no apparent interest in learning an instrument or performing, either solo or as part of a group, and also those who traditionally have not been able to. There are many reasons for this:

- home environment, where music is not valued
- negative comments in the past, damaging self perception
- peer pressure
- other interests
- lack of self confidence
- limited availability of instruments
- parental lack of finance
- parents unable to manage several children's activities at once

These children too can be included with a bit of imagination. In my experience, there have been very few children who do not wish to participate in musicking (cf. Small, 1999). The main factors I have seen are peer pressure, other (usually sporting) activities taking priority and limited availability of instruments.

We have been fortunate in our area that the County Music Service has had a strategy for making instruments available and that a child starting on one instrument is very often given the opportunity to change later on if necessary, or even to add new instruments as they progress. More difficult to deal with are the issues of peer pressure and the impact of other activities.

We often hear of the learning of instruments being dropped due to pressures of work (GCSE, etc.) in secondary school, but in the primary phase too, children cite their involvement in sports or dancing as reasons for giving up.

We have used Pupil Premium finance to offer bursaries to children on free school meals and, on a few occasions, to buy instruments. This has gone a long way to allow inclusion of children from backgrounds where there is financial hardship.

The perceived importance of music in school has made it 'cool' to play or sing and thus reduced the problem of peer pressure. Some children who have chosen to pursue other activities ahead of music come now to ask if they can help in the performance as stage managers, front of house or in other roles. The process of making school music 'cool' takes time to achieve, and the support of county music staff and, crucially, parents has been key to its success.

In attempting to include as many children as possible it is essential to work with each individual child and meet them where they are. There has been resistance to the inclusion of some children from staff, from parents and from the children themselves for many reasons. Staff have concerns ranging from the potential impact of disruptive behaviour, to the relevance of musicking to children with physical or learning difficulties; instrumental teachers initially had concerns about the early inclusion of new learners and about starting ensemble playing with the range of instruments. Some parents are worried about their own commitment or about allowing potentially disruptive practising at home and some of the children have confidence issues ('Will I have to perform on my own?'; 'I'm scared of being in a concert.'; 'I'm not good enough…').

Staff concerns have been alleviated over time; 'disruptive' children feel included and empowered and therefore embrace their musicking with a focus and attitude not usually evident in the classroom situation and we have been including children with various medical and learning difficulties for the last five years with great success.

Olivier Urbain states, 'For me it is crucial to feel that "this person is inherently precious" ' (Urbain, forthcoming). This is also a central tenet of my work with the orchestra.

Some principles

Allowing agency

Agency, or allowing children some choice in what they do and control over it, can be argued to lead to increased engagement, inclusion and hopefully enjoyment of the learning process (Green, 2002). A study of Australian students found that they had strong ideas about the choice of repertoire:

> The choice of pieces came in for criticism from some of the children, with general agreement that the repertoire should include "tunes that kids know, like off the movies," and also a suggestion that some of the music should be chosen by the band members themselves. (Pitts & Davidson, 2000: 79)

Lucy Green also talks about pupil choice in her 2002 research study:

> Playing music of one's own choice, with which one identifies personally ……. and having fun doing it must be high priorities in the quest for increasing numbers of young people to benefit from a music education which makes music not only available, but meaningful, worthwhile and participatory. (Green, 2002: 216)

This assertion seems to encapsulate a desirable philosophy for an orchestra. It suggests that providing choice for the students, through a restricted list of repertoire from which they choose, in addition to arranging music specifically for them, based on their free choice, is a suitable approach for a primary orchestra, and this is the model I chose to adopt.

Relevance

Closely linked to agency is relevance. It goes without saying that any form of learning is far more effective if it is relevant to the learner. Music is no different. Gruhn (2006) asserts that

> there is a big gap between extra-curricular activities and the way music is taught in the classroom, and between musical experience in real life and musical experience in a school setting.

Making musical experiences in the school setting more relevant to those in 'real life' can have a positive effect on the take-up of opportunities offered at school.

Green (2002, 2008) asserts that classical music is far removed from children's lives and identities and warns that to give classical music to primary age children is likely to switch off their interest and engagement. While I accept that a broad musical repertoire is essential, my own view is that the manner of delivery of classical music to children can make it relevant to them.

A study by Rusinek (2008) found that by setting a goal of a concert to work towards, disaffected students became enthusiastic about the process of preparing for the concert, and that the school administrators 'noted that the adolescents appeared to be agents of their learning [… and] the social character of the music learning promoted responsibility'.

Creativity

Allowing children this freedom to create is a challenging shift from the didactic 'teacher as expert' (cf. Grasha, 1994) style of teaching often found in English schools. Christopher Small, an early advocate of creative music-making in education, wrote:

> if we acknowledge the creative power of children in art, we must also recognize their ability to create other forms. (Small 1977: 216)

The use of instrumental improvisation has been trialled successfully in school for children from ages 6 to 11 in a whole-class setting. All classes involved in these trials have been offered penny whistles, and where children are learning other instruments they have found these sessions valuable in introducing a new style of playing as well as integrating their other learning into a classroom setting. These improvisation sessions offer the opportunity to compose using rhythm, pitch and timbre without any constraints other than imagination. They are fun as well as valuable learning experiences.

Social aspects

The way music is delivered in our school is carefully structured to emphasize the social aspect of musicking. Work is shared with the rest of the school in assemblies, performances for individual classes and with the wider community through concerts in local churches, secondary schools and care homes. Children are paired as 'desk partners', sharing a music stand in orchestra sessions with a peer, often from a different year group, and this has led to new friendships with older and younger children. Shared lunches with other schools' musicians at gatherings arranged by school, the local schools' partnership and events organized by our local secondary school, add to the social aspects of musicking and cross-establishment friendships have arisen from these events.

> Music education across all stages should support students, educators and audience to find the self in each of us and create a spacious social and individual environment rich in opportunity for the development of a fluid and responsive self-understood and self-owned identity open to future possibilities and which is creative and 'alive' in the present moment. (J. Leigh, in conversation with the author, 2010)

Some examples

Over the last few years, we have included children with cerebral palsy, autism, ADHD, cystic fibrosis and cochlear implants. Their participation benefits not only themselves but the whole school community, and has led to some truly amazing and rewarding opportunities for musicking in a complete social sense.

There was some surprise from the parents of children with cochlear implants when we suggested that learning an instrument might be an option for them. Our first pupil (who started on flute) is still playing eight years later and now also plays alto sax. We broke down parental reservations by buying the child a copy of Evelyn Glennie's *Rhythm Song* and then inviting her parents in for a discussion about our ideas. We currently have a violinist playing with us who, along with his family, refused to accept that his hearing problem could prevent him from playing.

Several 'disaffected' and 'disruptive' children have found a way into musicking through learning brass instruments provided by the school with a teacher well known in the brass band circles of our area. These children continue to play up to the present and conversations with their class teachers suggest that the disruptive behaviour in class has reduced.

Inclusion is achieved by matching instruments to children's talents as defined by their specific disabilities, for instance, using classroom percussion such as bells that can be fitted around the wrist for children with cerebral palsy and finding the correct instrument (based on individual preference) for children with hearing problems.

A recent end-of-term concert provides an example of how we try to implement our aims and principles in order to maximise the involvement and engagement of all children. In the lead up to the concert, the children asked if they could work on 'One Way Or Another' by Blondie (One Direction). We discussed the potential problems of range, key, etc. and they decided to give it a go. I worked up a small ensemble version from a piano score and played it through at one of the orchestra rehearsals. Over the next few weeks, we worked together to build a full version in 16 parts for the range of instruments available to us, with the (child-led) proviso that each section must share elements of the tune. This led to discussion of the characteristics of the different instruments and the subsequent distribution of the tune in the final version in an appropriate way. The children then took it a step further by suggesting that we should teach the song to the choir and perform it as a collaboration – a huge project involving around 120 children and a first for the school and the children. This came to fruition in July 2013 with great success.

Other Musicking

In order to maximise involvement I have remained open to incorporating as many forms of music and as many ways of creating opportunities for progression as possible. From the core provision of the orchestra, we have developed a range of other provision, including:

- a pop group and a staff pop group
- opportunities for children to conduct the orchestra
- a jazz group

I am pleased to say that the initiative for some of these developments has come directly from the children.

In addition, we have tried to promote involvement of all by creating a 'music-rich' environment which includes, apart from the National Curriculum provision, visiting groups of instrumental teachers and other performing groups, including my own string quartet, the Kildale Quartet. There is also a wide range of recorded music played in assemblies and during lessons, and groups after school in several styles of dance. There has been a conscious effort to create an atmosphere in school that is conducive to including all children and staff in many forms of response to music, and from this has grown an expectation amongst many of the children that they will either play an instrument and join the orchestra or pop group, or sing in the choir at the appropriate time. The effect of this is that children move into KS3 confident in their musical identity and therefore with an expectation that their musicking will be continued and expanded in secondary school. There is a very small drop-out rate during transition, contradicting the national trend.

Conclusions and thoughts for the future

I hope I have started some thoughts about our approach to inclusion – namely, inclusion of as many pupils as possible in musicking, and including high-quality opportunities for learning music in as many styles as possible both for pupils and staff. Over the last ten years I have found that the efforts we have put into inclusion have led to the Music Service and others responding positively and gradually the range and quality of our music provision have spiralled until we have reached the situation described above. However, we are still looking for ways to include still more and improve the experience we offer to our children.

For the future, we have plans to extend the provision of musicking in KS1 as well as the expansion of the jazz and pop work and adding in a more structured approach to world musics in order to tap into children's different musical preferences. We are also looking at further ways of using Pupil Premium funding to include still more children on the FSM register and provide a wider range of musicking throughout school.

Music is uniquely placed in the curriculum to engender collaboration, meaningful and positive social interaction between everyone in school. Inclusion of everyone, all pupils, staff and the school community can lead to rich and rewarding experiences for all that will stay with them for the rest of their lives.

References

Grasha, A. (1994) A Matter of Style: The teacher as expert, formal authority, personal model, facilitator, and delegator. *College Teaching*, 42(4): 142-149.

Green, L. (2002) *How Popular Musicians Learn*. Aldershot: Ashgate Publishing.

Green, L. (2008) *Music, Informal Learning and the School: A new classroom pedagogy*. Aldershot: Ashgate Publishing.

Gruhn, W. (2006) Music Learning in Schools: Perspectives of a new foundation in music teaching and learning. *Action, Criticism & Theory for Music Education*, 5(2) http://act.maydaygroup.org/articles/Gruhn5_2.pdf (accessed 27.07.2013).

Pitts, S. & Davidson, J. (2000). Supporting musical development in the primary school: An English perspective on band programmes in Sydney, NSW. *Research Studies in Music Education*, 14: 76-84.

Rusinek, G. (2008) Disaffected learners and school musical culture: an opportunity for inclusion. *Research Studies in Music Education*, 30: 9-23.

Small, C. (1977) *Music, Society, Education*, Hanover: University Press of New England.

Small, C. (1999) Musicking: The Meanings of Performing and Listening. A lecture. *Music Education Research*, 1(1).

Urbain, O. (forthcoming) Inspiring Musical Movements and Global Solidarity: "Playing for Change", "Min-On" and "El Sistema". in *Peace and Policy*, 15.

Focus on 'Harder to Reach' young people: the work of Wigmore Hall Learning's resident outreach ensemble, Ignite

Kate Whitaker and Ursula Crickmay

Ignite is a group of professional musicians that was brought together by Wigmore Hall Learning to lead on its creative outreach programme, as well as performing as an ensemble in their own right.

In forming Ignite in 2008, Wigmore Hall Learning aimed to create an ensemble of chamber music players who could work adaptably in a range of challenging environments, whilst reflecting Wigmore Hall artistically in their approach. At the time, Wigmore Hall Learning was working in a range of different settings – hospitals, youth clubs, family centres – where the environment was very unpredictable, and working with people from very diverse backgrounds, many of whom had never heard of Wigmore Hall and certainly wouldn't describe themselves as interested in chamber music. A lot of work during projects was going into bridging an artistic and cultural gap, and it was hard to find genuine shared ground where creative work could happen. In addition, it was hard for Wigmore Hall through a series of short-term projects to make the most of the knowledge and trust that would have to be built up from scratch each time.

In discussion with Jackie Walduck, who founded the project with Wigmore Hall, we developed the idea of having an ensemble based within the Learning programme who would work together primarily through improvisation. The ensemble would collaborate together, and sometimes with other artists too, to devise music and perform it. On projects they would take the same approach, forming an ensemble with the project participants to devise and perform music. This would provide an artistic integrity to the work: rather than a classical ensemble working outside of their usual performance environment, this would be an ensemble whose very purpose was creative work and collaboration, so they would be developed as an ensemble as much through working in a hospital as they would through working in a practice room or concert platform.

Ignite frequently use 'One-Page Scores' as starting points for their work. This is when a composer provides just 'one page' of material – often the compositional 'backbone' of the piece – and the players have to develop the performance from this. Composers who have written one-page scores for Ignite include Luke Bedford, Stephen Warbeck, Jason Yarde, Param Vir and Joe Cutler. New commissions this year are from Martin Butler and Kerry Andrew and were performed at Wigmore Hall as part of Ignite's Aperitif concert on 4 June 2013.

Community Partnerships

Ignite work across the breadth of Wigmore Hall's Learning programme, but for their core programme it has been important that partnerships with community settings are long-term rather than one-off, in order to build rewarding relationships. The key partnerships that have developed for Ignite have been with the Cardinal Hume Centre, who work with homeless young people and badly housed families, as well as local people with little or no income; Turtle Key Arts, who pioneer programmes involving participation in the arts for all with an emphasis on disabled, disadvantaged, or socially excluded people; and Chelsea Community Hospital School, described below. All of these organisations work with harder to reach groups, and are specialists in their field. This means that Wigmore Hall Learning and Ignite can work together with them to design and provide bespoke projects suited to the needs of the individuals involved, and that these individuals already have trusted relationships with the organisations.

Key focus: Chelsea Community Hospital School

Chelsea Community Hospital School (CCHS) is a community special school which delivers education for children and young people aged 4 to 18 while they are in hospital. It also provides places for a number of students who cannot access mainstream school due to their medical conditions or learning difficulties. The Hospital School has four sites across Kensington & Chelsea and Westminster: Chelsea and Westminster Hospital, a large general hospital specialising in a range of chronic and acute conditions; Collingham Child and Family Centre, a referral unit for children and young people between the ages of seven and thirteen, who have complex emotional, behavioural and mental health problems; The Royal Brompton Hospital, which specialises in chronic and acute heart and lung conditions; and St. Mary's Hospital which has a large paediatric unit, including a bone-marrow transplant ward.

The children and young people Ignite work with at CCHS can be defined as 'harder to reach' for a number of reasons. In some cases, chronic health conditions may mean that these young people have spent long periods of time out of school and thus will not have received the same educational and extra-curricular opportunities as their peers. They may have been isolated from their peers either by factors caused by the physical effects of their condition, or through bullying, meaning that some of them are unwilling or unable to re-integrate into mainstream education. Many of the longer-term students have a complex array of needs, which may combine physical and mental health difficulties, and some of them can present with challenging behaviours. Some students also have complicated or difficult home lives. All these factors can contribute to low self-esteem, isolation, and an unwillingness to engage or participate, making them 'harder to reach'; although this is by no means always the case – and with the right support and activities, positive experiences can be created and long-term benefits provided. This is the ethos of the hospital school, and the different centres provide a nurturing and therapeutic environment in which children and young people can learn and develop.

Collingham Child and Family Centre provides the most intensive support as students are usually attending the Centre for an average of four months, many as residential patients, and are referred specifically by community Child and Adolescent Mental Health Service teams as they have particularly severe mental health problems. Often these children and young people have been excluded from at least one school, although many are extremely bright. During a young person's time at the Centre, teachers work closely with their parents or carers, school and the Local Authority, to develop an agreed reintegration plan. Staff members at the Centre have training in the management of challenging behaviour, and are aware that if children behave in an unhappy and disturbed manner it is essential that there is an understanding of the meaning behind their behaviour and a consistent and sensitive plan to support the child.

Work in the hospital school, and at Collingham specifically, is complex and requires a high level of cooperation and communication between hospital staff (including teachers, support staff, nursing staff and the wider hospital community), the Ignite musicians, and Wigmore Hall Learning project management. In preparation for working with these particularly vulnerable groups of young people, Ignite musicians and project staff attended training with CCHS to learn about the philosophy of the school; risks and resilience factors affecting mental health; introductions to mental health issues that are common at the Centre including depression and anxiety, ADHD, eating disorders and autistic spectrum disorders; and an understanding of how these might influence people's behaviour. Each project also has a high level of reflective practice built in, giving staff members and musicians time to analyse sessions and interactions, as well as planning pathways for individuals and enabling honest feedback and communication on both sides. These sessions are on-going through the projects, culminating in an evaluation meeting at the end of each individual project, and ensure that work is of the highest quality, as well as meeting the needs of participants.

The 'creative ensemble' model in context

Ignite has now done three years of work in Collingham and projects have followed a developmental trajectory, each project building on knowledge, experience and relationships formed in the last. This has been enabled by grasping deeper understanding of the experiences of the young people and forming strong relationships with the staff, but has been particularly facilitated by the use of Ignite's 'creative ensemble' model of working.

As described earlier, the creative ensemble model involves participants becoming part of a group of musicians with the aim of creating new music together. There are several factors which make this immensely suited to working with 'harder to reach' young people, the most salient of which I will outline below.

- *It is an equaliser:* it doesn't split the group into teachers and learners; rather the whole group – young people, teachers, nurses and musicians – are all learning and creating together on an equal footing.
- *It enables self-expression:* no musical styles are imposed - the starting points for pieces are as likely to come from participants as from the ensemble, and are developed as a group. The participants are encouraged to find their own musical voice, whether that manifests through making up a new drum rhythm or conducting a whole group of people.
- *It respects personhood:* the musicians don't know what difficulties the child or young person has; they are purely engaging with them as an individual in a creative, not a medical, context.
- *It helps to build self-confidence:* playing a glockenspiel tune or shaker rhythm on your own might not sound like anything much, but playing it alongside professional

musicians of whom you have control can be an immensely rewarding experience, helping children to realise that they are making a valued creative contribution and that big, complex pieces of 'actual music' can be built from small beginnings.

- *It is flexible:* in turbulent environments, the best laid plans can go out of the window in a number of minutes! Working through improvisation means that the musicians can be responsive to new directions the participants might take them in.
- *It is inclusive:* it doesn't matter if a participant has never played an instrument before or is a violin virtuoso; there will be a way for them to contribute within the group. This is particularly helpful in an environment which provides for young people with a range of abilities and age groups.

An Ignite workshop typically begins with participants, staff and musicians taking seats together in a circle, very much creating their own 'chamber group'. This set-up creates a sense of equality from the outset, as well as providing for easy verbal and non-verbal interaction; for example through eye-contact and gesture. The group will then kick off with musical warm-ups designed to put everyone at ease and help them to get to know one another. These give everyone involved a chance to explore an instrument, as well as using their voices; building up rhythmic, listening and group-work skills through, for example, call and response games, taking solos or directing the group. Warm-ups are quite stylistically neutral and have more to do with thinking about musical 'ingredients' such as rhythm and sound as starting points. Getting teachers and support staff involved at this point can also help to provide a relaxed atmosphere, and young people often feel more inclined to put themselves out there if a teacher has shown enthusiasm to do so. Repetition of these tasks over a number of weeks helps to build confidence and in some settings participants even start making up their own warm-up games to share!

After warming up, the group either work as a whole or split up into smaller groups to create some music of their own. Ignite might introduce a series of notes, or a basic rhythm or groove for the participants to build upon; or the young people might have strong ideas of their own for how they want to start the music, sometimes using pictures, video or stories as starting points for inspiration. For example, a recent project focusing on 'elements' used a different classical element (earth, air, water and fire) as a starting point each week, using pictures of icebergs or videos of fire to generate ideas for musical atmospheres and melodic lines. Sometimes the young people would come up with completely unrelated ideas too – the great thing about a creative ensemble approach being the flexibility of Ignite to incorporate these easily into the development of a piece: the aim always much more to encourage creative expression than to force ideas into an existing scheme.

During workshops members of the group can pick instruments they would like to try and are encouraged to think about the sounds and textures they can create. Exploration is gently supported by the Ignite musicians, lending ideas; picking up on musical cues; or sometimes taking very specific instructions! Improvisation is encouraged through duets with Ignite members, or by giving participants an opportunity to solo or direct others, and these ideas are developed into new sections of music, slowly building into a piece. In some settings the group will compose together, whereas in others the young people respond very well to 'owning' a piece each, developed with the help of the group.

Recording and listening back is used as an important reflective tool throughout each project, helping participants to build on their ideas as well as being able to show things that they are proud of to others inside and outside the group.

Through these processes, participants are enabled to take part as composers, performers and conductors; both musically expressing their individuality and being able to contribute sensitively to the ideas of others.

Case study - Tom

The positive effects of Ignite's model of working may be best illustrated by use of a case study from a Collingham project. (All names have been changed to protect the identities of the young people.)

Tom is a very intelligent young man of 12 or 13 who had been a student at Collingham for a number of months. At the first session of the project he came into the room with a book, took a look around, pulled a chair out of the circle defined for the workshop, took it to the back of the classroom and sat reading. Instead of forcing him to re-join the circle, a member of staff and a musician went to sit with him, gradually drawing him into warm-up activities and enabling him to participate in the group whilst allowing him to be physically separate. When it came to the first musical activity Tom was put into a small group with the same staff member and musician, and had chosen to play a hand drum. Initially reluctant to do anything, once he realised he had creative control Tom came up with a complex sequence of musical events, directing the adults and chastising them humorously if they got things wrong. He also tested the boundaries by hitting the drum as hard as possible, making some incredibly loud noises and clearly expecting to be reprimanded. However, the musicians responded in kind; reflecting his gestures and channelling them into something positive – part of a piece of music. By the end of that session, Tom had composed his piece and shared it with the group – showing obvious delight and devious grins during the fortissimo section!

This gradual integration was patiently repeated over the course of the project, with a key moment happening when Tom challenged Ignite's cello player to play one of the 'demos' on the classroom's keyboard, saying that it was one of his favourite pieces of music. Although it was a complete tangent from the workshop, the cellist rose to the challenge admirably, playing along to the tune in perfect unison to barely hidden astonished looks from Tom, gaining the respect of this young man. From that point forward, if not always easily, Tom was more readily engaged in activities – not only interested in creating his own music, but contributing to the group as a performer for others, and more willing to take new ideas on board. The flexibility of the sessions which had allowed him his time and the opportunity to be listened to in the group context could now 'hold' him, whilst providing ways for him to see how he could let others take the lead.

In his final session, Tom conducted a recording of his piece being played by the whole group which was recorded for the project CD.

Conclusions

We have found that the creative ensemble model of working used by Ignite includes several key elements which make it ideal for working with harder to reach young people.

The examples given have highlighted the importance of several of these factors including equality, flexibility, communication, empathy, inclusivity, interactive creativity and through these the promotion of self-expression, personhood, and self-confidence. In addition to this, it takes the core values of chamber music – working collaboratively in small creative groups – out of Wigmore Hall and into our local community, engaging a wider range of people with this art form and the Hall itself through first-person experience. Working closely with partner organisations with knowledge of and relationships with the young people is also vital to provide the informed and supportive environment for quality and focussed work. Long-term relationships with partners also mean that work can continue to improve. We are delighted to say that Chelsea Community Hospital School has recently been awarded a Gold Arts Mark, partially as a result of our partnership work, and Wigmore Hall Learning and Ignite look forward to more of this valuable and important work with them in the future.

Further information:
Ignite and the Wigmore Hall Learning programme: www.wigmore-hall.org.uk/learning
Chelsea Community Hospital School: http://www.cchs.org.uk/
The Cardinal Hume Centre: http://www.cardinalhumecentre.org.uk/
Turtle Key Arts: http://www.turtlekeyarts.org.uk/

A lily of a day

Andy Murray

A lily of a day,
Is fairer far, in May,
Although it fall, and die that night;
It was the plant and flower of light.

(Ben Jonson)

This chapter is about a troubled person I first met when he became my neighbours' new 14-year-old foster child. It tells how his unexpected musical dedication and achievement forged a lasting bond between Mark (not his real name) and myself. Twenty years on, we are again back in daily contact, but regrettably there is no happy ending.

My interactions with Mark were outside my professional duties and my mainstream teaching experience. Readers should bear in mind that I am not a specialist in hard-to-reach education. This article is intended more as an illustration of the significance of music to one hard-to-reach individual than as an example of good practice.

When we first met, people like Mark, who had been statemented with 'emotional and behavioral difficulties', were segregated off into self-contained EBD special schools. I had taught a wide spectrum of pupils in my mainstream secondary career. Mark was indeed different but he certainly didn't like the public EBD label and his school held little worth in his mind.

While he always looked impeccably smart and neat, Mark was rebellious. He listened to Gangsta rap and, aged 14, was already regularly taking drink and drugs. I didn't know it then, but thirty or so previous placements with various foster parents and children's homes had all been unable to accommodate Mark's challenging behaviour.

On our first meeting, Mark was quite shy and he said nothing at all. His new foster father, Tony, rang my doorbell and introduced me as "Andy, the music teacher". While they sipped tea, I played them a couple of TV ditties on my piano.

I was in their house the next day and Mark silently wiggled his fingers, miming piano playing. I asked if he "wanted a go" on my piano and he nodded. Tony said we could go to my house for a "piano lesson" if I was happy with that. It was more than I had offered, but yes, I went along with it.

At last Mark spoke. He said that his Nan had shown him how to play 'Chopsticks' and he played us that ubiquitous C, Am, F, G piano riff (I know it as *Heart and Soul*). "Well done Mark" I said casually, noticing that he reacted in a way that made me suspect that praise was rare. I then demonstrated several pieces myself, in a variety of styles. After I played the first movement of Beethoven's *'Moonlight'* sonata Mark unexpectedly announced that he would like to learn to play it. I'd wrongly presumed, from his street-wise look and manner, that Mark would not want to learn anything classical.

Mark knew nothing about music notation. I thought that learning the opening few bars of the 'Moonlight' might be possible, but that successfully learning the whole movement seemed very unlikely, especially with no practice piano at home. But I didn't want to deny him an opportunity so I said I'd teach him one bar at a time and we'd only take on a new bar when he could remember how to play everything so far. I wasn't really expecting this regime to last for long.

I was wrong again. Mark kept ringing my doorbell—every day. Progress was understandably at a slower pace than I was used to, but Mark was very tenacious. His persistence prevailed when I thought he might find things too hard. Slowly and gradually we built the piece up, some bars taking several days to conquer.

With no knowledge of notation or letter names, we learnt new material by noticing the physical finger patterns against the fixed layout of black and white piano keys. These passages were memorised in sequence, initially along to a spoken commentary of reminders. Identifying specific piano keys became a little easier after I explained letter names, but recall of these was never totally reliable.

Over many weeks, Mark kept up a daily routine of piano visits that surpassed any previous regular commitment. Against a background of otherwise chaotic behaviour, this was a new indicator that Mark could focus with purpose on something longer term, despite the goal being highly aspirational. The normal practice with instrumental beginners is to teach short manageable pieces that are contrived to progress technique gradually. I'm not sure that this approach would have offered enough motivation to Mark. It was important to him that he was learning a 'proper' piece by a recognised composer.

At the piano, Mark was by now playing with real emotion and sensitivity with no need for coaching from me. Interpretation was just natural and integral to him. In some passages he would stare deep into my eyes, expressing feelings that he did not try to put into words. Perhaps this served as a therapeutic experience that contributed to him coming back for more, but Mark has never confirmed this.

I began to hope that these positive new musical developments might herald wider changes in Mark's life, perhaps infusing calm into other areas of his behaviour. In fact, as we came to know each other better, away from the piano, his self-control with me began to evaporate.

Mark was already quite well-practised at over-stepping boundaries by stealth. With me, he began innocuously, e.g. sliding down the stairs, then gradually progressed through escalating levels of play-fighting, culminating in painfully clamping the skin of my chest between his teeth. This sort of behaviour was entirely new to me and it took me by surprise. At the same time, it exposed a level of need that encouraged me to want to help further.

I spoke to his foster parents about what was happening and this was when they told me about Mark's care history. They said they were battling hard with his will themselves and I admired what they were doing. Their sanctions sometimes involved 'groundings' that ruled out Mark's piano visits. I found myself thinking that maybe his music should be a right not a privilege, but I can see arguments for both sides.

I contacted Mark's case worker, saying I'd like to put my meetings with him onto a more formal footing (child protection practices now make this happen much sooner). She suggested that I could become a session worker and get paid for the time I spent with him.

I wasn't wanting to be paid, but I did think that a wider support network might be a good thing, for everybody's safety and security.

I thought Mark would like this idea too, but yet again I was wrong. When I told him, Mark reacted angrily with accusations of betrayal—as if I were siding with the enemy. I explained that the circumstances of our lessons wouldn't actually need to change at all. But this made no difference. Mark detested Social Services and he didn't want me linked with them in any way.

Social Services had been given the unenviable task of removing Mark, aged 5, from his mother when she could no longer cope with him (Mark says she told him he was going away on a holiday). Of course he now realises what happened, but still craves his mother's love and hates Social Services. Emotion seems able to prevail over anything.

I abandoned the session worker idea and told Mark that piano visits could continue, but that some other things would need to change. We managed to put a stop to the biting and other excesses. I don't recall exactly how, but I do remember it involved a sanction of denying eye contact (Mark craved attention) and quickly showing him the front door when things became unacceptable. Time spent at the piano was never really a problem, though.

I was worried that focusing on one piece might become too tedious. We started looking at other excerpts, like the openings of Beethoven's *Für Elise* and Satie's *Gymnopédie No.1*. We also tried Satie's *Gnossienne No.1*, where Mark really relished playing those bold acciaccaturas in the melody. Sometimes we'd improvise a duet: I would play a bass and chords backing and Mark would improvise a melody over. He loved adding trills and twiddles; there was just something about ornaments that appealed to his personality.

Broadening the musical scope in this way was much more like the educational experiences I was familiar with and Mark seemed to enjoy it too. I also sometimes played other pieces just for him to listen to. Once he knew a tune, Mark would improvise lyrics and sing along with the piano. This is something that many people find quite difficult to do spontaneously, but it seemed second nature to Mark. He sang well in tune, he was creatively 'loose', and he just 'kept going' with an intriguing mix of association and dissociation. I still remember how he improvised on Schubert's *Impromptu No.2*:

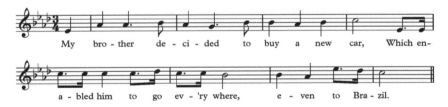

Notice that, after setting off, Mark adapts Schubert's rhythms to his unfolding fantasy lyrics while still preserving the underlying melodic shape. Mark's brother didn't actually have a car, though it might indeed have let him go anywhere. But 'enabled' was certainly not in Mark's everyday vocabulary. And how did Brazil pop out?

Mark just seemed to enjoy the experience of 'letting go' and wondering what would happen, both in words and on the piano, and maybe in life too. In a different existence he might have made a good jazzer.

Eventually, the day arrived when we reached the final two chords of the '*Moonlight*' sonata, which seemed relatively so simple but yet so meaningful. This was followed by a week or so in which we aimed to do away with the memory-jogging commentary that Mark still relied on in a few places.

Then, at last, after many near misses, Mark performed the whole movement from beginning to end with no mistakes. It was truly an incredible achievement. I wish I had made a recording. I heaped praise on him and he glowed with pride. We invited his foster family in to listen. Mark made a few mistakes under the added pressure but they too heaped praise on him.

If this article were a fairy tale it would now end by saying that this was the breakthrough that Mark needed; that he put his difficult past behind him, settled down and lived happily ever after. Unfortunately, reality is not this rosy.

Mark is now 35 years old. We lost touch for several years, but he now rings my doorbell again almost every day, or I ring his. I now count him as a close friend and I do my best to support him in those life skills that continue to elude him. The interim years have brought a few modest achievements, but in Mark's own mind negatives obscure positives. Things have not really gone well for him in so many ways. Mark now has a serious liver condition and doctors have told him that he has only weeks to live if he doesn't stop drinking. Mark can't stop drinking and he is now facing up to the real prospect of death.

Music once opened a new window onto Mark's soul. But it was no self-fulfilling magic wand. After his foster placement broke down I still kept in touch and visited him in subsequent placements. But of course those piano visits were not sustainable in the same way. On reaching the age of 16 Mark was given a flat of his own and some good friends of mine generously gave him a piano. Unfortunately, funding substance misuse became more of a priority than his musical inclinations and Mark sold his piano.

Low esteem for his school experience, coupled with his unwillingness to engage with formal support mechanisms, makes me question whether professional interventions could have had any musical impact on Mark at all. Those piano visits arose through a chance informal coincidence that blossomed for a while, but was not sustainable through changing circumstances. Ironically, mechanisms that could have survived the changes were simply not acceptable to Mark in the first place. I guess this is a real dilemma of hard-to-reach education.

So that big success we once celebrated has turned out to be a flash in the pan: a 'lily of a day' in the Ben Jonson quotation that heads this article. Something wonderful to remember that is now gone.

There was no measured transference resulting from Mark's piano visits, but I am convinced that they made a positive difference. Although the learning could not be maintained, Mark still enjoys re-living those childhood experiences and occasionally playing what he can still remember. His unexpected ability to play something at the piano that sounded so profound helped to raise his esteem with his friends and, more importantly, with himself.

Whenever Mark needs encouragement in the face of adversity I remind him of what he once proved he could achieve when he really put his mind to it. He has never faced a challenge as big as the one that now confronts him.

Reaching Ben

Emily Sahakian and John Finney

In this chapter Emily Sahakian and John Finney tell the story of Ben (not his real name), a sixteen-year-old 'disaffected' student in the final year of his GCSE Music course. Ben has not in the past been easy to teach or to reach, but here we read about his music teacher Miss Sahakian discovering Ben's hidden voice and how through building an I-Thou relationship (Buber, 1970) combining the musical and the human, Ben is reached. Commentary is added by John Finney in an attempt to better understand the transformation of Ben.

A Story

Ben is a year 11 student from a troubled family, where there are several fathers but none of them a father figure. Relationships in this family are tense, and Ben likes to stay out of the house as much as possible. As a result, he is influenced by drinking, smoking and drug culture, and this has been the case for a large part of his teenage years.

Ben is currently finding school difficult. His behaviour, language and attitude to learning are challenging, and so Ben is not a student that teachers enjoy having in their lessons. He can be intimidating, and is dominated by the pressure to live up to the persona that his peers expect from him. This reputation is what defines him, and it will not be challenged by any kind of authority. However, Ben has been moving further up the school report system, and so he knows that he is on his last chance to prove to the school that he is willing to turn things around. He is mature enough to realise that his GCSEs do matter, and that to push things so far as to be excluded from school would be a foolish move.

My first interaction with Ben was when he was a year 9 student who had been pushed to be in the band for the current school musical. His instrument is electric guitar. I had never taught him, and so he did not have any experiences of me being an authority figure. He soon labelled me as 'safe', and I did not really see much of the Ben I had heard about from teachers. This boy was troubled, yes, but also longing to be known, and was eager to chat, make me laugh and feel that he was valued by me. That was our only shared time that year.

Later in that year Ben opted to take GCSE music. He knew that it wouldn't be his kind of music (which in public he is very specific about defining: a mixture of house, club dance and garage), but he also thought that it would be better to do a subject which he could vaguely connect to, rather than another boring one. He had also been told that he plays the guitar to the standard necessary for the course. Ben didn't quite realise that the terminology and theory needed for the course would be difficult, and his successive failed tests at the start of the year led to a cloud of negativity towards his musical ability that continually hovered over him. This did not dissuade him, however. Even though he was given the option of changing to a different course at the beginning of the year, he was adamant that he wanted to stick with music - 'I may be a total dunce at all the theory crap, but I still wanna do this.'

In his music lessons, Ben is visibly torn between wanting to do well in the subject and wanting to maintain his reputation. He will at all times be listening to his 'own' music through his headphones, even whilst composing, and he makes a great effort to appear uninterested in all aspects of any lesson. I allow him to be, and for that reason our relationship is a positive one. He does any work I tell him to do without a fuss (as long as he can appear uninterested), and is never confrontational, so our dynamic is peaceful.

It is time for us to record his ensemble performance after school. He has been reluctantly practising a guitar part to be performed as part of a band. The drummer and bassist have had enough of playing the same part over and over, waiting for Ben to get a good take. It is evident that even with a lot of practice, Ben will probably still play this piece out of time and with many mistakes, so I decide to end the recording session, and set about trying to find an easier piece that he could learn quickly. As I am looking, Ben comes into my office with a nervous look on his face. He says

> 'Miss, could I like, er, sing something for this ensemble thing? Would be way flipping easier than this guitar crap.'

I ask him if he likes singing.

> 'Well I don't like singing like some gay, but I can have a go.'

I choose for now to ignore the implications of his use of the word 'gay' and go on to ask him whether he knows any duets and what could he sing?

> 'Right don't judge me or anything Miss, it's not as gay as it sounds, but I like, you know that song 'Something Stupid', you know by Frank Sinatra. It's cheesey as -----, mind, but I reckon that'd turn out alright.'

I find the song online and print it out. I smile to myself about the song choice – such a paradox! We go to the piano to try it out and he looks panicked.

> 'Miss, if someone finds out that I've been singing I will literally kill you.'

I give him a starting note and ask if he knows the song well enough to just sing it without going through the notes.

> 'Yeah, well I sing along to this cheesey crap in my room. It's proper classic, all them singers – Frank Sinatra, Dean Martin, Perry Como. That's proper talent. I keep that to myself mind.'

I am bemused and ask whether he sings often?

> 'Yeah. It kinda keeps me company, and it expresses what I feel. I'll do it, as long as no one can hear me.'

We start the song and I sing the melody along with him. He knows it perfectly. I wonder if he can sustain the melody with the girl's harmony part underneath. He does. We burst out laughing at the repeated 'I love you's at the end of the song. The moment is more beautiful than awkward.

We do a recording. The first take is perfect. We feel all the same nuances and expressions in the song. The balance is just right. I am amazed - this is the best singing that I have heard all year from a boy. I ask him how he has managed to keep this amazing voice so hidden? He is surprised that I am so delighted, but brushes his happiness off.

'Miss I didn't think we could do that song, that's been like a secret ambition. I thought it would be way difficult with all them harmonies. Didn't think it would sound so good.'

Ben stays for another half hour. He wants to keep singing the song. I have reports to write, but this is of so much more value. As he leaves he says

'Miss, is there any way, like, you could put that on a CD? I think my mum would be well happy with that. She'd probably cry or something.'

This after-school episode was the start of a mutual and silent understanding that took place during all our interaction. Once, I breached this silent understanding by suggesting in front of a few others in the class that he sing a Frank Sinatra song for his solo performance. This was met by a defiant 'no thanks Miss, I'm not singing some gay song.' I understood from that point onwards that his singing was a very private thing, to be heard only by myself and maybe his mum. His eclectic taste was also never to be mentioned in public. However, when working together, the many masks that Ben had been wearing seemed as if they were being removed. At first this was just through the music: being able to delight in certain bars of harmony, or loving how a certain lyric could express an exact emotion. But this opened the door to his expression of his longings and desires for his life. He was unhappy with the mess that he was in and wanted to see a way out. He saw that his lifestyle would not get him anywhere. His younger brother was following in his footsteps, and Ben knew that he had to sort himself out before his brother made the same mistakes as he did. He valued our conversations, and my advice.

'It's kinda refreshing to have a teacher that you can actually talk to without having to be careful what you say. And you're interested in what I'm saying even though I tell you lots of crap.'

He said that when he's older he'd probably say something cheesey to me along the lines of 'thanks for believing in me'.

Ben came to spend many after school sessions in the music department, not to record something for his GCSE, but for musical enjoyment in itself. He says it keeps him out of trouble, and out of the home. He brings in songs that he wants to sing, and we sing them. He is becoming interested in composition, and has discovered Gaelic folk music. He is currently composing a folk song, and his visible excitement whilst composing it is a joy to see. He does this all after school of course; he would not dare work on it during lesson time. And when he composes after school, his headphones come out.

Allowing Ben to 'be', and believing in him before anyone else believed in him, has, in a small way, brought about changes in attitude. I have listened to that first recording often, so has he. He is going to record an album.

Commentary

How are we to think about this story of Ben being reached, a story about Ben coming to a place where he is willing and wanting to be known? What can we learn from the story told? Perhaps this shouldn't be attempted. The joy of stories is that they speak for themselves and in many different ways to many different people. Enough said perhaps. The reader therefore may not wish to go further. However, while explanations of Ben's becoming known are beyond our scope, we can offer some interpretations that may serve to promote a little further understanding. These may be helpful and even lead to thought about issues of relevance to music education in general. But first, and if we are concerned with the reaching of 'hard to reach' children through music, two matters come to mind in the case of Ben. First, the place of music in constructing Ben's various identities and the protection of his masculinity, and second, the teacher's condition of profound empathy in engaging with this.

Masculinity

While Ben's teacher introduces him as 'in many ways a stereotype of a 'disaffected' student' and certainly not easy to reach, predictably Ben exhibits many of the attributes of a masculinity protected (Brod & Kaufman, 1994). As part of this Ben has presented a deceptive musical persona, with a public guitar-playing identity yielding to a hidden vocal one, a club dance/garage one yielding to a popular American song one. For Ben singing is an intensely private matter that provides solace and sanctuary.

> 'It kinda keeps me company, and it expresses what I feel. I'll do it, as long as no one can hear me.'

Singing has been frequently been perceived as a feminine activity and something that can bring masculinity into question (Green, 1997; Harrison, 2008) as part of music itself being constructed as a feminine subject (Coomber *et al.,* 1993; Green, 1997; Cooper, 2010).

Fear of the feminine as a way of understanding male disaffection and underachievement has been addressed by a number of researchers in recent times. Mac an Ghaill (1994), Salisbury & Jackson (2003), for example, have shown how the stigmatistion of homosexuality within youth culture and in school has become a significant factor in the construction of masculinity.

> Boys who are indentified as different – through their clothing, their voice, their mannerisms and gestures, their interests, their behaviour, their friendship networks, have often been exposed to homophobic abuse, most consistently from other boys. (Younger & Warrington, 2005: 27).

These are dangers, the source of fears and cause for boys to work hard at their masculinity. Ben tells his teacher of the dangers in being labeled 'gay' and only in the privacy of the music room can the mask be allowed to fall. In the public forum of the classroom the mask is put on again, 'no thanks Miss, I'm not singing some gay song.' The risk of exposing a voice that is soft, refined, expressive of feeling, showing sensitivity and caring for others, seen as feminine characteristics and possibly reflective of mother, from whom his repertoire of privately learnt songs may have originated, is too great. In yielding up his guitar image (masculine) and accepting a vocal one (feminine) Ben may be accepting a part of himself previously denied.

Musical relationships as human relationships

One recurring conviction feeding the early idealism of those coming to initial teacher education is that music, unlike any other subject in the curriculum, can be accessed by all children and young people. Music is within the reach of everybody. These aspiring music teachers may well have in mind some of the barriers encountered in achieving in maths, science and subjects demanding particular kinds of cognitive literacy. Music, they know, is more than cognition. It is emotion too. They also know, through their own positive experiences of music education, that this in some significant part depended upon a knowing relationship with a music teacher where learning music was embedded in a relationship – teacher-pupil-what is being learnt. Music was a subject where learning made sense when it broke through the impersonal relationships and protocols of the school. The music teacher commonly experienced school as a place where they were able to benefit from small group or individual learning and close relationship with their music teacher. Beyond school a common experience may well have been in a one-to-one instrumental learning relationship. In the learning of music the teacher will have experienced an I-Thou relationship.

The I-Thou

Martin Buber (1970) proposes two fundamental orientations in human relationships, the I-Thou and the I-It. The I-Thou is characterised by a mutuality between subject and object while in the I-It there is the exercise of some control, some distance or objectification existing between subject and object. The I-Thou doesn't classify, pigeon-hole, make hierarchies. It doesn't reduce what is there to be known in its fullness, in its uniqueness. Feeling and intuition are more fully drawn upon and in Buber's words allowing for 'an opening of our hearts to hear what experience has to say' (ibid). The I-Thou relationship anticipates dialogue and on-going conversation where each addresses the other in the expectation of being a part of a symmetrical relationship (Bauman, 1992). Another way of understanding this is to consider the significance of empathy as a key component of a teacher's role and as shown above in the reaching of Ben.

Empathy

That teachers have 'an overwhelming desire to support, care for and relate deeply to their pupils' (Cooper, 2004) was a finding of research setting out to better understand the role of empathy in teacher-pupil relationships and its relevance to moral modelling. In depth study of the work of sixteen empathic teachers enabled Cooper to classify empathy in a four-part model while recognising the complexity of the concept and the many factors bearing upon it. There is empathy that is fundamental, that which is functional, that which is profound and that which is feigned. Fundamental empathy works at the level of basic interaction and having the characteristics of what is required to initiate a relationship. With frequency this becomes functional empathy, typical of the working conditions of the school where a class of 30 is being related to, while feigned empathy is an act lacking in sincerity. Of most interest to us here is profound empathy which Cooper defines as encompassing

> a rich understanding of others in their social, historical and relational contexts … Teachers who show profound empathy create an extremely rich mental model of individuals in their minds which they can relate to closely, both emotionally and cognitively. They draw upon all their experience and experience of other people and the clues emanating from pupils to interpret their feelings and understanding. (Cooper, 2004: 16)

One-to-one and small group teaching are places where profound empathy can be developed and flourish. We see this clearly in the case of Ben and his music teacher, growing from fundamental empathy at the initiation of the relationship in year 9 to a profound level of empathy as they make music together.

Cooper's research shows how the constraints of the school, its managerialism, the fragmented and rigid curriculum and its assessment structures, as well as general working conditions, leave teachers frustrated in their role as moral models. It is where students experience functional and feigned empathy that many of those hardest to reach like Ben are lost. Ben is not somebody who teachers enjoy having in their lessons, yet his music teacher, through sustaining an empathic attitude in the face of his disaffected classroom behaviour, has been able to move to a relationship based on profound empathy.

Returning to Buber's I-Thou, Ben is in an I-Thou relationship both with the songs of Frank Sinatra and now with his teacher. Relating to each other though the music opens up the possibility of dialogue where listening to each other 'requires a [particular] set of skills, those of closely attending to and interpreting what others say before responding, making sense of their gestures and silences as well as declarations' (Sennett, 2012: 14). Ben discloses that

> 'It's kinda refreshing to have a teacher that you can actually talk to without having to be careful what you say. And you're interested in what I'm saying even though I tell you lots of crap.'

Roland Chaplain writes about male students making a strategic withdrawal, disengaging in the cause of protecting self-worth (Chaplain, 1996). Such students show a learned distrust of teachers in general. They don't expect to be listened to, really listened to in a manner that is genuinely dialogic (Wegerif, 2011).

Another thought

In looking at single cases, like the one described here, thoughts about wider issues quickly come to mind, matters that the case might shed light upon. We have already speculated that here might be a case of protecting masculinity, with Ben breaking through this to reveal what may have been a previously undisclosed musical identity. This might lead us to think more about the many-sided musical identities of young people.

In this case we can reasonably assume that Ben would not have brought a recording of Frank Sinatra to school whether to work with formally or less so. I wonder what would have been brought had he been invited to do so? This may lead to consider, given that musical identities are so complex and multiple, whether consideration of student musical identities and their musical preferences, often leading to the doctrine of starting from where the student is, what is their music, is necessarily worthwhile. This may distract from what is more fundamental about encountering music of any kind where there is dialogic space in which to respond openly and with generosity and where there is an empathic teacher at hand. Here is a pedagogy yet to be fully discovered. Ben's music teacher is working on it.

The story continues

Ben taught my year 8 class today. He wanted to skip ICT so in jest I said that he could come and teach my lesson. He was so keen! He made a PowerPoint, found some videos, and devised a reggae practical task for the year 8s. I managed behaviour while he taught the lesson. He was nervous, but engaging, and all children were being musical. It was an 'outstanding' lesson, and 28/30 hands went up for 'put your hand up if you think Mr X will make an amazing teacher.' He was *so* elated - he didn't stop talking about it. The headphones, hoody-jumper and chains around his neck remained firmly in place throughout.

In my heart the most significant issue that has stayed with me is the musical relationship that I had with this one child. I could make time like this for many more children, not just him. But I am bound by meetings, rehearsals, and general school admin. If this relationship has made more of a difference in Ben's time at school than any of his other teacher relationships, then shouldn't this type of transformative pupil-teacher working be the aim of all teachers? So many more children would leave school feeling valued and having an aspiration. Ben told me a few weeks ago that he was seriously considering being some kind of teacher - he said it felt really fulfilling when he was teaching my year 8s. A small-scale investment has made at least a fantastic memory for him, and at best a changed life.

Ethical note

Throughout the time Ben's music teacher worked with Ben, pastorally and musically, her Head of Department had an oversight of the process and remained a close presence.

Reporting the story of Ben raises ethical questions. Ben is the centre of interest. How does he feel about this? Is it done with his approval? Ben's music teacher asked Ben if the story could be told and made public albeit with anonymity – no location disclosed and with Ben as a pseudonym. This he agreed to. He wondered what all the fuss was about.

References:

Bauman, Z. (1992) *Postmodern Ethics*. Blackwell Publishing: Oxford.

Brod, H. & Kaufman, M. (1994) *Theorizing Masculinities*. London: Sage.

Buber, M. (1970) *I and Thou*. Walter Kaufmann: New York.

Chaplain, R. (1996) Making a strategic withdrawal: disengagement and self-worth protection in male pupils. In J. Rudduck, R. Chaplain & G. Wallace (eds.), *School Improvement, what can pupils tell us?* London: David Fulton Publishers.

Coomber, C., Hargreaves, D. & Colley, A. (1993) Girls, boys and technology in music education. *British Journal of Music Education,* 10: 123-34.

Cooper, B. (2004) Empathy, Interaction and Caring: Teachers' Roles in a Constrained Environment. *Pastoral Care in Education,* 25(3): 12-21.

Cooper, L. (2010) The gender factor: teaching composition in music technology lessons to boys and girls in year 9. In J. Finney & P. Burnard (eds.) *Music Education with Digital Technology*. London: Continuum.

Green, L. (1997) *Music, Gender, Education*. Cambridge: Cambridge University Press.

Harrison, S. (2008) *Masculinities and Music: Engaging Boys and Men in Making Music*. Newcastle: Cambridge Scholars.

Mac an Ghaill, M. (1994) *The Making of Men: Masculinities, Sexualities and Schooling*. Buckingham: Open University Press.

Salisbury, J. & Jackson, D. (2003) *Challenging Macho Values: practical ways for working with adolescent boys*. London: Falmer Press.

Sennett, R. (2012) *Together: The Rituals, Pleasures and Politics of Co-operation*. London: Allen Lane.

Wegerif, R. (2011) Towards a dialogic theory of how children learn to think. *Thinking Skills and Creativity,* 6: 179-190.

Younger, M. & Warrington, M. (2005) *Raising Boys' Achievement: Issues, dilemmas and opportunities*. Maidenhead: Open University Press.

Al's Journey

Graham Dowdall

This brief study looks at a group of young people with moderate to severe learning disabilities and particularly focuses on the journey of one young lad in this group whose development through the project has reinforced for me the value of this work.

I am not a trained music therapist but rather an experienced community musician with some instinctive knowledge of the therapeutic benefits of music and a lot of experience of witnessing how taking part in meaningful music-making can make a huge contribution to the quality of someone's life. One thing that is clear to me is that effective participatory music activity with disabled people operates increasingly on the cusp between traditional music therapy and community music where musical, social and therapeutic aims operate side by side.

The perceived benefits for young people with learning disabilities, both mild and more profound, of being involved in music-making include physio-therapeutic benefits from singing and playing instruments, gains in perception, memory and learning, as well as mood enhancement, both calming and stimulating. Additionally taking part in group music sessions has social, communication and listening benefits and the extra and harder to define reward of being creatively self-expressive clearly offers the same benefits to disabled young people as it does for anyone given this opportunity.

Background

This project took place in a Special School described as being for 'very special children'. It takes children aged from 2 to 19 with a range of difficulties including severe learning needs and complex disabilities, and includes two dedicated classes for pupils who benefit from a highly structured environment, many of whom have Autistic Spectrum Disorder. It is quite a large school but one, nevertheless, where relationships are personal and it is clear that the individual needs of the children are not subsumed by institutional or administrative drivers.

I have had the privilege of running an after-school club with some of the older young people ranging in ages from 13 to 19. We have a core group of around 7 or 8 children supported by between 2 and 4 support workers, some of whom are Teaching Assistants. The group is disparate both in age and also in the range of disabilities that they manifest – a couple are in wheelchairs, one with very limited control and mobility, the other has some control of his upper body and also has autism. We have two lads with Down's Syndrome who are very different characters – Ad is the oldest member of the group at 19 and is very shy but relatively verbal whilst P is outgoing, jocular but non-verbal. Most of the rest of the group have varied but quite severe forms of Autism. This wide range of abilities and challenges demands a wide range of different activities and so I have developed a repertoire that mixes songs, both familiar and less so, soundscapes, creative improvisation, rhythm work and other approaches. Most of the group are non-verbal or just verbal, some have no physical disabilities while others have very limited mobility, so it is important that activities are accessible and enjoyable for all but also challenging where appropriate.

Activities

A project like this needs to be about fun and recreation, but should also have serious learning built into it. The group needs a certain amount of familiarity so we repeat some activities like 'hello' songs each week but also try to develop the work and stretch the young people in a safe, warm and supportive environment. Over two terms of this project a great culture has developed where the group is warm and inclusive – the participants look out for each other and assist the least able, they joke and tease each other and myself and they have developed a great sense of ownership where they feel they can make choices and demands about repertoire and activities.

A typical session would start with a warm-up song which encourages stretching and shaking as well as breaking the ice. This song has become known as 'Nose' because it includes touching the nose in its activities. We then follow up with a song where we go around the group saying hello to each in turn by name. It has become important for the group that everyone including adult helpers is named and welcomed even if they arrive late.

We usually then share out instruments, letting the young people choose their favourite instrument for that day. Some are unable to express choice so the support workers and myself may suggest and offer an instrument. Ad (see above) usually goes through a ritual of not wanting an instrument, whilst we all know he really wants an Agogo bell, so a game emerges which finishes with laughter as we play "My name's Ad, I play the bell" as a rhythm and he excitedly grabs the bell. Others might be more assertive and come and choose something from my case, or might mime an action to describe their instrument of choice. We will often then try to build a rhythmic piece from the names of the people in the group which helps them to remember each other and to focus on the number of syllables in a given name. Another activity could be playing and stopping, exploring dynamics and speed or turn taking and solos.

We have a range of well known and less well known songs that we sing, with the group again choosing as much as possible. Most of these are accompanied with backing tracks, so that I can move around and engage with the individuals, but also with digital drum pads that the group can use to trigger relevant sound effects for the song. For instance *In the Jungle* (The Lion Sleeps Tonight) is accompanied by animal and forest sounds and has become known in the group as 'Animals'. *We Will Rock You* uses distorted guitars. The drumpads allow the group to engage with a wide pallet of sounds from my laptop and to explore quite different sound worlds quickly and easily - one minute we could be playing heavy rock, the next quite ambient soundscapes.

I have been bringing in an iPad too, which is a really popular activity, using Apps that can access interesting sounds without physical dexterity. Managing the access to a single iPad is a challenge but can be a good lesson in turn-taking for those who find this hard.

One lad, G, who has profound and multiple disabilities with very little movement at all, has really been able to engage on the iPad and we have witnessed him struggle to slide a finger across the screen to access different notes. It is clear he is trying to express himself and we are witnessing some hand-eye co-ordination as well as being convinced that he is making musical choices.

Another activity we engage in is using a microphone through a delay effect with very long feedback – this means that any sound the young people make will echo before finally decaying into the next contribution. We pass the microphone round and pretty much everyone has a go. T, who is wheelchair bound and has autism, is normally very quiet – he can make sounds but not confidently. When he first heard his voice back from the echo he was transfixed and started to vocalise with himself loudly and with clear intent. His classroom assistant had never in five years heard him so vocally demonstrative. We now do this regularly, allowing T a longer time as the benefits are so clear for him.

I think it is important that despite the group's shared learning disabilities we can offer musical activities that might engage the taste of any typical teenager and also some easily accessible 'silly' songs that give them a sense of safety and comfort. The familiarity of repeated activities is appreciated by the young people with autism and there is an expectation that we will always include particular pieces. Interestingly these favourites aren't just the familiar songs but also songs like *The River is Flowing* or *Marawathana* that we use for calming towards the end of the session.

Al's journey

In the first session Al, who has autism and is semi-verbal and aged around 15, sat next to a support worker but declined any instrument except for a second or two. He appeared disengaged and we weren't sure if the sessions would be of value to him.

Over the next couple of weeks he came slowly out of his shell and exhibited a good sense of rhythm when offered and encouraged to play a drum. He would play in time for a few minutes at a time and was clearly becoming more a part of the group session.

I then started to notice how closely he looked at my mouth when I was singing and over a few weeks I could observe how he was trying to copy the movements of my mouth on both familiar and unfamiliar songs and a few weeks later started to make sound and actually sing along with me, exhibiting tunefulness as well as approximations of words both in English and other languages. He now sings along enthusiastically on most songs especially, it seems, those he has learnt more recently.

During rhythm sessions he started to take a leading role, keeping an excellent pulse and became more and more attentive to the names in the group, looking around and modelling the names of the others as we tried to build rhythms from the names. On one occasion I asked him if he could play people's names solo, which he did – looking at each member of the group as he modelled their names. Thereafter, he asked to do this as a regular activity.

He also started to request songs using his own derived hand signals to describe them – for instance a monkey gesture for *In the Jungle*. This started to include songs we hadn't ever tried. One week he made a gesture that looked like a fish but after questioning turned out to be a request for *Yellow Submarine*!

During most sessions I have offered the group the chance to conduct using a few simple hand signals to control our improvisation. Al took up this role eagerly and as well as using those signals I had given, he invented some incredibly descriptive ones of his own including setting speed with arm gestures, inviting solos and fluttering hand gestures to encourage approaches to playing.

It has been quite astonishing to witness Al's progress on all fronts but I was truly amazed to hear from the assistant head in an email that in the week after my term ended they had held a session anyway and that Al had effectively led the session – choosing and leading songs and other activities that we have used in previous weeks – using hand signals rather than verbal commands. The staff weren't sure how a session would run without me but from the start Al took control, insisting on a structure, and pacing the session from 'hello' songs to a lullaby at the end. Apparently he even introduced a 'goodbye' song he had heard in school where he sang to each member of the group at the end and this has now joined our repertoire.

To witness at first hand how over a relatively short period one young person can go from virtual non-engagement to effectively leading a session despite the absence of language, and the huge rise in confidence as well as skill that this manifests, has been truly humbling and if I ever felt a need to justify the value of participatory music work with young people in very challenging circumstances then Al's story delivers that in spades.

Since this occasion I have been back twice, after a long break, to the Music Club and I have found that the culture has been sustained. When a guest ran a one-off session, Al was pretty assertive about activities he wanted to co-lead and on my return I encouraged him to lead a couple of songs, which he did really confidently. Even though he doesn't have extensive language, Al certainly has communication and leadership skills to add to his excellent rhythmic sense and huge sense of humour – a pretty good tool kit for any aspiring music leader let alone one with a fairly profound learning disability!

'I am the Moon'

Ros Hawley

'Am I dying Mum?' is not the question any parent wants to be expected to answer in their lifetime. Through my work as a musician in hospital as part of the Music for Health team at The Royal Northern College of Music, whilst working with a play specialist, I encountered a family who went through this very experience.

Music had played an important role as part of a creative, interactive and normalising experience for J, a young teenage boy, over a 3-year period, during his regular stays in the hospital, and music increasingly became a part of his family's engagement with him and the hospital right up until his death. My chapter uses the experience of working with J to reflect on the practice of being a musician in hospital, and what being 'hard to reach' means within this context, where circumstances beyond anyone's control can make it harder for a child or young person to be able to engage and interact with the world outside: where the everyday normalities of life become ever more distant and a new 'normality' begins to take over.

As a musician working in hospital, any preconceived idea of what 'normality' may be is challenged; finding ourselves working in highly sensitive and acutely emotional situations, an open mind is needed to be able to receive and assess information presented, and an understanding of the wider context in which you find yourself working is crucial. The musician has to work with whatever is 'normal' for the situation and for the patient, and to know how to respond. Sometimes, 'normal' means 'hard to reach'. For a long-term patient, accessing what *they* want to do, when *they* want, is a goal that becomes ever harder to reach.

The hospital is not a 'normal' environment for music; it is pretty unusual and unexpected to see a musician playing by the bedside of a young patient, or singing, or creating music together, and not what you may expect to experience during your stay as a patient. Whilst the Arts in Health movement has been established for several decades, and gained a wealth of documentation and research to support the impact and value of interactive and participatory work within the healthcare environment, music in hospital is a relatively new, younger cousin, just beginning to stretch its wings and gain recognition as a movement within the UK. This work is neither teaching nor the practice of music therapy; it stands in a ground somewhere between performance and participation, drawing on skills and techniques from both areas, which need to be adapted to appropriately fit the environment of the hospital. The musician not only has to be a highly skilled instrumentalist – using their own instrument, voice and carefully selected percussion instruments confidently and creatively - they need to have excellent observational and communicative skills in order to create open and interactive 'spaces' for patients to feel comfortable to step in to; the analogy of 'less is more' is often very fitting in this context: the musician needs to listen just as well as they can 'speak'.

The hospital environment itself can already present a very full acoustic soundscape; depending on the ward setting, there may be the sound of machines beeping, children crying, TVs playing, doctors on their rounds, nurses talking to family members, or administering treatment to patients, physiotherapy taking place, and tired and frustrated younger siblings may be letting off steam at the end of a long and boring afternoon. The musician has to carefully place themselves both physically and musically within this already busy and constantly changing environment, considering how, where and when to begin music and who with. It may not be a good time for music – what if someone is asleep in the bed nearby, or the consultant comes to see the family you are with? What if a patient is hungry, or in pain? Every sound we add as a musician in this context layers on top of this existing 'normality': it is not our job to make the sound world more chaotic than it already is, and we have to be extremely careful not to do this.

Having said all this, however, the environment of the hospital *can* benefit enormously from the intervention of musical interaction. With J, the presence of musicians gave *him* a framework to interact, participate, listen and enjoy, taking him out of his present surroundings and into a neutral space where responses, ideas and thoughts could be freed from the clinical surroundings that dominated his life in hospital. Music can soften the edges of the hospital; musicians are neutral – they are not medical, or clinical – but can be essential in providing a connection, or re-connection, with some element of normality, or an outlet for feelings, expression, creativity and *fun* – all important factors on our road to wellbeing and recovery, and often having an immediate and uplifting impact on mood, awareness and state of mind – easy to reach if you can access activities that promote such opportunities.

J's experience of working with us at the hospital over 3 years gives a good insight into the range of situations and musical interactions that a musician may find themselves involved in when they work in hospital. J unwittingly provided excellent training for our Music for Health students on placement through his work with us – keeping our classically trained musicians on their toes by challenging them to find particular sounds on their instruments for his compositions and improvisations, and confidently taking charge of structuring the music he made, clearly and precisely instructing the students as to what he wanted to hear and how it should be played. The students were already dealing with the strange experience of taking part in making music, in a hospital, around the bedside of a patient, who was at times attached to various drips and bits of equipment; having to then think and respond spontaneously and creatively – and instantly – and enter someone else's musical world presented an unusual but exciting challenge. We had to make ourselves *easy* to reach in order to be responsive to J's creativity.

An excellent listener (J's condition meant that he had very little vision and this constantly surprised our students as he was often seen walking up and down the wards and would find or follow musicians when they were on the ward with ease), J would listen intently to musicians performing on the wards as part of the hospital concerts programme or in atrium concerts. I have one very clear memory of him choosing to sit between us as we performed a lunchtime concert - at this stage it was wonderful to observe that J was comfortable and confident enough in his relationship with us to just sit between the two of us as we performed, and it was a pleasure for us to have him sat with us as we played. We had to be aware of J's enjoyment at being close to the musicians and position ourselves so that he could gain the maximum benefit from the experience. We had to be flexible and generous with both our physical and musical space.

J had excellent control over when music was appropriate for him. He had become accustomed to us coming to visit him if he was in hospital; we would regularly stop by his room and get the instruments out, compose music and make recordings; he had also gained confidence in asking us to learn some of his favourite songs so he could sing and us accompany him (he did a mean Rudolph version at Christmas time singing alternative lyrics!). One day he had to have a blood test that he was not looking forward to and had discussed with the play specialist about the musicians coming into the treatment room with him whilst he had it done; at the last minute, he changed his mind, going off for his test leaving us in his room; he returned, said something along the lines of 'Glad that's over' and resumed the music session just like that. In our debriefing afterwards one of our students observed that it was clear to her that J separated his musical time from being in hospital – when he was 'in music' he wasn't 'in hospital'; to have musicians playing whilst the test took place would have muddied the two worlds. It was important for us *not* to be present at times just as much as it was important to be present.

There were times when J was not so well; the play specialist would always let J know that we would be in that day and he would always have the right to say he didn't want to see us. This is an important part of our work – the patient always has the right to say no; there is very little else a patient can often say no to, and the framework of musical interaction provides an autonomous relationship between musician and patient and allows the patient to have control. As it happened, J was always open to us visiting him, even on bad days. One wonders if the musical interactions fulfilled two important roles here - escape from present circumstances and consistency of relationship/activity. As the world outside becomes harder to reach, those activities where you feel you have time to have fun, be distracted, be creative, be entertained and meet others become paramount – but can also become ever harder to reach. As a musician in hospital it is important not to expect or prescribe - what you created one week may not be appropriate the next, and the skill lies in being able to judge how to create an appropriate and enriching experience in a range of ways, from sharing in a lively group composition session to singing a lullaby gently by the bedside whilst the patient listens and relaxes. They may be too tired to join in for very long or at all but it may be important that you are there. The musician needs to be able to read the situation and respond instantly – to have empathy for the patient's needs and know they may change at any time.

J was a very sociable young man who loved company. He was very much a 'top dog' in the hospital due to his frequent stays and spoke to many people as if they were old friends. His world had increasingly become that of the hospital and he was increasingly detached from his school and his home life many miles away. His stays in hospital had meant that he had a very grown up ability to interact with adults whilst still being a child dealing with emotions of anxiety, vulnerability and the unknown. One of his skills was in enabling younger children to join in with musical interactions on the wards; in this role we would facilitate his leadership of the situation; he liked to encourage the children to choose instruments to play and choose children's songs that they would enjoy; our role was to make this happen within a secure framework. Again J showed the musicians how to respond sensitively to the dynamic created between the children. In this instance the musician has to understand when to take the lead and when to facilitate and support; and to be free from judgement as to what repertoire is appropriate – it may not seem 'normal' for a teenage boy to be singing children's songs and nursery rhymes but facilitating this opportunity brought great pleasure and pride for J, and great enjoyment for all involved. One of the happiest examples of this was J singing nursery rhymes whilst cuddling his little sister with family all around him – J created a space for his family to be just that through the musical activity he chose to do: a sensitive situation where the musician is the outsider – the only ones not in the family, but given the privilege of being a part of the experience by facilitating the musical interaction between patient, sibling and parent. The musician has to judge what an interaction needs from them - emotionally and musically. The musician needs to be wholly present, but not conspicuous, allowing the family space to interact together.

Towards the end of his life, J became increasingly harder to reach - his illness made it more difficult for him to participate in the way he had previously. His resilience meant that even after experiencing bouts of being very poorly, he still raised his hand to touch the Indian bells he had become familiar with as we played for him. When his mum had been told that J would not be leaving intensive care, and that he was very poorly, she asked if we would to go in and play for him by his bedside. This was a huge challenge for us, but a professional duty at the same time and a huge honour to be asked to play at such an acutely emotional time. We were at this point not just playing for J, but for his mum too, and for all the other times we had made music with him, and with his mum. Our role again at times like this is to be consistent – to always be there if needed, to provide a connection through familiarity and understanding, to do what is needed at the time. To do this the musician has to have emotional strength, integrity and a sense of professionalism that enables one's own emotions not to get in the way of the work you need to do. The musician needs to have good support in order to be able to deal with the emotional challenges that can arise; using a practice model of working largely in pairs helps enormously in our work.

Later that day J's mum asked us if we would play at his funeral. It is important to stress here that this is not a normal part of a musician's role but given the unique person that J was, and the increasing involvement we had had with him and his family, particularly during the last weeks of his life, it felt like a natural and important final task. At this point our focus was for J's mum, for what she needed; the need for music had moved to her and she took comfort in knowing that music had been there for J when he was in hospital, and had also been part of their experience together in the hospital – it had united them in a way outside the constant reminder of healthcare and hospital. For us as musicians working in hospital, this stage of our journey with J and his mum highlights the need for the musician to have humility, strength and consideration for the needs of others - particularly at such a vulnerable and painful time.

Near to the time of his death, J asked his mum if was dying. On knowing the answer to his question, J told her, that when he died, she had to remember him as the moon, not the stars, as the moon was bigger and shinier than the stars. He would continue to shine down on her from the sky. How much harder can a child be to reach than when they become the moon?

Musicians working in hospital are not miracle workers; sometimes we won't be able to make things better. But what we can do is provide unique musical memories that can be treasured forever and never forgotten – snapshots of a moment in life with fun, laughter, creativity, and expression at its heart, where life, even for a moment, isn't hard to reach at all.

Further Reading and Information

Websites

www.rosfishmusic.com

www.musique-sante.org

www.limeart.org

musicforhealth.wordpress.com

Articles

Preti, C. (2009) Music in hospitals: Defining an emerging activity. In K. Stevens *et al* (Ed.), 2nd International Conference on Music Communication Science (ICoMCS2) (pp. 79-82): University of Western Sydney.

Preti, C. & Welch, G. F. (2011): Music in a hospital: The impact of a live music program on pediatric patients and their caregivers. *Music and Medicine,* 3(4), 213-223.

Preti, C. & Welch, G. F. (2012) The inherent challenges in creative musical performance in a paediatric hospital setting. *Psychology of Music.* doi: 10.1177/0305735612442976

Bouteloup, P. (2008) 'Et Je coupe le son'. Spirale (Erès, 2008) No.45.

Reports

RNCM/ Oakland, J. (2012) Music in Health: A thematic evaluation of practitioner experiences of work, training and professional development.

University of Salford (2012) RNCM Medical Notes Project at The Royal Manchester Children's Hospital: Outcomes for children, families, musicians and hospital staff. Final Report. ISBN:978-1-907642-33-7.